GOLD experience
2ND EDITION

STUDENT'S BOOK

B1
Preliminary
for Schools

CONTENTS

Unit	Reading	Grammar	Vocabulary
Starter **Happy days**	**topic:** a great day **task:** matching	articles past simple comparative and superlative structures	science entertainment the natural world travel free time
1 Identity page 9	**topic:** identities **skill:** matching information **task:** multiple matching	present simple and present continuous (p12) adverbs of frequency, time phrases (p14)	personality adjectives adjective + preposition collocations
2 Get the message page 21	**topic:** communication **skill:** understanding overall meaning **task:** multiple choice	past simple and past continuous (p24) -ing form (p26)	language and communication verb + preposition collocations
3 The future is now page 33	**topic:** the future of music **skill:** skim-reading a text **task:** gapped text	the future: *will, going to*, present continuous, present simple (p36) modal verbs for advice and suggestions (p38)	technology in the home phrasal verbs
4 Taking part page 45	**topic:** unusual sports **skill:** identifying phrases with similar meanings **task:** multiple matching	present perfect (p48) past simple and present perfect (p50)	sport
5 In the spotlight page 57	**topic:** growing up in the spotlight **skill:** understanding what is being tested **task:** signs and notices; multiple choice	zero, first and second conditionals (p60) *unless, in case, if I were you* (p62)	entertainment

Listening	Speaking	Writing	Switch on
topic: holiday photos **task:** matching	**topic:** summer holidays **task:** collaborative task	**topic:** my personal best **task:** paragraph about an experience	
topic: cities **skill:** understanding agreement and disagreement **task:** multiple choice	**topic:** giving personal information **skill:** giving reasons and examples **task:** introductions – social interaction	**topic:** a personal profile **skill:** getting started, reacting, finishing **task:** email	**video:** no more boys and girls **project:** prepare a presentation
topic: a summer camp **skill:** predicting information **task:** sentence completion	**topic:** communicating **skill:** organising your description **task:** describing a photo	**topic:** mistakes **skill:** creating an atmosphere; using strong adjectives and adverbs **task:** story	**video:** school interpreters **project:** make an information poster
topic: buying something new **skill:** identifying differences **task:** multiple choice (pictures)	**topic:** the future of technology **skill:** giving and asking for opinions, agreeing and disagreeing **task:** collaborative task and discussion	**topic:** living without technology **skill:** giving advice and making suggestions **task:** email	**video:** app entrepreneurs **project:** design an app
topic: enjoying sport **skill:** listening for the question **task:** multiple choice	**topic:** watching and doing sport **skill:** saying when you are not sure **task:** describing a photo	**topic:** a new sport **skill:** linking ideas **task:** article	**video:** top spin **project:** plan a campaign
topic: music **skill:** identifying agreement **task:** multiple choice	**topic:** live music **skill:** dealing with unknown words **task:** describing a photo	**topic:** an evening of entertainment **skill:** making positive comments, describing problems **task:** article	**video:** in search of fame **project:** write a fact file

CONTENTS

Unit	Reading	Grammar	Vocabulary
6 Down to earth page 69	**topic:** our blue planet **skill:** referencing in a text **task:** gapped text	the passive: present simple and past simple (p72) *have/get something done* (p74)	the natural world order of adjectives
7 Travellers' tales page 81	**topic:** ways of travelling **skill:** matching details **task:** multiple matching	defining relative clauses (p84) modals of obligation, prohibition and necessity (p86)	travel verb and noun forms
8 Time out page 93	**topic:** developing patience **skill:** finding synonyms **task:** multiple choice	reported speech (p96) indirect questions (p98)	hobbies and interests
9 Life experiences page 105	**topic:** summer bucket list **skill:** identifying linking **task:** gapped text	past perfect (p108) *used to* (p110)	feelings *-ed* and *-ing* adjectives
10 Summertime! page 117	**topic:** holiday jobs **task:** multiple choice, open cloze, multiple-choice cloze		

Grammar file   page 124   **Activity file**   page 156
Extend vocabulary   page 144   **Audioscripts**   page 167
Exam file   page 146

Listening	Speaking	Writing	Switch on
topic: young people who change the world **skill:** avoiding distractors **task:** multiple choice	**topic:** being environmentally friendly **skill:** turn-taking **task:** collaborative task	**topic:** a place to visit **skill:** thanking, inviting, accepting, refusing **task:** email	**video:** ocean culture **project:** design a community
topic: travelling the world **skill:** identifying the type of information missing **task:** sentence completion	**topic:** travel problems **skill:** referring back to what someone said **task:** discussion	**topic:** holiday tips **skill:** creating interest **task:** article	**video:** surf around the world **project:** prepare a research-based presentation
topic: unusual hobbies **skill:** avoiding distraction **task:** multiple choice (pictures)	**topic:** talent shows **skill:** making and responding to suggestions **task:** collaborative task and discussion	**topic:** celebrity hobbies **skill:** paragraph openers **task:** article	**video:** domino art **project:** write a video script
topic: experiences **skill:** listening for advice **task:** multiple choice	**topic:** living on a desert island **skill:** describing likes and dislikes **task:** discussion	**topic:** a day out **skill:** ordering events **task:** story	**video:** finding your voice **project:** debate a topic
topic: work experience **task:** notes completion, multiple choice	**topic:** various **task:** all parts	**topic:** various **task:** email, article, story	

Look at the photo and discuss the questions.
1 Who do you like to spend your free time with? Why?
2 How would you describe your perfect weekend?

STARTER

Happy days

READING
read blog posts about a great day

SPEAKING
talk about your summer holiday

LISTENING
listen to people talking about holiday photos

WRITING
write about your best moment

Power up

1 Work in groups. Find five things you have in common with the other people in your group (e.g. something you both like/dislike, a skill you share).

Read on

2 Match the phrases (1–5) with the photos on page 7 (A–E).

1 A future scientist
2 Our new pet
3 My first performance!
4 Friends are the best!
5 Mmm … my favourite drink!

3 Read the posts on page 7. Find someone who:
1 thinks something is attractive. ....
2 has just celebrated a special day. ....
3 met someone successful. ....
4 will return home soon. ....
5 felt different to how he/she expected. ....

4 Match the topics (1–5) with the posts on page 7 (A–E). Add five words for each topic.

1 science
2 entertainment
3 home life
4 travel
5 free time

IT WAS A GREAT DAY!

A EMILY
I was the last one on the stage, and they had cameras there! I wasn't as nervous as I thought I would be, but I'm pleased with the results.

B ADRIANA
The best day ever! My project won first prize and guess who gave the prize? My hero – the owner of a big technology company!

C DANNY
After shopping for hours and spending all our birthday money, Sam and I had a hot chocolate at Willy's Café. Yummy!

D MADISON
Our last day in Germany. This trip was more amazing than I ever imagined. I'm going to miss all my new friends.

E RYAN
Meet the newest member of our family. Isn't she gorgeous?

5 Complete the blog post with 'a', 'an', 'the' or no article (–).

Blogging about your hobbies

I'm a huge fan of collecting **¹**............ football stickers and so, when **²**............ visitor to the school suggested that we start **³**............ interesting blog on something, my hobby was **⁴**............ most natural choice. Being **⁵**............ blogger has **⁶**............ lot of good things about it. For a start, I'm better at writing now, and **⁷**............ good communication is really important. It also needs **⁸**............ time and someone who is organised. These are also **⁹**............ kinds of things that really help in **¹⁰**............ life, and I'm happy that I'm doing something to develop them. I've also met a lot of new people, through **¹¹**............ emails and comments. Most blogging communities are very friendly places. In fact, some of **¹²**............ people I have met through blogging are really nice!

6 Did you have a good summer? Look at the list of holiday activities. Which sentences are true for you?

Last summer I:

A	went walking in the countryside.	....
B	learnt a new skill.	....
C	travelled to a new place.	....
D	played a new game.	....
E	had a barbecue with friends.	....
F	tried a new food or drink.	....
G	took lots of photos.	....
H	swam outdoors.	....

Listen up

7 🔊 S.1 Listen to eight people talking about their holiday photos. Match the speakers (1–8) with the activities in Ex 6 (A–H).

Speak up

8 Work in pairs. Take turns to give your partner more information about the sentences you chose in Ex 6.

Starter Happy days

Speak up

9 Work in pairs. Think about your summer holiday and discuss the questions.
1. What was the best thing you did on your last holiday? Why?
2. What new place did you go to (e.g. a new shop, a new street)? What did you think of it?
3. Are you very active in your free time? Why/Why not?
4. Do you prefer to be in the city or in the countryside when you have free time? Why?

10 Work in pairs. Some family friends are coming to visit next month. They have two children your age. Which activity do you think all the family would enjoy the least? Why? Can you agree on the best one?

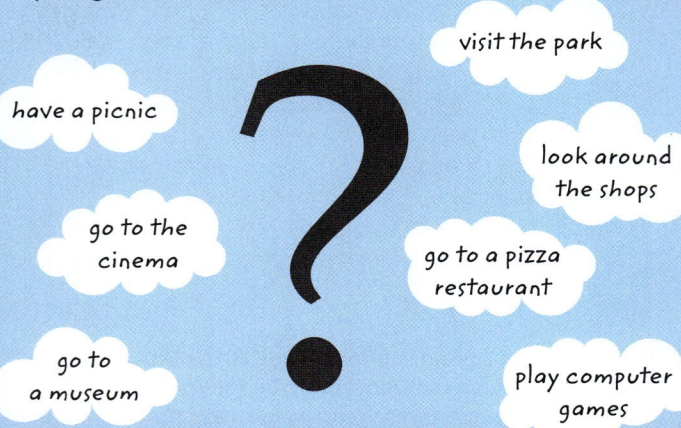

have a picnic · visit the park · go to the cinema · look around the shops · go to a pizza restaurant · go to a museum · play computer games

game on
Write four sentences about your last holiday – two that are true and two that are false. Then work in pairs and read your sentences to your partner. He/She must guess which sentences are false.

Write on

11 Write two sentences about:
1. something you saw on TV or at the cinema and enjoyed.
2. something new you tried.
3. somewhere you like going.
5. someone new you met recently.
4. something you do really well.

12 Read the advert and the student's paragraph below. Then write a paragraph about yourself. Write about 100 words.

My personal best!

We want to use our website to show the world what great students we have in our school. Tell us about your personal best moment!
- When did it happen?
- What skills did you use?
- What did you do?
- Why was it your best moment?

'When I was at primary school, we all had to come to school dressed like a person from our favourite book. I really loved Little Red Riding Hood, so I decided to dress like her.

My mum found me a photo on the internet to copy and my dad helped me. It took us all weekend and I didn't get everything right the first time!

There was a competition at school the next day and I got a prize! You might think it's not a big thing, but I learnt that you get much more out of things when you spend a lot more time preparing.'

"Be who you are."

Look at the photo and discuss the questions.
1. Can you think of three words that describe your personality?
2. Do you behave differently in different situations? Think about:
   - with your family.
   - with your friends.
   - at school.
   - with strangers.

Identity

READING
topic: identities
skill: matching information
task: multiple matching

GRAMMAR
talking about the present: present simple and present continuous
adverbs of frequency, time phrases

VOCABULARY
personality adjectives
adjective + preposition collocations

LISTENING
topic: cities
skill: understanding agreement and disagreement
task: multiple choice

SPEAKING
topic: giving personal information
skill: giving reasons and examples
task: introductions – social interaction

WRITING
topic: a personal profile
skill: getting started, reacting, finishing
task: email

SWITCH ON ▶
video: no more boys and girls
project: prepare a presentation

1 Identity

READING

Power up

1. Work in pairs. Read the instructions about how to make an identity box. Look at pictures A–C and answer the questions.
   1. What is an identity box?
   2. What kind of person do you think owns each box? Why?
   3. What does each box show?

How to make your own identity box

Find a box you love and put things in it to show who you are. Take a photo of your box to show to your friends or put on your profile.

Read on

2. Read about the five people below. Find the key words in each profile. What hobbies does each person have?

MARLA   1

I live with my family in São Paulo – a huge city! I'm learning how to play the guitar at the moment. I feel really happy when I hang out with my friends after school.

SANDIP   2

I live in a village near the mountains with my parents and all my cousins. I spend a lot of time outdoors but I also like reading at home. I want to be an author.

SANDRA   3

I live in the city with all my brothers and sisters. We're very musical – we always fight about who gets to play! We go to a lot of shows. We're taking part in a TV programme.

COCO   5

I know everyone because I live in a very small village. I like cooking for my family. I travel a lot and I'm a member of several clubs. I like organising people.

PAOLO   4

I'm living with my grandma by the sea this summer but I go back home every weekend. I love being outdoors and I do lots of sports.

10

3 Read the exam tip and complete the tasks.

exam tip: **multiple matching**

Make sure **all** the information matches, not just some of it.

What do we know about Marla in Ex 2? Choose the correct information.
1 city / village
2 likes music / sports
3 likes being alone / with friends

Read descriptions B, C and G below. Find all the information that matches Marla's profile. Which box belongs to her?

4 e Read the descriptions of identity boxes below. Match the identity boxes (A–H) with the people in Ex 2 (2–5).

5 Find words or phrases in the descriptions that have these meanings.
1 an area of land between hills and mountains: ....
2 spend time with: ....
3 small pieces of paper with pictures or writing: ....
4 the area behind the main thing that you are looking at: ....
5 a person that belongs to an organisation: ....

Sum up

6 Work in pairs. Cover the descriptions. What did the students put in their boxes? Why?

> Coco: she put a saucepan in her identity box because she likes cooking.

> Sandip: he put the book in his box because he wants to be an author.

Speak up

7 Plan your identity box. Work in pairs and discuss these things.
1 Choose five things to put in your box. Why did you choose them?
2 What objects, photographs, music, etc. would you choose to show your life? Think about these things.
   • your family
   • your hobbies
   • where you live

IDENTITY BOXES   We found these boxes. Whose are they?

A This box is a paper box. In it there is a photo of a family and eight children. They are standing near a house at the bottom of a valley. There is also a pair of walking boots and a book with the title 'How to Write'.

B This box is a big silver box with a lot of patterns on it. Inside there's a photo of a girl. There is a CD by a pop group and a photograph of my friend playing the guitar. There is also a small model of the Eiffel Tower.

C This box is painted with lots of colours. Inside there's a programme for the theatre, a page from an entertainment guide and a photo of several boys and girls. They are walking on a bridge in a big city and one boy is holding a guitar.

D This is a wooden box with a recipe book and a wooden spoon inside. There's a picture of a girl standing next to a woman on a TV show. The box also contains a pair of new tennis shoes.

E This is a very messy box. Inside the box there is a picture of a family at the seaside in swimsuits. There are also several shells and a mirror. There's a book called 'Teach Yourself to Play Guitar' and a picture of a boat.

F This box has got stickers of different places all over it. Inside there's a photo of some little houses around a square and there is a river nearby. There's a small saucepan and a diary with lots of timetables and notes in it.

G This box has been painted with pictures of skyscrapers and huge buildings. There's a CD of a pop singer and a card with the address of a music teacher. There's a photo of a large group of students, all laughing together in a park.

H This is a very big box. It has a basketball in it and a photo of a boy with a surfboard and an old lady smiling. There's another photo of a football team on a bus with mountains in the background.

Identity is like a puzzle: you need all of the pieces to complete the picture.

1 Identity

GRAMMAR

1 Read the grammar box and complete the examples with the correct form of these verbs.

go   like   spend   take part   want

explore grammar → p126

talking about the present

present simple

We use the present simple:

A for permanent states.

I **live** in a village in the mountains.

B for habits and repeated actions.

Every week, I ¹............................ to drama classes.

I ²............................ a lot of time outdoors.

present continuous

We use the present continuous:

A for actions that are happening now.

We're **talking** to her on a video call now.

B for actions that are happening around now.

I'm **learning** the guitar at the moment.

We ³............................ in a TV show.

present simple and present continuous

We can contrast regular or permanent activities with activities happening now, today or around this time.

I'm **living** with my grandma this summer but I **go** back home every weekend.

stative verbs

Some verbs don't often use the continuous form: *feel, hate, hear, know, like, love, see, think, understand, want.*

I **feel** really happy when I hang out with my friends.

I ⁴............................ reading at home.

I ⁵............................ to be an author.

2 1.1 Watch or listen to people talking about their lives. Read the questions (A–C). Which ones does each speaker (1–11) answer? Some speakers may answer more than one question.

A What are you doing at the moment that's different to what you usually do?

.... / .... / .... / .... / .... / .... / ....

B What do you usually do in the evenings?

.... / .... / .... / .... / .... / ....

C What do you love doing?

.... / ....

3 1.2 Watch or listen again and complete the sentences.

1 On Tuesdays I .... a commercial dance class.
2 In the evenings I .... sport, such as tennis or football.
3 I usually .... my dinner.
4 I .... my friend's cat because her and her family are on holiday.
5 As it's the winter season, I .... hockey every Friday night for my local club.
6 I .... a film a day to learn more about acting styles.
7 At the moment I .... hard for my exams that I have in, like, the next couple of months.
8 I .... a lot more dancing because I've got a dance competition, a choreographics competition, coming up.

4 Complete the conversation with the present simple or present continuous form of the verbs in brackets.

 Hi, Tamsin. How are you?

 I'm fine. What ¹............................ (you/do) at the moment?

 Well, it's five o'clock in the afternoon in Argentina. I ²............................ (sit) outside.

 Lucky you! It's ten o'clock at night here! What time ³............................ (your classes/finish)?

 School ⁴............................ (end) at two o'clock. That's why I ⁵............................ (relax) now!

 My school day ⁶............................ (start) at nine o'clock and it ⁷............................ (not finish) until five o'clock.

 ⁸............................ (you/study) now?

 Yes, I am. I ⁹............................ (do) my English homework but I'm fed up with it!

 Never mind. At least you ¹⁰............................ (practise) your English now!

Speak up

5 Work in pairs and tell each other a few things about yourselves that the other person might not know.

My favourite food is cereal.

I'm learning to play the drums at the moment.

VOCABULARY
personality adjectives

1 Match these adjectives with their meanings.

A clever   confident   funny   lively   sporty
B bossy   lazy   noisy   rude
C calm   serious   shy

Someone who:
1. always tells other people what to do is ....
2. doesn't like working is ....
3. is happy and active is ....
4. makes loud sounds in an annoying way is ....
5. speaks or behaves in a way that isn't polite is ....
6. makes people laugh is ....
7. is intelligent is ....
8. believes he/she can do things well is ....
9. likes activities such as ball games or team games is ....
10. thinks about things a lot and doesn't laugh much is ....
11. is often nervous with people they don't know is ....
12. is relaxed and not angry is ....

2 Look at the adjectives in Ex 1 again. Answer the questions.
1. Why do you think they are organised in different groups?
2. Can you add any more words to any of the groups?

3 Choose the correct words to complete the conversation.

A: Hi, Ella. What are you doing?
B: Nothing. I'm staying at home today.
A: You're so **¹bossy / lazy**! Come on, there's a baseball game at the park.
B: You know I'm not very **²rude / sporty**, Matt. I'm staying here.
A: Ella, you should go out. It's bad to stay inside all day.
B: Stop being so **³bossy / clever**. I need to relax and be **⁴calm / shy** for my exams next week.
A: All right. Take it easy! Are you feeling **⁵confident / serious** about the exams?
B: Yes, I am. But I need to revise. Now go to the park and leave me alone.
A: OK, but don't be **⁶clever / rude**!
B: Sorry, Matt!

4 🔊 1.3 Listen and check your answers.

explore language

adjective + preposition collocations

Some common adjective + preposition collocations are: *good/brilliant at, bad/terrible at, bored/fed up with, excited about, interested in, afraid/frightened of, keen on*.

We use adjective + preposition + noun.
She's also **interested in languages**.
I'm **fed up with this song**.

Remember: you can use some *-ing* forms as nouns.
Jake's brilliant at **cooking**.

5 📧 Read the language box and then the article. For each question, choose the correct answer.

How personalities develop

If you're a teenager, you know that the way you behave and feel in different social situations changes as you get older. So, you might be interested **¹**....... a new study about how teenagers' personalities develop. From about thirteen years old, it becomes more important to **²**....... in a way that means other people will like you. Also, we start to become **³**....... on, and more serious about, our work and study. We become good at **⁴**....... rules and we want to complete tasks that we started much more than when we did when were younger. The big question in the study was whether our friends affect our **⁵**....... towards others. The results show we choose to hang out with people who are like us, but that does not mean we change because of them. In fact, we stay the same – we just choose friends who are **⁶**....... to us!

1	A	at	B	with	C	in	D	for
2	A	appear	B	try	C	act	D	stay
3	A	prepared	B	active	C	careful	D	keen
4	A	achieving	B	following	C	keeping	D	doing
5	A	performance	B	behaviour	C	activities	D	ways
6	A	matching	B	similar	C	same	D	like

Speak up

6 Work in groups. Ask questions using the collocations in the language box. Can you find someone for every adjective?

> Are you good at playing the guitar?

Where do cows go at the weekend? To the mooovies!

1 Identity

LISTENING

Power up

1 Think about a city you know. How does it make you feel? Why? Use these words to help you.

excited   happy   interested   pleased   relaxed   stressed

2 Work in pairs and compare your answers.

Listen up

3 Work in pairs and read the questions (1–6). Decide if each question is asking you to listen for an agreement (A), a suggestion (S) or feelings (F). Then find the key words in the options.

1 You will hear two friends talking about the weather in their city. What do they agree about?
   A The bad weather makes them feel sad.
   B They like the changes in the seasons.
   C The weather makes it hard to live in their city.

2 You will hear two friends talking about moving. How does the girl feel about moving to a new city?
   A amazed at how friendly the people are
   B happy about the different people she can meet
   C surprised by the variety of things to do

3 You will hear two friends talking about cities they want to visit. Which opinion do they share?
   A Istanbul has a great history.
   B Paris is romantic.
   C Singapore is exciting.

4 You will hear a grandfather talking to his granddaughter about changes in their city. How does he feel about the change?
   A He is pleased the city is easier to live in.
   B He enjoys the greater variety of people.
   C He is happy about the new buildings.

5 You will hear two friends comparing the city and the country. They agree that the city makes them
   A more friendly.
   B more serious.
   C more relaxed.

6 You will hear two friends talking about travelling in their city. What advice does the girl give?
   A The train is the fastest way to travel.
   B Walking is a good way to see new things in the city.
   C Travelling on the bus allows you to spend your time better.

4 Read the exam tip and complete the task.

exam tip: multiple choice (short texts)

Decide if you're listening for agreement or disagreement. You may need to listen for agreement words/phrases (e.g. *yeah, me too, it's true* …) or disagreement words/phrases (e.g. *not sure, hm* …, *but*).

Look at the questions in Ex 3. In which conversations do you expect to hear the phrases above?

5 🔊 1.4 Listen to the conversations. For each question in Ex 3, choose the correct answer.

6 🔊 1.5 Listen again and check your answers.

7 Read the grammar box and choose the correct words to complete the rules.

explore grammar ➥ p126

adverbs of frequency, time phrases

Adverbs of frequency go **¹before / after** the verb *be*.
I hate autumn – it**'s always** so windy.

Adverbs of frequency go **²before / after** other main verbs.
My brother **usually stays up** late at weekends.

Other time expressions usually go **³at the end / in the middle** of a sentence.
I meet up with my friends **at the weekend**.

8 Put the words in the correct order to make sentences.

1 we can see / once a month / a full moon
2 it isn't / in June / usually / dark
3 in the river / I like swimming / now and then
4 Tom and I / once a week / go skating
5 often / it / rains / in the middle of the day
6 always / tired / am / on Friday evenings / I

9 Write true sentences about yourself using the prompts (1–6). Use one of these words or phrases in each sentence.

every week/weekend   most days   now and then   often
once/twice/three times a year/week   rarely   usually

1 hang out with my friends   4 watch a movie
2 go on holiday   5 study
3 take part in a sport   6 read a book

Speak up

10 Work in pairs. Compare your sentences from Ex 9. How are you similar? How are you different?

You are more likely to give true answers to questions when you text than when you talk face to face.

SPEAKING

Power up

1 What answers would you give to these questions?

What's your:
1. name / family name / full name / surname?
2. first name / second name / middle name / nickname?

Speak up

2 Work in pairs. Take turns to ask for and give the information to complete the table. Spell any difficult words. Check that the information is correct.

How do you spell the town? K-O-N-Y-A.

Personal information

Name:	
Address:	
Town:	
Postcode:	
Email:	

useful language
giving reasons and examples

because one reason is (that)
as for example

3 1.6 Listen to Elsa and Chen answering these interview questions. Who gives the best answers? Why?
1. Where do you live?
2. Where do you come from?

4 Work in pairs. How could the students in Ex 3 improve their answers? Think about information, descriptions and reasons they could add.

5 1.7 Listen to Elsa and Chen answering another interview question. Who gives the best answer this time? Why?

What do you enjoy doing in your free time?

6 Work in pairs. Read the useful language. How could the other student in Ex 5 improve their answer? Think about examples, opinions and reasons they could add.

7 e Work in pairs. Take turns to answer the questions in Ex 3 and 5.

8 Work in pairs. Student A, turn to page 156. Student B, turn to page 162. Follow the instructions.

Speaking extra

9 Work in pairs. Ask and answer the questions. Give reasons and/or examples.
1. How do you get to school every day?
2. What's your favourite subject?
3. What do you like doing at the weekend?
4. Who do you like to spend time with?

1 Identity

WRITING

Power up

1 Work in pairs. Take turns to talk about these things.
1. something you love
2. something you're interested in
3. something you're keen on
4. something you can't stand

> I'm interested in pop music.

> I don't like playing video games.

2 Read the advert and Sofia's notes. Then read Sofia's email below. Match the paragraphs of the email (1–4) with the notes (A–D).

Tell us about you!

Channel 1 is making a programme about life for young people around the world. We want to know more about you and the place you live. We will come and film you and your family.

For this programme, you can be 14–17, so lots of teenagers can take part!

We want to know what you are like and what kind of things you enjoy.

Why should we choose you?

Send us your profile in an email.

A tell them
B talk about my personality
C say what
D give a reason

From: Sofia

Hi,

1 I'm Sofia Pérez. I'm fifteen and I come from Colombia. My life is quite unusual because we live near the beach. There aren't many people here, so my family is very important to me.

2 Some people think I'm quite shy but, in fact, I'm a confident person. For example, I'm good at making friends.

3 We have a lot of horses, so I'm also keen on horse-riding. I usually ride on the beach every morning. Also, it's great having barbecues and we love telling stories in the evenings!

4 Choose me because I'm a typical teenager but I live in a very different place. Not many people have this kind of lifestyle these days.

I hope to hear from you!

Sofia

3 Read the language box. Find four phrases with 'quite' and 'very' in Sofia's email.

explore language

quite and very

We can use *quite* and *very* before adjectives. We use *very* to make an adjective stronger and *quite* to make an adjective less strong.

He's **very funny**.   I'm **quite lazy**.

If there is an article (*a/an*) before the adjective, then *very* and *quite* go before the article.

It's **a very good** film.   It was **quite an interesting** story.

We don't use *quite* or *very* with extreme adjectives (e.g. *mad, passionate, furious, terrified*).

I was ~~very~~ terrified!   My mum was ~~quite~~ furious!

Plan on

4 Complete Jakob's notes with these phrases.

a very old   quite an exciting   quite interested   very funny   very keen on

1. I'm from Krakow in Poland. There are a lot of things to do here. It's .... city.
2. My grandparents live in .... part of the city. I know a lot of Warsaw's history.
3. I'm not .... maths. I'm not very keen on science.
4. I'm .... in acting. I like singing. I don't enjoy dancing.
5. Choose me. I'm a .... person. I can make you laugh.

5 Join the sentences in Ex 4 with 'and', 'but', 'or', 'because' or 'so'.

game on

Work in pairs. Close your books. Make a list of all the adjective + preposition collocations you remember from this unit. Take turns to say an adjective. Your partner has to give the correct preposition. You each get one point for each correct preposition.

Write on

6 Read the advert in Ex 2 again. Think about what you can say about yourself. Follow these steps to plan your email.
1. Make notes for each point you need to write about. Use Sofia's email in Ex 2 to help you.
2. Think about your descriptions. Think about adjectives and the language you can use to make them stronger or less strong.
3. Work in pairs and check your ideas.

7 Read the exam tip and complete the task.

exam tip: email ➔ p150

Make sure you write about **all** the content points (for example, where you live, what you enjoy, what you are like and why they should choose you). Always give some extra information about each point.

Look at your notes in Ex 6. Have you included all the points? What extra information can you add for each point?

8 e Write your email in about 100 words.

Improve it

9 Work in pairs. Read your partner's email and make notes about these points. Then talk about how you can improve your email.
1. Did your partner write about all four points?
2. Does each point have extra information?
3. Did your partner use 'quite' and 'very'?

The eastern chipmunk can stay inactive at home for the longest – up to a year. (Guinness World records)

SWITCH ON

No more boys and girls

1 Work in pairs and answer the questions.
1 When you were a young child, what did you want to be when you grew up? What job did you want to do?
2 What were your favourite toys when you were younger?

2 ▶ Watch the clip. What's the main thing that the children have learnt by the end of the experiment?

3 ▶ Watch again. Are these sentences true (T) or false (F)?
1 Scientists agree that boys' and girls' brains are different. T / F
2 When they're young, girls are just as strong as boys. T / F
3 Javid gives the girls a teddy bear, and the boys a robot. T / F
4 At the end of the experiment the boys' behaviour is worse. T / F
5 At the end of the experiment the girls' self-confidence has improved. T / F

Project

4 Work in groups to prepare a presentation on how a new school in your area can be more gender-neutral. Follow these steps.
1 Work in groups. Discuss how these things could be more gender-neutral. Then try to come up with some ideas of your own.
   - classrooms and school environment
   - classes
   - school uniform
   - after school activities
2 In your groups, present your ideas to the class. Make notes on the other groups' presentations.
3 Have an open discussion as a class. Agree on a list of changes that you would like to make at school.

INDEPENDENT LEARNING

Think about your learning

1 Look at the ways you can assess your own work. Do you prefer any of these ways of looking back at your work? Why?
1 looking back at what I did well
2 thinking about what I can do better
3 checking my work with my classmates
4 making a plan for improving

2 Work in pairs. Do you think it is important to assess your own work? Why/Why not? How is that different to getting feedback from the teacher or your classmates?

3 Work in the same pairs. Compare your answers to Ex 1 and discuss these questions.
1 What kind of things can I check in my work?
2 How can I know what I did well and where I need more practice?
3 When is it helpful to get feedback from my classmates?

4 Work in pairs again. What can you do after you have checked your work yourself or with a classmate? What things can you plan to do to help you practise or improve? Make a list of ideas together.

redo my work
find extra activities to practise

5 Complete the sentences.

1 I like to assess my own work because ....

2 I find it difficult to assess my own work because ....

3 I can ask a classmate to help me assess my ....

UNIT CHECK

Wordlist

Personality adjectives
bossy
calm
clever
confident
funny
lazy
lively
noisy
rude
serious
shy
sporty

Adjective + preposition collocations
afraid of
bad at
bored with
brilliant at
excited about
fed up with
frightened of
good at
interested in
keen on
terrible at

Adjectives for emotions
happy
pleased
relaxed
stressed

Other
achieve (v)
active (adj)
activity (n)
appear (v)
background (n)
behaviour (n)
follow (v)
hang out with (v)
keep (v)
matching (adj)

member (n)
performance (n)
same (adj)
similar (ad)
stay (v)
try (v)
valley (n)
way (n)

Extra
fight (v)
friendly (adj)
identity (n)
mirror (n)
saucepan (n)
shell (n)
sticker (n)

Vocabulary

1 Choose the correct answers to complete the sentences.

1 You're so .... ! Stop telling me what to do.
   A serious   **B** clever   **C** bossy   **D** lively

2 My cousin's very .... He always gets good marks in his school exams.
   A shy   **B** clever   **C** sporty   **D** bossy

3 Rebecca doesn't speak to many people at parties. She's not very ....
   A confident   **B** funny   **C** rude   **D** quiet

4 My cousins are very .... They never help my aunt do jobs in the house.
   A noisy   **B** calm   **C** lazy   **D** sporty

5 My brother loves telling jokes, but they're never very .... !
   A confident   **B** calm   **C** lazy   **D** funny

6 Why are you always so .... ? Come on, smile!
   A serious   **B** lively   **C** noisy   **D** bossy

7 Helen never says 'please' and 'thank you'. She's very ....
   A lively   **B** rude   **C** confident   **D** shy

8 Our family is very .... We often go swimming or cycling at the weekend.
   A funny   **B** sporty   **C** lively   **D** lazy

9 My dad's always very .... He never gets angry!
   A calm   **B** lazy   **C** bossy   **D** lively

10 She's very .... , so it wasn't easy for her to make new friends when she first moved here.
   A sporty   **B** lively   **C** clever   **D** shy

2 Complete the text message with prepositions. Use the wordlist to help you.

When I first arrived at my language school in Paris, I was really bad [1]............ speaking French. Now, two months later, my French still isn't perfect, but I'm not afraid [2]............ trying! I was also very shy at first, but now I think I'm quite good [3]............ talking to new people. And I love hanging [4]............ with my new French friends. I'm also very interested [5]............ the museums and in finding out more about this beautiful city!

3 🔊 1.8 Complete the conversation with *Adjective + preposition collocations* from the wordlist. Listen and check your answers.

A: I'm really [1].......................... the school trip.

B: Me too. I'm [2].......................... school at the moment – I need a day off!

A: Yes, me too. I seem to be [3].......................... most of my subjects this year.

B: That's rubbish! You're not [4].......................... maths, and you're [5].......................... science – you get great marks!

A: Well, science is the only thing I'm [6].......................... .

B: This school trip will be great for you then – it's the National Science Museum!

19

UNIT CHECK
Review

1 Choose the correct words to complete the sentences.
1. Alice **thinks / is thinking** of travelling to South America this summer.
2. Manu **doesn't see / isn't seeing** his friends every day after school.
3. **Do you understand / Are you understanding** the exercise?
4. I **look / am looking** for my camera but I just can't see it anywhere.
5. We **don't enjoy / aren't enjoying** going to the beach when there are lots of people.
6. Oh no! **It's raining / It rains** and I haven't got my coat.
7. Katie's quiet. **Does she play / Is she playing** a game on the computer?
8. The Year 7 students **learn / are learning** French this year.
9. Kevin **gets / is getting** ready for his birthday party – he's very excited!
10. I **don't know / I'm not knowing** where Kelly is. Why don't you call her?

2 Put the words in the correct order to make sentences.
1. play / now and then / Mark and Hannah / volleyball
2. after school / play / three times a week / I / sport
3. get up early / I / at the weekend / usually
4. go / my friends and I / once a month / to the cinema
5. go / once a year / on holiday / we
6. goes / Anna / most weekends / shopping
7. have lunch / always / we / on Sundays / with our friends
8. go / never / on weekdays / I / to bed late
9. late / Chris / is / for school / often
10. my dad / work / on Fridays / finishes / at 4.00

3 Complete the sentences with the present simple or present continuous form of the verbs in brackets.
1. Neil isn't at school today. He .... (not feel) very well.
2. I .... (not ride) my bike every day.
3. My sister .... (have) blonde hair and blue eyes.
4. That smells really nice! What .... (you/cook)?
5. Amy and Sarah .... (want) to go on holiday to Italy or Spain.
6. Harry .... (live) with his grandparents while his parents are decorating their house.
7. I .... (not understand) this maths problem.
8. Adam and Chris .... (listen) to some music on their phone at the moment.
9. Hurry up! Your friends .... (wait) for you downstairs!
10. We .... (not go) to the cinema very often.

4 🔊 1.9 Choose the correct sentence in each pair. Listen and check your answers.
1. A What? Why are you laughing? What's so funny?
   B What? Why do you laugh? What's so funny?
2. A Do you visit always your grandparents at the weekend?
   B Do you always visit your grandparents at the weekend?
3. A Jason doesn't want to come with us today.
   B Jason isn't wanting to come with us today.
4. A Can you stop that noise? I try to revise for my test.
   B Can you stop that noise? I'm trying to revise for my test.
5. A I don't think that's a very good idea.
   B I'm not thinking that's a very good idea.
6. A What happened? Why does Ella cry?
   B What happened? Why is Ella crying?

5 e Read the advert and for each question, write the correct answer. Write one word for each gap.

A new kind of club

Do you want to do something different after school? Many of you play sports or learn music but we think it's time to start a new club **1** .... helps other people. There are many younger children at the moment who **2** .... trying to read but find it difficult. Are you interested **3** .... helping them? We hope so!

We are looking for students who would like to do this. Just spend one hour **4** .... Wednesdays and read with the children – it's easy! After the 'class', we are **5** .... to have some juice and biscuits and chat. We start next Wednesday in Room 312 at 4 p.m.

At **6** .... moment we are still organising all the chairs and tables we need. Come along and help us!

6 Write a paragraph about how you do and don't enjoy spending your free time.

"Are you a good listener?"

Look at the photo and discuss the questions.
1 How do you prefer to communicate with your friends?
2 When do you and your friends usually talk?
3 What kind of things do you talk about?

Get the message

2

READING
topic: communication
skill: understanding overall meaning
task: signs and notices; multiple choice

GRAMMAR
talking about the past: past simple, past continuous
-ing form

VOCABULARY
language and communication
verb + preposition collocations

LISTENING
topic: a summer camp
skill: predicting information
task: sentence completion

SPEAKING
topic: communicating
skill: organising your description
task: describing a photo

WRITING
topic: mistakes
skill: creating an atmosphere; using strong adjectives and adverbs
task: story

SWITCH ON ▶
video: school interpreters
project: make an information poster

2 Get the message

READING

Power up

1 English is a national language in countries 1–5. Which other language is spoken in each country? Match the countries with the languages (A–E).

1 Canada   A Zulu
2 Ireland   B Inuit
3 New Zealand   C Gaelic
4 South Africa   D Maori
5 Wales   E Welsh

2 Work in pairs and discuss the questions.
1 Think of three good things about speaking a language which few other people speak. Are there any problems?
2 What languages are spoken in your country? Do you know any other countries where those languages are spoken?

Read on

3 Read the texts. What kind of texts are they? What is their purpose?

1

Opportunity for Maori reporter on school paper

Year 10 students with high grades who are interested should contact their teacher.

2

From: **Aisha**   To: **Charlotte**
Subject: **Gaelic article**

Hi Charlotte,
I tried to send this article to your brother, but I've lost his contact details. Could you do it?
Aisha

4 Read the texts in Ex 3 again. For each question, choose the correct answer.
1 What does the notice say about applying to the school newspaper?
  A Students can apply through their teachers.
  B Students that get low marks can apply.
  C The position is available to all students.
2 What does Aisha want her friend to do?
  A pass something on to someone
  B send someone's email address
  C share something in the news with her

5 Read the article on page 23 quickly. Which minority languages are mentioned? Which does the writer speak?

6 Read the exam tip and complete the task.

> **exam tip: multiple choice (long text)**
> Remember that the last question tests the meaning of the whole text.
> How does the article argue that languages with few speakers are important?

7 Read the article again. For each question, choose the correct answer.
1 What does the writer say about English in the first paragraph?
  A It is the most popular language in the world.
  B It is one of several British languages.
  C It will become more important than it is now.
  D It has been replaced by other languages.
2 How did the writer feel about Welsh when he was younger?
  A annoyed about the quality of Welsh programmes
  B angry because he had to translate all the time
  C confused about when to use the two languages
  D disappointed because he had to learn a third language
3 What does the writer say about Gaelic speakers?
  A They find it hard to talk to relatives.
  B Many choose to stop speaking the language.
  C They understand that English matters more.
  D Too few speakers train in the field of education.
4 The writer mentions 'smugglers' Cant'
  A because it was frequently used in the past.
  B to show that languages have already been lost.
  C because it was a good thing that it died out.
  D to suggest how some languages can be saved.
5 What would the writer be most likely to say?
  A Children need to learn languages they can use internationally.
  B There should be more support for languages in danger.
  C English may possibly die out too one day.
  D Entertainment is the best hope for saving languages.

Endangered languages?

English is an international language spoken by an increasing number of people around the world. In many English-speaking countries though, English isn't the only language. In the UK, for example, people speak Welsh, Gaelic and a few other old languages. Because these languages aren't international, people pay less attention to them. So what does this mean for children who grow up speaking them as their mother tongue?

I grew up in Wales. My family spoke English, but the Welsh language was everywhere. When you were driving around Wales, all the road signs were in English and Welsh. As a child, I hated reading everything twice! We had Welsh television programmes too. While everyone in England was watching fashionable American TV shows, we were learning about local farming in Welsh! At secondary school I was dreaming of going to live in Paris, when I realised that instead of Welsh lessons, I needed French lessons. No one spoke Welsh outside Wales. Now I'm older I feel differently. Welsh is a part of my identity and, besides, we have better Welsh TV now!

In parts of Scotland some children grow up in families where grandparents still speak Gaelic. Gaelic has even fewer speakers than Welsh, and few are confident that this part of their culture will survive. It's difficult when English is everywhere else in the country, but teaching subjects in Gaelic in schools helps. However, often there aren't enough Gaelic-speaking teachers. Unless families continue to speak the language at home too, these languages won't survive.

In fact, many old languages are disappearing in the UK. People on the Isle of Man spoke Manx for centuries until the last native speaker died in the twentieth century. The same thing has happened to Cornish. Cant was a language spoken by smugglers who were bringing goods into the country illegally, or travellers and criminals. It allowed them to keep secrets from the police but it too has disappeared. Languages, even if they are spoken by very few people, have a history and culture, and it's a shame to see them go. If we care about saving forests and animals, we should care about saving languages, too.

8 Find words or phrases in the article that have these meanings. The first letter of each word is given.

1. connected with several countries (para 1): i........................
2. grow in size or number (para 1): i........................
3. look or listen carefully (para 1): p........................ a........................
4. popular, especially for a short period of time (para 2): f........................
5. from or happening in the area you live in (para 2): l........................
6. understand or begin to understand something (para 2): r........................
7. become impossible to see or hear any more (para 4): d........................
8. give someone the opportunity to do something (para 4): a........................

Sum up

9 Work in pairs. Talk about:
1. what life was like for the writer as a young child.
2. how the writer's opinions have changed.
3. a thing that might help small languages survive.

> The writer sometimes found the TV shows annoying because …

Speak up

10 Work in two groups. Read the statement below. One group argues for the statement, the other argues against it. Try to think of as many reasons as possible. Take turns to share your ideas.

'We should try and keep all languages alive.'

> In my opinion, languages contain a lot of information about the past. …

> It's expensive to translate everything into two languages. …

There are no specific words that mean 'yes' or 'no' in the Irish language.

2 Get the message

GRAMMAR

1 Read grammar box 1 below and complete the examples with the correct form of these verbs.

dream   grow up   learn   realise   speak   watch

explore grammar 1 → p128

talking about the past

past simple

We use the past simple for finished actions or situations in the past, past habits, regular past events or past actions that happened one after the other.

I **¹**............................ in Wales.
My family **²**............................ English.

past continuous

We use the past continuous to describe actions in progress in the past, especially when another action (past simple) interrupts the first one (past continuous).

While everyone in England **³**............................ fashionable American TV shows, we **⁴**............................ about farming.
I **⁵**............................ of going to live in Paris when I **⁶**............................ that I needed French lessons.

2 ▶ 🔊 **2.1** Watch or listen to people talking about actions in progress. Which of these things do they talk about?

A   what they were doing last night
B   what they were doing when something else happened
C   what they were doing when they met their best friend

3 ▶ 🔊 **2.2** Complete the sentences with the past simple or past continuous form of the verbs in brackets. Watch or listen again and check your answers.

1 Last night at six o'clock I .... (walk) to my nan's house.
2 I .... (clean) my room about a week ago and I .... (get) a phone call from my nan saying that my dog broke his leg.
3 I .... (play) hockey and afterwards I came home and .... (have) some food.
4 I .... (practise) my drama lines for my drama exam and my mum .... (call) me, saying my cousins were coming round this weekend.
5 I .... (be) out shopping with my friend when I .... (hear) there was a sale in my favourite shop.
6 I .... (do) my homework and my auntie .... (ring) to tell us that she had her baby.

4 Read grammar box 2 below. Then read paragraph A in Ex 5 and choose the correct answer for question 1. Why isn't the past continuous form used?

explore grammar 2 → p128

verbs not used in the past continuous

Some verbs, particularly about sensing and knowing (e.g. *know, like, hate, look, hear*) are stative and are not used in the past continuous.

As a child, I **hated** reading everything twice!

5 Choose the correct verb forms to complete the interview. Are there any other examples of stative verbs in the text?

A Where did you go and why?

My grandparents are Mexican, but before this summer, I **¹was not understanding / did not understand** much Spanish. So my brother and I **²were going / went** to my grandparents' house in Mexico to change that.

B How did you learn?

When we arrived, our grandparents **³were waiting / waited** to greet us at the airport in the town of Merida. We didn't use any books to learn Spanish, but we didn't need them. We **⁴were going / went** with our grandmother to the local market every day, where we **⁵were choosing / chose** something tasty for our dinner that day. One day, we **⁶were listening / listened** to Mexican songs on the radio while we **⁷were cooking / cooked** together, and I realised I could understand all the words!

C What did your grandfather teach you?

Most weekends we **⁸were exploring / explored** interesting places around town with my grandad. One day, he **⁹was shutting / shut** the car door on his finger. I **¹⁰was hearing / heard** him say a new word. 'What does that mean, Grandad?' I asked. 'You don't need to know that word,' he told me! I'm not bilingual yet, but I'm good at communicating in Spanish now.

game on

Write one true sentence and one false sentence about last week using the past simple and past continuous. Work in pairs and swap sentences. Can you guess which sentence is true?

In some parts of Mexico, grasshoppers, ant eggs and caterpillars are popular foods.

VOCABULARY
language and communication

1 Work in pairs. What two pieces of advice would you give a student starting to learn English? Why?

2 🔊 2.3 Complete the conversations with these verbs. Listen and check your answers.

> explain   mean   pronounce   repeat
> say   speak   translate   understand

1. **A:** Listen and .... after me: success.
   B: Success.
2. **A:** How do you .... 'difícil' in English?
   B: 'Hard' or 'difficult'.
3. **A:** What does 'challenge' .... ?
   B: Something new, exciting or difficult.
4. **A:** Can anyone .... Italian?
   B: Yes, I can.
5. **A:** How do you .... this word?
   B: P-R-O-U-D. Proud.
6. **A:** Can you .... this word into Turkish?
   B: Yes, that's 'mutlu'.
7. **A:** I don't .... this grammar point.
   B: Don't worry, I can .... it again.

explore **language**

verb + preposition collocations

A listen to, talk to, speak to, explain (something) to someone

Who were you **talking to**?

B talk about, speak about something

They were **talking about** sport.

Note: We say **something** to someone, but **tell** someone something.

3 Read the language box. Choose the correct verb to complete the sentences.

A tell, talk
1. **Tell** / **Talk** us a story.
2. She didn't **tell** / **talk** me the answer.
3. If I have a problem, I **tell** / **talk** to my friends.

B say, speak
4. **Say** / **Speak** the alphabet in English.
5. We **say** / **speak** two languages at home.
6. My sisters **say** / **speak** in very quiet voices.

C hear, listen
7. Please **hear** / **listen** to your teacher.
8. **Hear** / **Listen**! This song is amazing!
9. Can you **hear** / **listen** me now?

4 🅴 Read the blog post. For each question, choose the correct answer.

When in **Rome**, ...

This time last year my dad and I were getting onto a plane to take us from our home in Canada to Italy. My teacher had often **¹**........ us stories about her life when she lived in Rome, and I couldn't wait to experience all that myself. I'd taken Italian lessons, but it was difficult to **²**........ notices and things into English because they used so many words I didn't know. I spent ages preparing questions, but whenever they gave the answers or **³**........ their ideas, it just came out so fast!

Fortunately, the hotel staff could **⁴**........ both Italian and English, and they helped us a lot. In fact, I found it easier to **⁵**........ to them than other people in Italy. One day, my dad hired a car and we were driving around. We stopped at the red light, but all the cars behind started beeping at us. My dad was getting really upset. Eventually, the driver behind came up to **⁶**........ to my dad. 'Signore,' he said, very politely, 'In Italy the red lights are more of a suggestion than a rule!'

1	**A** spoken	**B** said	**C** told	**D** explained
2	**A** talk	**B** mean	**C** listen	**D** translate
3	**A** explained	**B** spoke	**C** understood	**D** pronounced
4	**A** tell	**B** say	**C** speak	**D** talk
5	**A** say	**B** talk	**C** hear	**D** listen
6	**A** pronounce	**B** speak	**C** translate	**D** tell

Speak up

5 Which English speaking country would you like to visit? Why? What would you do there?

game on

Work in pairs. Take turns to say a verb from Ex 2 or 3. Your partner makes a sentence with the verb. Which verbs don't collocate with *to*?

Listen.   You never listen to me.

Our Italian holiday car! 😍

2 Get the message

LISTENING

Power up

1 Do you think these are good ways to learn something new? Why/Why not? Which one would you prefer?

do a course   get an app   look online   read books
talk to other people   watch someone else

Listen up

2 🔊 2.4 Listen to Rick talking about a camp he went to last summer. What type of camp was it?

3 Read the exam tip and complete the task.

> **exam tip: gap fill**
>
> Predicting the word before you listen (e.g. The last date = a day) will help you to focus.
>
> Look at the sentences below. What kind of word is missing in each gap (a number, a place, etc.)?

Rick's SUMMER APP CAMP

The last date Rick could apply for App Camp was ¹................. .

Rick joined the app course for ²................. .

Rick's app is called ³................. .

Rick got the idea for his app when he was arranging a ⁴................. .

Rick's app came in second place and he won a ⁵................. .

As part of the course, Rick's group visited a museum of ⁶................. .

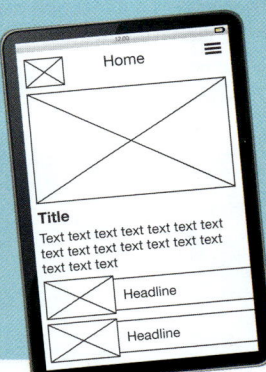

4 e 🔊 2.5 Listen to the rest of Rick's talk and complete the sentences in Ex 3. Write one or two words or a number or a date.

5 🔊 2.6 Listen again and check your answers.

explore grammar → p128

-ing form

We use the *-ing* form:

A as the subject or object of a sentence.
   Applying takes time – it's a popular camp.

B after prepositions.
   You don't end **up forgetting** to text someone.

6 Read the grammar box and complete the app reviews with the *-ing* form of these verbs.

celebrate   choose   code   eat   learn
make   recommend   waste

The best apps out there

StudyFriends
Working with other students on projects lets you get to know their work pretty quickly. If you like ¹................. other people's success, the StudyFriends app lets you do just that! ²................. a co-student couldn't be easier and you can let everyone else know just how wonderful they are!

Yeti Monster
³................. is one of the most useful skills out there. ⁴................. to write your own code is simple with the Yeti developer's kit. It lets students of all ages create their own apps. This app will save you from ⁵................. time on typical mistakes.

HealthMap
⁶................. the right choices for your health can be difficult in your teens. With this app, ⁷................. the healthiest options is easy – just scan any barcode and the app will tell you the calorie count and other information about the food you are planning on ⁸................. .

Speak up

7 Work in pairs. Imagine you went to a specific kind of summer camp (e.g. a performing arts camp or a sports camp). Take turns to interview your partner about your experiences at the camp.

I usually call my friends at 12.59. I like to have a bit of one-to-one time!

SPEAKING

Power up

1 Which of these people do you speak to most days? Which do you never speak to? Why?/Why not?

> best friend   bus drivers   other people in queues
> people on public transport   shop assistants   teachers

2 Work in pairs. Choose one of the topics below (1–3) to talk about for thirty seconds. Use these question words to help you plan your answer. Make notes before you start.

> who   what   where   when   why

1 someone you see every day but never say hello to
2 the person you find it easiest to talk to about problems
3 someone you would like to speak to one day

explore language

describing a photo

giving an introduction
I think this photo shows a typical scene in a …

introducing the people
There are three people in this photo, and a few others in the background.

saying where the photo was taken
I guess that this photo was taken in (a shop/street) because of all the (objects/buildings) around the people.

saying what the people are doing
The woman is definitely (buying something) because …
I'm pretty sure that the man (is lost) because …

3 Read the language box. Work in pairs to talk about photo A for one minute. Make notes before you start.

1 Where are they? How do you know?
  ....
2 What objects can you see? What adjectives describe them?
  ....
3 What do the people in the photo look like? What adjectives describe them?
  ....
4 What are they wearing? What are they doing?
  ....

4 🔊 2.7 Read the exam tip and complete the task.

exam tip: describing a photo ➔ p147

Remember that you need to speak for one minute. If it helps, use fifteen seconds to:
1 introduce the idea.
2 describe the place.
3 say what the people look like.
4 say what the people are doing.

Listen to a student describing photo A. What else could she talk about to fill the sixty seconds?

Speak up

5 e Work in pairs. Student A, turn to page 156. Student B, look at photo B on this page. Follow these steps.
  1 Take turns to describe your photos in approximately one minute.
  2 Time your partner as you listen. Did he/she speak for one minute? If not, what else could he/she talk about? Look at your notes from Ex 2.

Speaking extra

6 Tell the class about a conversation you had with someone you didn't know. What were you doing? What happened?

2 Get the message

WRITING

Power up

1 Have you ever said something funny when you didn't mean to? Why was it funny?

2 Work in pairs. Read the student mistakes. Can you correct them?

1 I never used to like olives but now they are starting to grow in me.

2 Being a shop assistant is hard. You have to smell all the time.

3 First, cut all the vegetarians into small pieces.

4 On Sundays we often have lunch or suffer with my grandparents.

5 Put the flower and eggs in a bowl and add some water.

6 I never buy recipe books, I borrow them from the bookshop.

7 What is your favourite plate to eat at a restaurant?

3 Look at the situations in Ex 2 again. What were the students trying to say? What did they actually say?

4 Have any of these things happened to you when you were speaking in another language? Where were you when it happened? What were you doing?
- You forget a word.
- You go red.
- You panic and say nothing.
- You say the wrong word.

5 Which tense do we use:
1 when we talk about the main events in a story?
2 to say what we were doing at a certain time in the past?

6 Complete the story with the past simple or past continuous form of the verbs in brackets.

Sunday roast?

Last year I ¹.................... (stay) with a wonderful family in England. The mum was really kind and ².................... (cook) brilliant food. One day we ³.................... (eat) a traditional Sunday lunch of roast chicken with potatoes and vegetables, and a brown sauce called 'gravy'. It was delicious. While we ⁴.................... (eat), I ⁵.................... (try) to make conversation and said, 'This kitchen is really good'. Everyone looked surprised. 'It's old now,' said the mum. 'My husband ⁶.................... (do) it a few years ago.' Then I ⁷.................... (realise) the word I wanted to say was 'chicken'. I always confuse 'kitchen' and 'chicken' because they sound alike. When they finally understood, they all ⁸.................... (laugh).

'False friend': a word in a foreign language that is similar to one in your own, but doesn't mean the same thing.

7 Read the language box. Then find strong adjectives and adverbs in the story in Ex 6.

> ### explore language
>
> **strong adjectives and adverbs**
>
> We use strong adjectives to make our writing more interesting.
>
> awful   brilliant   delicious   disgusting   fantastic
> furious   hilarious   huge   terrible   wonderful
>
> We can also use an adverb to make an adjective stronger.
>
> **really** kind   **very** big   **extremely** dangerous
>
> We don't use *very* or *extremely* with strong adjectives. We use *absolutely*.
>
> ~~very fantastic~~   **absolutely** fantastic
> ~~extremely brilliant~~   **absolutely** brilliant

8 Find words in the sentences that can be replaced with these words.

> delicious   disgusting   fantastic   furious   hilarious   huge

1. The film was very funny. We laughed all the way through it.
2. The pasta was very bad because I cooked it for too long!
3. I took a tour around the Hollywood stars' homes – they were really big.
4. My brother was very angry when I broke his new phone.
5. Our holiday was really good. I didn't want to come home!
6. This soup is very good. Did you make it?

9 Work in new pairs. Retell your story from Ex 4, using a range of past tenses and strong adjectives. Did it sound different? How?

Plan on

10 Read the writing task below and answer the questions.

1. Where must the sentence given in the task come in your story?
2. How many words do you need to write?
3. Who are you writing for?

> Your English teacher has asked you to write a story. Your story must begin with this sentence:
>
> > 'I glanced around and everyone in the room was looking at me.'
>
> Write your **story** in about **100 words**.

> ### exam tip: story ➡ p154
>
> Are you writing a story? First, think of an idea that could follow the sentence given in the task (e.g. Why were they looking at you?). Then plan it (e.g. When? Where? Who? What happened in the end? What past tenses can you use?).

11 Read the exam tip. Then read the ideas for sentences that could follow the one given in the writing task. How could the story develop? Use the exam tip to help you.

1. I was speaking English in the classroom and made a big mistake.
2. I was singing in a school concert when I forgot the words.
3. I was giving a class presentation and the electricity went off.

12 Choose an idea from Ex 11. Answer the questions to plan your answer.

1. When did it happen?
2. Where did it happen?
3. Who was there?
4. What was the main action?
5. What happened in the end?

Write on

13 e Write your story in about 100 words.

Improve it

14 Read your story and follow these steps to improve it.

1. Find the adjectives. Can you think of a place to add two more?
2. Can you improve on any of the adjectives (e.g. nice → delicious, big → huge, good → amazing/fascinating)?
3. Check the past tenses. Did you use the past simple and past continuous? If not, can you find a place to put them both in?

SWITCH ON ▶

School interpreters

1 Work in pairs and discuss your favourite words in English. Why do you like them? Is it because of what they mean, how they sound or because you think they are funny?

2 Work in pairs and follow these steps.
  1 Choose an English word from a dictionary (that nobody in your class will know).
  2 Write one wrong definition and the real definition.
  3 Show your word and your definitions to another pair. Can they guess which one is correct?

3 ▶ Watch the clip. What are the benefits of learning to be an interpreter?

4 ▶ Watch again and answer the questions.
  1 How many different nationalities live in London?
  2 Where is Konstantin from?
  3 Why does Konstantin like being an interpreter?
  4 Why does Dagmara think learning to be an interpreter is a good thing?

Project

5 Work in pairs to create an information poster for a new student at your school. Follow these steps.
  1 Talk about these things and make notes.
    • places you need to show them
    • people they need to meet (teachers, fellow students, etc.)
    • helpful information about your school
    • something funny that has happened at school
  2 Create your poster. Make it as detailed as possible. Add a map and route around the school and information from your notes.
  3 Share your posters and vote for the best one.

INDEPENDENT LEARNING

Setting goals

1 Read what four students say about their learning goals. Which student do you think will be more successful? Why? What can each student do to achieve these goals?
  1 'I want to get better.'
  2 'I need to learn ten new irregular past verbs by next week.'
  3 'I want to learn new words.'
  4 'I want to be able to comfortably speak for one minute.'

2 Read the statements below. Do you agree with them? Mark each one (1–6). Then work in pairs and discuss your answers.

1 = strongly agree	4 = slightly disagree
2 = agree	5 = disagree
3 = slightly agree	6 = strongly disagree

3 Work in pairs again and make a list of things you would like to improve in your English.

  1 It's enough to do the homework the teacher sets. ....
  2 If I work on things I find difficult, I'll get better. ....
  3 I know where I need to practise more. ....
  4 I know what to do to find help to improve. ....
  5 I will easily see if I've improved or not. ....

Why would you like to improve those things?

I would like to improve my vocabulary so I don't always use the same words.

4 Set two goals for yourself. Think about what you find difficult at the moment. How will you try to improve? How will you check that you are making progress?
  1 I want to ....
    I will do this by ....
  2 By the end of next month, I want to
    ....
    I will do this by ....

UNIT CHECK

Wordlist

Language and communication
explain (v)
hear (v)
listen (v)
mean (v)
pronounce (v)
repeat (v)
say (v)
speak (v)
talk (v)
tell (v)
translate (v)
understand (v)

Strong adjectives and adverbs
awful (adj)
brilliant (adj)
delicious (adj)
disgusting (adj)
extremely (dangerous/kind/etc.) (adv)
fantastic (adj)
furious (adj)
hilarious (adj)
huge (adj)
really (dangerous/kind/etc.) (adv)
terrible (adj)
wonderful (adj)

Other
allow (v)
app (n)
celebrate (v)
choose (v)
code (v)
disappear (v)
do a course (phr)
dream (v)
fashionable (adj)
grow up (phr v)
increase (v)
international (adj)
local (adj)
look online (phr)

pay attention (phr)
realise (v)
recommend (v)

Extra
criminal (n)
culture (n)
go red (phr)
make conversation (phr)
panic (v)
say nothing (phr)
smuggler (n)
survive (v)

Vocabulary

1 Complete the sentences with words from the *Language and communication* section of the wordlist in the correct form.

1 I really need someone to .... the meaning of this word to me.
2 I don't like it when people .... really quickly. I can't understand what they're saying.
3 My history teacher used to .... us jokes all the time.
4 The quality of the recording was really bad. I couldn't .... what the people were .... about.
5 When people .... unkind things, they don't always .... them.

2 Match 1–6 with A–F to make sentences.

1 I translated the word 'sugar' as 'salt'. The cake I made was absolutely
2 I was passing notes under the table to my friend and the teacher was really
3 Talking to people you don't know online can be extremely
4 The awful joke my brother sent was absolutely
5 My pen pal is really
6 I couldn't stop laughing. That meme you sent was

A terrible. Not even a five-year-old would find it funny.
B furious with me.
C brilliant. She's passed all her exams with top grades!
D dangerous, so it's best to stick to people you know.
E hilarious, especially the cat!
F disgusting. That'll teach me!

3 🔊 2.8 Listen to six sentences. When you hear the beep, write the correct word from the *Other* section of the wordlist.

1 .... 4 ....
2 .... 5 ....
3 .... 6 ....

4 🔊 2.9 Listen and check your answers.

5 The verbs in bold are in the wrong sentences. Put each verb in the correct sentence.

1 How do you usually **recommend** your birthday? Do you have a party? ....
2 We want to take our cousins out to dinner. Can you **translate** a good restaurant? ....
3 Stop talking and **do** attention to what I'm saying! It's important! ....
4 I'm sorry, I didn't hear the question. Can you **choose** it, please? ....
5 I know what the word means but I can't say it! How do you **repeat** it? ....
6 Mike doesn't speak German, so he asked me to **celebrate** the letter into English for him. ....
7 My dad's painting all the walls yellow, but I'm going to **pronounce** a different colour for my room. I don't like yellow very much. ....
8 I want to learn how to design apps, so I'm going to **pay** a course in the summer. ....

31

UNIT CHECK
Review

1 Choose the correct words to complete the sentences.
1. While my sister **finished / was finishing** her homework, I **put / was putting** the dishes away.
2. My mum **helped / was helping** me to find a website after I **asked / was asking** her.
3. The TV documentary **came / was coming** to an end while I **slept / was sleeping**.
4. I **take / was taking** notes while I **watched / was watching** the programme on TV.
5. I **thought / was thinking** that the homework **seemed / was seeming** quite easy.
6. This time last year I **studied / was studying** at a Spanish school and I **lived / was living** in Valencia.
7. I **broke / was breaking** my watch while I **played / was playing** tennis.
8. My brother **played / was playing** his drums while I **tried / was trying** to study for my French exam!

2 Read the answers and complete the questions.
1. A: .... last night?
   B: Yes, I was studying at 8 o'clock.
2. A: .... the film?
   B: No, I didn't like the film at all.
3. A: .... the football match last night?
   B: Yes, we were watching the football match together.
4. A: .... yesterday?
   B: No, I didn't go out. I wasn't feeling very well.
5. A: .... at six o'clock?
   B: Of course I was sleeping! I got up at nine.
6. A: .... this morning?
   B: No, she didn't call me because she didn't have my number.

3 Write these verbs in the correct group.

believe   feel (cold or hot)   feel (= think)   have (a pet)
have (dinner)   like   look forward to   own   stop   take
think (about a problem)   think (= have an opinion)   want   watch

state	action

4 Complete the joke with the past simple or past continuous form of the verbs in brackets.

Daniel ¹.......................... (drive) through Dublin when he ².......................... (lose) his way. A woman ³.......................... (walk) along the street, so Daniel ⁴.......................... (get out) of the car and ⁵.......................... (speak) to the woman.

'Excuse me,' he ⁶.......................... (say), 'Can you tell me the quickest way to get to Cork?'

The woman ⁷.......................... (look) at Daniel and ⁸.......................... (ask), 'Are you on foot or in the car?'

'In the car,' Daniel replied.

The woman ⁹.......................... (smile). 'Ah well, that will be the quickest way to get there.'

And then she ¹⁰.......................... (walk) off.

5 🔊 2.10 Listen and check your answers. Do you understand the joke?

6 e Read the article and for each question, write the correct answer. Write one word for each gap.

Lost in translation?

Some conversations are hard. You've upset a friend. Someone has posted unpleasant comments about you online. Before starting any conversation in situations like these, there are a ¹.......................... things you should think about. Start by asking yourself ².......................... the worst part is. The conversation might not be as bad as you ³.......................... expecting. You don't always have to be right. Sometimes it's more important to stay friends. Then choose the right time to speak. It helps to make sure the other person is in a good mood, particularly ⁴.......................... your conversation is about something personal. Avoid using words like 'you', which can make you look angry, and don't focus ⁵.......................... complaints that are connected to other things. Finally, ⁶.......................... you are listening, remember that we all feel hurt and fear differently. Just because you feel fine doesn't mean others do too.

7 Write a blog post giving young people advice on how to communicate better.

"Technology is about people."

Look at the photo and discuss the questions.
1. What can you see in the photo? What does it do?
2. What's the most important piece of technology that you use? Why?
3. Does technology help or stop you connecting to the world? How?

The future is now

3

READING
topic: the future of music
skill: skim-reading a text
task: gapped text

GRAMMAR
talking about the future: *will*, *going to*, present continuous, present simple
modal verbs for advice and suggestions

VOCABULARY
technology in the home
phrasal verbs

LISTENING
topic: buying something new
skill: identifying differences
task: multiple choice (pictures)

SPEAKING
topic: the future of technology
skill: giving and asking for opinions, agreeing and disagreeing
task: collaborative task and discussion

WRITING
topic: living without technology
skill: giving advice and making suggestions
task: email

SWITCH ON ▶
video: app entrepreneurs
project: design an app

3 The future is now

READING

Power up

1 Work in pairs and discuss the questions.
1 What kind of music do you usually listen to?
2 Where do you get that music from?
3 How do you prefer to listen to music?

2 Work in pairs. Read the title of the article and discuss the questions.
1 What's the topic of the article?
2 What do you think it might say about these things?
- access to music
- music format (e.g. CDs, mp3)
- listening to music
- music concerts
- music videos
- writing music

Read on

3 Read the exam tip and complete the task.

> **exam tip: gapped text**
> Read the text quickly to understand what it's about. It will help you complete the task. You can:
> - move your eyes left to right and down quickly to pick out key words (e.g. verbs and nouns).
> - read the first line of each paragraph.
>
> Read the article quickly using one of the ideas above. Which things from Ex 2 does the article mention?

4 e Read the article again. Five sentences have been removed from the article. For each question, choose the correct answer. There are three extra sentences which you do not need to use.

A Users can take things away if they like.
B However, a few bands are trying them out at a festival next month.
C All of these things are great ideas.
D It won't be able to do it alone though.
E They store music, play it and record it.
F But none of those things came true.
G If musicians need help with this, I'll do it.
H The technology will also stop those people from sending the music to others.

5 Find words or phrases in the article that have these meanings. Are they adjectives, adverbs, verbs or nouns?
1 seen at the same time it is happening (e.g. music) (para 2): ....
2 happening often (para 2): ....
3 getting the result you want (para 2): ....
4 without anything or anyone else coming in between (para 3): ....
5 make (para 4): ....
6 say that something will happen before it happens (para 5): ....
7 a group of musicians (para 5): ....
8 so good that you can't believe it (para 5): ....

Sum up

6 Work in pairs. Explain in your own words how the article suggests these things will change the way we make or listen to music.
- virtual reality
- file-sharing technology
- intelligent machines

Speak up

7 Work in pairs. Which changes in the article do you think would be good? Which wouldn't? Why?

8 What other changes in music would you like to see? Make a list of ideas. Present your best idea to the class.

34   Did you know that people who play a musical instrument develop bigger, better connected brains?

The future of music

Changing technology gives us new ways to record and play music. Twenty years ago, musicians typically made music in recording studios and we listened to it on CDs. A few years later, more musicians used their laptops and we used MP3 players to listen. Now everyone can use smartphones. [1]............................ So, how will technology change the music industry in the future?

Music videos are a great way to tell a story about a song. In future, we'll watch music videos in virtual reality and be a part of that story. We'll also regularly watch live virtual reality concerts from our own homes. We'll put on our headset just before the concert starts and be ready to go. Virtual reality concerts might not be common at the moment. [2]............................ If successful, these concerts are likely to become very popular.

Musicians are always looking for new ways to connect with listeners of their music. New technology, known as a 'block chain', will allow musicians to share new songs directly with fans. [3]............................ This means musicians will no longer lose money through file sharing. Some artists are going to try out this technology soon.

Finally, we won't only listen to music made by humans. It'll be possible for a machine to learn how to write songs too. [4]............................ It'll need us to help it so it'll be a team activity. Humans and machines will work together to produce, hopefully, great music.

Of course, the great thing about the future is that none of us really knows what will happen. In the past, people predicted no more guitar bands, no more rock music and no more radio. [5]............................ What we do know about the future is that, with all these incredible developments in technology, music's going to be exciting!

3 The future is now

GRAMMAR

1 Read the grammar box. Match the future forms in bold in the sentences (1–6) with the uses (A–F).

1 In future, we'**ll watch** music videos in VR.
2 We'll put our virtual reality headset on just before the concert **starts**.
3 A few bands **are trying** them out next month.
4 Some artists **are going to try out** this technology.
5 If musicians need help with this, I'**ll do** it.
6 What we know is that, with developments in technology, music'**s going to be** exciting.

explore grammar → p130

talking about the future

will

We use *will*:

A for predictions based on our personal opinions.
   I think the music I like **will change** in future.

B for offers and immediate decisions.
   Don't worry, I'**ll lend** you some money for the concert ticket.
   It's quiet in here. I'**ll put** some music on.

going to

We use *going to*:

C for intentions or things we're planning (but we haven't decided the details yet).
   The boys **are going to start** their own band.

D for predictions based on outside information.
   You don't like rap, so you **aren't going to like** this song.

present continuous

E We use the present continuous for arrangements with other people (we've agreed when, where etc.).
   I'**m meeting** Abi at the concert at 8 p.m.

present simple

F We use the present simple for scheduled or timetabled events.
   The concert **finishes** late tonight.

2 3.1 Watch or listen to people talking about the future. Match the speakers (1–9) with the question they are answering (A–C). One speaker can be used more than once.

A What are your plans for this evening? .... / .... / .... / .... / ....
B How do you think the way you listen to music will change in the future? .... / ....
C How do you think your musical tastes will change in the future? .... / .... / ....

3 3.2 Choose the most appropriate future form to complete the sentences. Watch or listen again and check your answers.

1 In the future I think people **are listening** / **will listen** to music the same way as they do now.
2 I listen to pop music but in the future I think it **will change** / **changes** to opera.
3 I'm not sure, so **I probably** / **I'll probably** watch TV with my family.
4 I don't think my music taste **is changing** / **will change**.
5 I think I **will change** / **change** my style of music in the future.
6 I'**m meeting** / **I'll meet** my uncle for lunch and **we'll go** / **we're going** to a Turkish restaurant.
7 I think more people **are starting** / **will start** listening to vinyls again.
8 Tonight I **go** / **am going to go** out with my friends to the cinema.
9 I **meet** / **I'm meeting** a friend for lunch in town.
10 Tonight **I'll iron** / **I'm going to iron** my clothes.

4 Read the article. Choose the correct verb forms to complete it.

A NEW TYPE OF ROCK STAR

On Friday, rock star Hatsune Miku ¹**start** / **starts** a tour of Japan, where she'll sing and dance. Thousands of fans ²**are** / **is** going to her concerts. ³**They'll** / **They won't** scream and call her name because they love her. This doesn't sound unusual for rock concerts, but it is, because Miku isn't real. She's a hologram, which is created by a computer program. Because the technology is possible now, experts believe more concerts like this ⁴**are** / **aren't** going to take place in future. Miku isn't ⁵**go** / **going to go** away any time soon and it's likely that new holograms will ⁶**come** / **to come** along and be even more popular than her in future.

Speak up

5 Work in pairs. Tell your partner about these things. He/She asks questions to find out more about your sentences.

1 something you'll offer to do for your parents tonight
2 an arrangement you have for the next few days
3 something you intend to do in the near future
4 a prediction about the next year

> I'll probably do the washing-up after dinner.

> Will you do it on your own or will someone help you?

VOCABULARY
technology in the home

1 Match these words with the photos (A–H).

coffee maker   dishwasher   fridge-freezer
kettle   microwave   remote control
smart TV   washing machine

2 🔊 3.3 Listen and match the sounds (1–6) with six of the photos in Ex 1 (A–H).

3 Match the phrasal verbs in bold with their meanings (A–H).
1 I never remember to **switch** lights **off** when I leave a room.
2 The electricity at home **goes off** during bad weather.
3 My parents often ask me to **turn** the TV **down**.
4 As soon as I wake up, I **switch** my phone **on** and check it.
5 When I need to **set up** a program on my computer, I ask someone else for help.
6 I **turn** the volume **up** when heavy metal comes on.
7 I **plug** my phone **in** at a coffee shop when my battery's low.
8 I never **shut** my laptop **down**. It's on all the time.

A start a light/machine working
B make the sound quieter
C connect equipment to electricity
D stop a light/machine working
E make the sound louder
F make something ready to use
G close a computer/program
H stop working

explore language

phrasal verbs

Some phrasal verbs can be separated.

Turn on the light.   **Turn** the light **on**.

When we use a pronoun, it must come between the verb and particle.

Plug it in first.   **Shut it down** now.

Some phrasal verbs cannot be separated.
The lights just **went off** for no reason.

4 Read the language box. Which phrasal verbs in Ex 3 can be separated?

5 Work in pairs. Are the sentences in Ex 3 true for you? Discuss.

> I never remember to switch off lights. My mum gets annoyed with me.

6 🇪 Read the article. For each question, choose the correct answer.

How **smart** is your home?

Smart homes have arrived. We say, '¹...... on the central heating,' and the room starts to get warmer. We tap a button on our mobile and our kettle boils. We tap another button and the air conditioning ²...... off. So, what's the future for smart home technology? Well, first we need to be able to ³...... all of our machines at home to one remote control. That will make it easier for us to ⁴...... up our machines so that they're ready to use and manage.

The machines in our houses are becoming more ⁵...... so that we use less energy and save money. In the future, this is going to happen more. Perhaps your TV will switch off when it senses you have fallen asleep in the future. Imagine that! However, there are some possible ⁶...... . For example, with our whole home online, we'll need to think hard about our security.

1 A Get   B Switch   C Try   D Keep
2 A goes   B puts   C takes   D gets
3 A tie   B start   C install   D connect
4 A fill   B set   C end   D pick
5 A efficient   B expensive   C relaxed   D hard
6 A topics   B discussions   C issues   D opinions

game on

Work in pairs. Take turns to draw a picture explaining one of the words or phrasal verbs on the page. Can your partner guess the word or phrasal verb?

Items like fridges, freezers, dishwashers and washing machines are known as 'white goods' in English.

3 The future is now

LISTENING

Power up

1 Which item from question 1 in Ex 3 would you buy? Why?

Listen up

2 Read the exam tip and complete the task.

3 🔊 3.4 Listen and for each question, choose the correct answer.

1 What does the girl decide to buy?
  A   B   C

2 What has a music player in it?
  A   B   C

3 Which book would the girl like?
  A   B   C

4 What app does the boy decide to download?
  A   B   C

5 What does the boy want?
  A   B   C

6 Which of the boy's things has stopped working?
  A   B   C

7 What does the girl collect these days?
  A   B   C

> **exam tip: multiple choice (pictures)**
> Before you listen, read the questions, identify what's in the pictures and predict words you might hear in the recording.
> Read question 1 in Ex 3. What is this conversation about? What words might you hear?

4 🔊 3.5 Listen again and check your answers.

5 Read the grammar box. Which phrase is followed by a different verb form to the others?

> **explore grammar** ➙ p130
>
> **advice and suggestions**
>
> We use *should* and *ought to* + infinitive for advice.
> What **should** I **buy**?
> He **should get** a new mobile.
> You **ought to get** a tablet.
>
> To make a suggestion, we use *why don't you/we* + infinitive, *how about* + noun/-ing or *you could* + infinitive.
> **Why don't you charge** your phone now?
> **How about downloading** this one?
> **You could upload** a photo of us.
>
> We use *shall I/we* + infinitive for offers and suggestions.
> **Shall I ask** her?   **Shall we watch** TV?

6 Complete the conversation with one or two words in each gap.

A: What kind of phone ¹_____ I buy?
B: You ²_____ buy something older. It might not even charge properly!
A: How about this one? It's got a good camera.
B: Great! You ³_____ make films on it!
A: Yes, that's true.
B: But maybe you ⁴_____ to think about it for a while. Why ⁵_____ you read some reviews?
B: Good idea. I could look online.
A: I'm good at research. ⁶_____ I help you?
B: Yes, that'd be great.

Speak up

7 Work in pairs and do this roleplay.

Student A: You want to buy a mobile but you don't know which one to buy. Ask Student B for some advice.
Student B: Student A wants to buy a mobile. Help him/her with some ideas.

SPEAKING

Power up

1 Work in pairs and discuss the questions.
1 If you had a robot, what would you like it to do for you?
2 Which of these words would you use to describe your imaginary robot? Why?

calm   convenient   creative   human
intelligent   time   trust   useful

Speak up

2 🔊 3.6 Listen to two people talking about different robots. What types of robots do they talk about? Which one do they think would be the most useful? Why?

3 🔊 3.7 Listen again and complete the extracts from the conversation.
1 **A:** In my ...., the robot pet would be useful. People could play with it.
   B: That's .... but it's not the same as a real pet.
2 **B:** In my ...., you couldn't really love a robot pet.
   A: I .... I think that a lot of robots are very cute.
3 **B:** What's your view .... the robot doctor?
   A: I don't think this would be a good idea. You couldn't trust it.
   B: I'm not ....
4 **A:** It could only check our bodies. I'd .... that's a problem.
   B: That's a .... point.
5 **A:** .... me, a robot that cleans my room would be really useful.
   B: You're ....

4 Read the useful language and add phrases from Ex 3 to each group.

useful language

giving opinions	asking for opinions
I think (that)	What do you think?
agreeing	**disagreeing**
I agree.	I can't agree.
That's right.	OK, but …

5 Read the exam tip and complete the task.

exam tip: → p148, p149
collaborative task and discussion

Listen carefully to what your partner says and respond before you give your own ideas.

Work in pairs. Choose three phrases from the useful language and give examples of how to use them.

6 e Work in pairs. Turn to page 158 and complete the task. Use as many phrases from the useful language as possible.

7 e Work in pairs and discuss the questions.
1 Would you like more technology in your life? Why/Why not?
2 Which do you think would be more useful: a robot to clean your room or a robot to do your homework? Why?
3 What's the best technology for watching a film? Why?
4 What do you think is most interesting about the internet? Why?

Speaking extra

8 Work in two groups. Read the comments below and discuss them. Persuade the other group to agree with you, giving reasons.

Group A: Think of reasons why the situations are good.
Group B: Think of reasons why the situations are bad.

- Robots will improve our lives.
- It won't be necessary to learn how to write with a pen.
- Children will learn faster and better from a computer at home.
- No one will need to learn how to drive.

The first industrial robot was created in the 1950s and was called Unimate.

3 The future is now

WRITING

Power up

1 Work in pairs. Read the notice and answer the questions.
1. Do you think it's a good idea?
2. Would you like to do it? Why/Why not?
3. How would you feel if you had to give these things up?

National Unplugged Day

This year's 'Unplugged' Day will be on Friday 22 November.

Each person gives up a gadget for the whole day.

What are **you** going to give up: your mobile phone, tablet, TV, games console or something else?

Plan on

2 Read Jamie's email to Mia and Mia's notes. Why is Jamie writing? What four things does Mia need to say in her reply?

From: Jamie **To: Mia**

Hi!

Sorry I didn't email last week. I had a terrible cold and was in bed all weekend. I feel much better now though. ← *show pity*

So, it's National 'Unplugged' Day in two weeks. I'm going to try and give something up. Which do you think is easier: giving up a phone or a games console for the whole day? And what will I do with my time instead? ← *say which one* / *suggest ideas*

What are you going to give up? ← *tell Jamie*

Jamie

3 Read Mia's reply. Does she include all four points from the notes?

From: Mia **To: Jamie**

Hi Jamie,

Sorry to hear you were ill but ¹I'm glad you're feeling OK now.

²I think you ought to give up your games console for National 'Unplugged' Day. You only use it for a couple of hours after school, so I don't think it'll be too difficult. ³You could go out to the park instead. ⁴How about organising a volleyball match with some friends or something? I'm sure they'd enjoy that.

I'm going to give up my tablet. It's going to be difficult ⁵because I use it to chat with my friends but I think I should try it. Hopefully, I can do it. After all, it's just one day!

Mia

4 Read Mia's reply again and answer the questions.
1. When Mia includes the information from her notes, does she include only that information or does she say a little more about it?
2. How many paragraphs are there in the email?
3. What is the purpose of each paragraph?
4. Is the email formal or informal? How do you know?

5 Which three highlighted phrases in Mia's email give advice or make a suggestion? What is the purpose of the other two?

> **exam tip: email** ➜ p150
> Use a variety of appropriate phrases in your email, e.g. phrases for giving advice or making suggestions. Avoid repeating the same one(s).

6 Read the exam tip. Then use these prompts to suggest five more activities that Jamie could do instead of playing on his games console.
1. You should …
2. You ought to …
3. Why don't you … ?
4. You could …
5. How about … ?

7 Work in pairs. Read Greg's email and discuss the questions.
1. Which gadget should Greg give up? Why?
2. What are you going to give up? Why?
3. Will it be easy or difficult? Why?

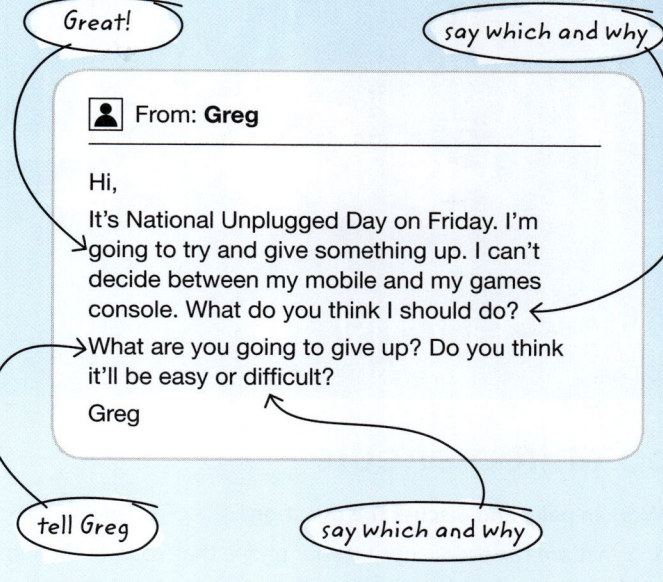

(Great!)
(say which and why)

> **From: Greg**
>
> Hi,
> It's National Unplugged Day on Friday. I'm going to try and give something up. I can't decide between my mobile and my games console. What do you think I should do?
> What are you going to give up? Do you think it'll be easy or difficult?
> Greg

(tell Greg)
(say which and why)

8 Plan your reply to Greg. Decide:
- what information to give about each of the four notes.
- how many paragraphs to include.
- the purpose of each paragraph.
- what phrases to use to give advice and/or make a suggestion to Greg.

Write on

9 **e** Write your reply to Greg in about 100 words. Include all the information in the notes in Ex 7. Follow your plan from Ex 8.

Improve it

10 Read your email and answer the questions.
1. Does it include all the information in the notes? Did you add a little more information to each one?
2. Did you organise your ideas clearly into paragraphs?
3. Did you use a variety of appropriate phrases for advice and suggestions?

11 Use your answers to Ex 10 to improve your email. Write it out again if necessary.

12 Read your email one final time. Look for other errors (e.g. grammar, spelling and punctuation). Correct them.

'Experience is one thing you can't get for nothing.' (Oscar Wilde, Irish author)

SWITCH ON

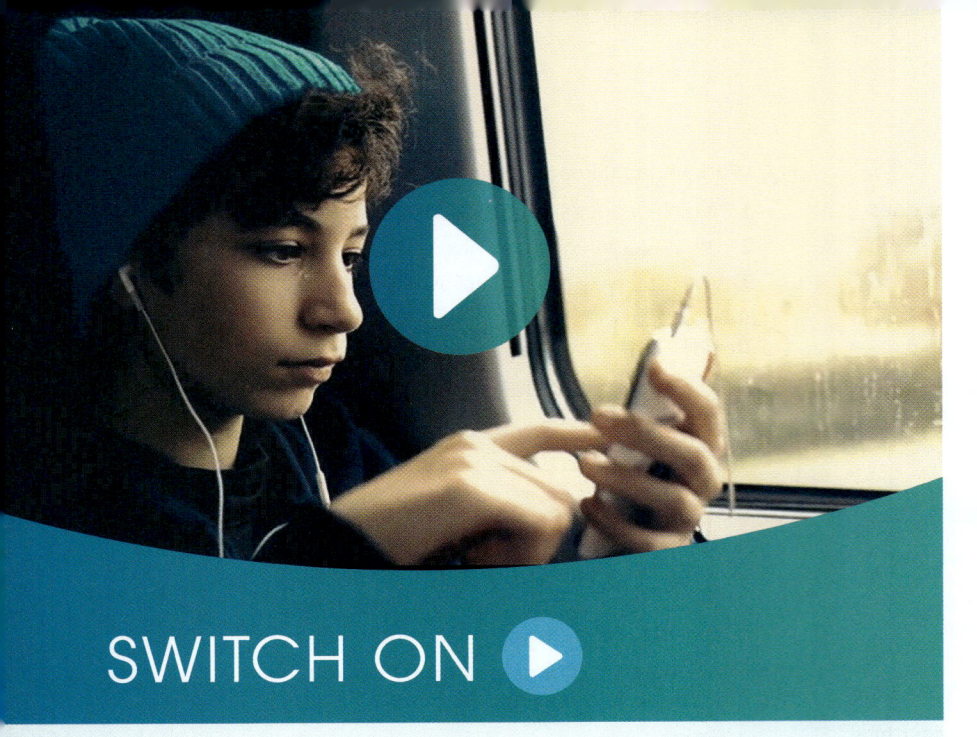

App entrepreneurs

1 Work in pairs and discuss the questions.
1. What are the three apps on your phone that you use the most?
2. Have you ever had a good idea for an app? If so, what is it?

2 ▶ Watch the clip and answer the questions.
1. What does Rajesh's app do?
2. What does Brandon's app do?
3. What does Emily's app do?

3 ▶ Watch again and complete the sentences.
1. Each student has forty-eight hours to .... a new app and prepare a presentation or ....
2. Next, mentors from big .... companies like Google help teams to develop their ideas by teaching them skills like ....
3. But this is just the start of their journey as tech ....

4 Which app would you be most interested in using: Mealr, NYC Loop or Empire Bash? Why?

Project

5 Work in groups to research and design a new app that can be used by young people in your town or area. Follow these steps.
1. Research apps for young people that already exist. Answer these questions.
   - What services do the apps provide?
   - How are they helpful for young people?
   - Why do you think young people might like/dislike these apps?
2. Plan your app. Is it a completely new idea or similar to an existing app?
3. What will your app look like? Design a logo and write a short description of it.
4. Present your app to the class.
5. Vote for the best app as a class.

INDEPENDENT LEARNING

Measure your progress

1 Look back at the Independent learning section for Unit 2 on page 30. What goals did you set yourself? How did you do?

2 Which of the things in the table can help you decide if you have achieved a goal? Tick the appropriate column.

	helpful	not helpful
performance in speaking and writing tasks		
test scores		
correct and incorrect answers in an exercise or test		
homework results		
what you found easy/difficult in class		
how confident you felt in class		
your effort		
the teacher's feedback		

3 Work in pairs and share your answers to Ex 2. Did you tick 'not helpful' for any of them? Why/Why not?

4 It is important to set goals that are very clear. Think about your reading skills in Unit 3. Complete these sentences with new goals for reading.

1. I think I did well in ....
   ....
2. I found ....
   .... difficult.
3. I need to work more on ....
   ....
4. I want to ....
   I'll do this by ....

5 Work in pairs. Share your goals from Ex 4. What new goals did you set?

UNIT CHECK

Wordlist

Technology in the home
coffee maker (n)
dishwasher (n)
fridge-freezer (n)
kettle (n)
microwave (n)
remote control (n)
smart TV (n)
washing machine (n)

Phrasal verbs
go off (phr v)
plug (your phone) in (phr v)
set (a new computer) up (phr v)
shut (a laptop) down (phr v)
switch (the light) on (phr v)
switch (the radio) off (phr v)
turn (the sound) up (phr v)
turn (the volume) down (phr v)

Smart homes
air conditioning (n)
battery (n)
central heating (n)
charge (a device) (v)
connect (v)
download (v)
electricity (n)
file sharing (n)
install (v)
machine (n)
online (adj)
robot (n)
tap (a button/an icon) (v)
upload (v)

Other
band (n)
common (adj)
convenient (adj)
creative (adj)
directly (adv)
discussion (n)
efficient (adj)
human (n)
intelligent (adj)
issue (n)
live (adj)
predict (v)
produce (v)
relaxed (adj)
successful (adj)
trust (v)
useful (adj)
view (n)

Extra
development (n)
give up (phr v)
music industry (n)
musician (n)
recommend (v)
studio (n)
suggest (v)
(vinyl) record (n)

1 🔊 3.8 Listen to eight people describing an object from the *Technology in the home* section of the wordlist. Which item is each speaker describing?

1 .... 5 ....
2 .... 6 ....
3 .... 7 ....
4 .... 8 ....

2 Rewrite the sentences. Replace the words in bold with the correct form of a phrasal verb from the wordlist.

1 This music's too loud. Can you **make** it **quieter**, please?

2 Can you **start** the dishwasher before you go out?

3 Where can I **connect** my mobile **to electricity**?

4 Have you **made** your new tablet **ready for use** yet?

5 Can you **stop the light working**? It's too bright.

6 Oh I love this song. **Make** it **louder**!

7 My laptop has **stopped working** for no reason and I don't know why.

8 Shall I **stop** the computer **from working**?

3 Complete the conversations with words from the *Smart homes* section of the wordlist.

1 **A:** You can .... their new song for free from their website.
   B: Really? Cool! I love that song!

2 **A:** How does this app work?
   B: Just .... this icon here, and wait for the 'ding' sound.

3 **A:** It's hot in here!
   B: I'll turn on the ....

4 **A:** Can I plug in my phone here, please? My .... is low.
   B: Of course.

5 **A:** And what does this .... do?
   B: It makes ice cream. Cool, isn't it?

6 **A:** The printer isn't working!
   B: You haven't plugged it in. Printers don't work without ...., you know!

4 🔊 3.9 Listen and check your answers.

5 Complete the sentences with words from the *Other* section of the wordlist in the correct form.

1 People will no longer go to .... music events. They'll just watch them online.

2 Robots will .... many of the things we own. Humans will lose jobs.

3 We won't have to be very .... Robots will do the thinking for us.

4 It'll be more .... to spend more time in the digital world than in the real world.

5 I .... that the world will be a safer place to be.

43

UNIT CHECK
Review

1 Choose the correct verb forms to complete the conversations.

1 **A:** Are you OK?
   B: No. Look at the time. **I'll / I'm going to** be late!
2 **A:** The game's nearly over and Nathan's won all the points.
   B: Yes, he has. **He'll / He's going to** win this match.
3 **A:** When will you be home?
   B: The concert **finishes / is finishing** at ten, so just after that.
4 **A:** I can't find my mobile.
   B: It's in the kitchen. **I'm going to / I'll** get it for you.
5 **A:** My tablet's not working.
   B: Wait a minute. **I'll / I'm going to** have a look at it.
6 **A:** **I'm meeting / I'll meet** Sam tonight.
   B: Oh, that'll be nice.
7 **A:** Do you want to go out tonight?
   B: No, thanks. **I'll / I'm going to** stay in and watch something online.
8 **A:** Jake knows a lot about computers.
   B: Yes, he does. Perhaps **he'll / he's going to** be a computer programmer.
9 **A:** Shall we go swimming?
   B: OK. The pool **is opening / opens** at 8 a.m.
10 **A:** **I'll start / I'm starting** guitar lessons tomorrow.
    B: Good luck!

2 Complete the sentences with the correct form of 'will' or 'be going to' and the verbs in brackets.

1 I .... (visit) the science museum with school next week.
2 I'm not sure if I have Tom's number. I .... (have) a look on my phone.
3 Look at this game – it looks great. I think I .... (ask) the shop assistant how much it is.
4 Oh no, I've forgotten my phone! I .... (have to) go back home and get it.
5 I .... (play) football with my friends after school.
6 Next week I .... (buy) some new headphones with my birthday money.

3 🔊 3.10 Listen to six conversations. What suggestion is given in each one?

1 ....
2 ....
3 ....
4 ....
5 ....
6 ....

4 🔊 3.11 Complete the conversations with these words. Listen again and check your answers.

about   could   go   going   I   ought   shall   should   you

1 **A:** I dropped my phone and the screen's broken. What .... I do?
   B: You .... to take it to a mobile shop in town. They'll help you.
2 **A:** I'd like a new ringtone.
   B: How .... this one? It's a singing baby.
3 **A:** I'd like to go shopping tomorrow. Why don't we .... together?
   B: Oh sorry, I can't tomorrow. It's my dad's birthday.
4 **A:** What .... we do on Saturday?
   B: How about .... to the cinema?
5 **A:** You should watch this video. It's really funny.
   B: Why don't .... send me a link? I'll watch it later.
6 **A:** It's hot in here. Shall .... open a window?
   B: Sure. You .... put the air conditioning on too if you want.

5 e Read the article and for each question, write the correct answer. Write one word for each gap.

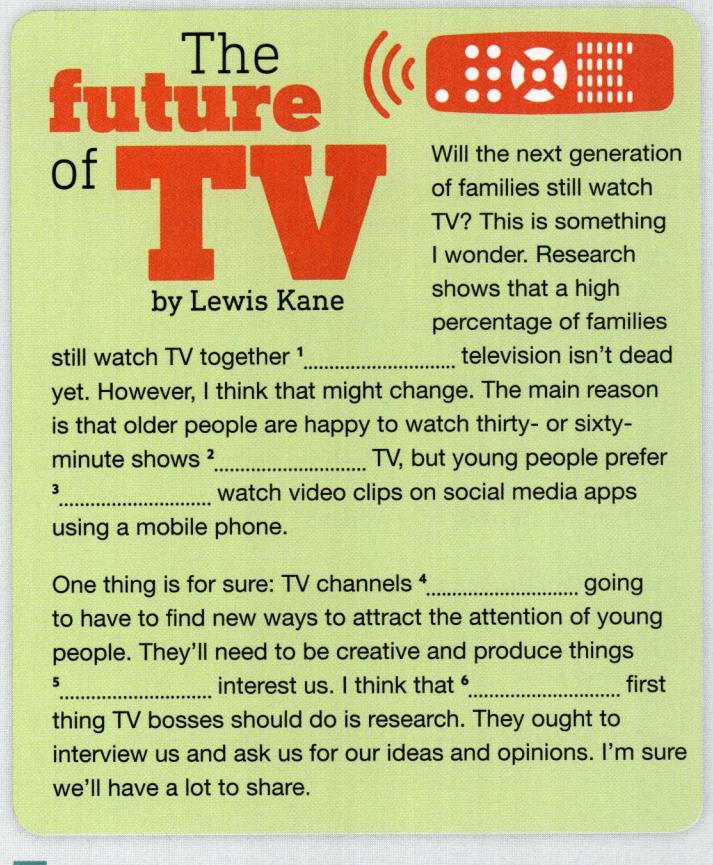

The future of TV
by Lewis Kane

Will the next generation of families still watch TV? This is something I wonder. Research shows that a high percentage of families still watch TV together ¹........................... television isn't dead yet. However, I think that might change. The main reason is that older people are happy to watch thirty- or sixty-minute shows ²........................... TV, but young people prefer ³........................... watch video clips on social media apps using a mobile phone.

One thing is for sure: TV channels ⁴........................... going to have to find new ways to attract the attention of young people. They'll need to be creative and produce things ⁵........................... interest us. I think that ⁶........................... first thing TV bosses should do is research. They ought to interview us and ask us for our ideas and opinions. I'm sure we'll have a lot to share.

6 Write a paragraph suggesting ideas for attracting younger viewers to TV channels.

> "I play my own game."

Look at the photo and discuss the questions.
1 What kind of sports do you find most enjoyable? Why?
   • sports with you and another person
   • sports with your team and another team
   • sports for you and your individual ability
2 How important is winning to you?
3 In what ways are you a competitive person?

4
Taking part

READING
topic: unusual sports
skill: identifying phrases with similar meanings
task: multiple matching

GRAMMAR
present perfect
past simple and present perfect

VOCABULARY
sport

LISTENING
topic: enjoying sport
skill: listening for the question
task: multiple choice

SPEAKING
topic: watching and doing sport
skill: saying when you are not sure
task: describing a photo

WRITING
topic: a new sport
skill: linking ideas
task: article

SWITCH ON ▶
video: top spin
project: plan a campaign

4 Taking part

READING

Power up

1 What sports can you do with this equipment? What sports don't require any equipment?

> goggles   helmet   net   racket   trainers   wetsuit

2 Can you think of any sports that are a bit unusual? Do you think many people play them?

Read on

3 Read the posts from five students who want to enter a sports competition. Which students like team sports?

1 Sandra
I like competitions where as many people as possible can play together. I've always played in team sports – I enjoy them a lot. I prefer really physical games that you can play outside. I'm very tough!

2 Luke
I cycle a lot. I've already won a few cycling competitions – but I'd like to do something in a team. I enjoy watching water sports and I think I'd like to try that – as long as it's something really fun.

3 Olivia
I've done gymnastics since I was little, so now I'd like to compete in a team running event that's fun and silly! Gymnastics has made me very strong and I'm a fast runner.

4 Joseph
I've tried team sports but I'm quite lazy, so I want to do something easy where I don't need lots of practice. I like silly games. And I don't want to buy any expensive equipment!

5 Hannah
I've just won a tennis competition, actually – but that was individual. I've never tried any team ball games, so I'd like to. Also, I want to do something outside as I live by the sea – something really active. I'm not keen on swimming, though.

4 Read the article on page 47 quickly. Match the photos (1–3) with three of the sports (A–H).

5 Read the exam tip and complete the task.

> **exam tip: multiple matching**
> Match phrases that have similar meanings.
> Look at post 1 in Ex 3. The student says she enjoys sports where 'as many people as possible can play together'. Which phrase in text B expresses this idea?

6 e Read the article about sports again. Decide which sport (A–H) would be the most suitable for the students in Ex 3 (2–5).

7 Find phrases in the article that have these meanings.
1 happen, especially if planned or arranged (text A): ....
2 continue (text B): ....
3 join in something (text C): ....
4 think that something is important (text D): ....
5 stay or move on top of liquid without sinking (text G): ....

8 Work in pairs. Take turns to describe a sport or famous sports event without saying its name. Try to use a word or phrase from Ex 7 in your description. Can your partner name the sport?

Sum up

9 Work in pairs. What information do you remember about each sport in the article?

Speak up

10 Work in pairs. Which sports in the article do you think are difficult/easy? Why? Which of them would you like to try? Give reasons for your answers.

> I don't think underwater cycling looks easy. It's hard to cycle underwater!

> I'd like to try toe wrestling. It looks like anyone can do it.

> Bed racing looks like fun. And I think it should be hard work to pull a big bed along!

Golf balls were once called 'feathery balls'. They were made of leather and filled with feathers.

Try these sports with a difference!

A Bossaball
Have you ever played volleyball? Well, Bossaball is similar to volleyball but also has elements of football, gymnastics and capoeira. It usually takes place on the beach on a specially designed inflatable court and has a trampoline on each side of the net. There are two teams with 3–5 players in each team. You might enjoy it!

B Kibasen
Have you ever wondered what sports Japanese kids play in school? It's a piggyback game played on a large field, with lots of teams all playing at the same time. The players beat the other team by being strong and keeping going till the end! But it's quite slow because you play until all teams are out except one.

C Underwater cycling
Can you imagine a race underwater on a bicycle? It's a difficult sport but you can do it in a swimming pool – or a lake. You take part as an individual on a specially designed bicycle. You need diving equipment and a wetsuit to take part. And you're not allowed to put your feet on the ground!

D Toe wrestling
Toe wrestling is like arm wrestling – but with your toes! You have to hold the other person's toe down for three seconds. You play against other people individually until someone has won. This event is taken very seriously by some competitors but anyone can join in. You don't need to train for it, so have a go!

E Shoulder wars
Or try shoulder wars. It's an informal game, which is played in water – mostly lakes or swimming pools. You play the game by riding on the shoulders of your teammates. You need to attempt to knock down and separate your opponents by pushing them into the water.

F Two-racket tennis
Two-handed, or two-racket, tennis is an unusual way to play the worldwide popular game of tennis. The game is played just like the traditional tennis game. The difference is that each player has a racket in each hand, so you can play with two forehands. Or two backhands if that's better!

G Bed racing
Yes, bed racing is a sport! The competitors push a bed along a route in teams of four or six, plus one on the bed. Each team provides their own bed, decorated in the theme for the year. The bed runs on four wheels, but also needs to be able to float. A typical race is 3 km long and includes going up hills and crossing a river.

H Jolleyball
If you can juggle, then jolleyball is a sport for you. It's a combination of volleyball and juggling – but mainly juggling. A game is played on a court similar to a badminton court, between two teams with two or three players each. Each player has to play with two balls and juggle between shots.

4 Taking part

GRAMMAR

1 Read the grammar box and complete the examples with the correct form of the verbs in brackets.

explore grammar → p132

present perfect

A a past action that has a result in the present
Gymnastics ¹............................ (make) me very strong.

B past experiences or situations that are still true
I ²............................ (try) team sports but I'm not very good.

present perfect with adverbs of time

A *just* for recent events
I ³............................ (just/win) a tennis competition.

B *already* for something that has happened before now
I ⁴............................ (already/win) a few cycling races.

C *ever* and *never* for any time up to now
I ⁵............................ (never/try) any team ball games.
⁶............................ (you/ever/play) volleyball?

D *always* for something that has been true all our lives
I ⁷............................ (always/play) in teams.

E We also use *for* and *since* with the present perfect.
I haven't tried a new sport **for** years. (a period of time)
I ⁸............................ (do) gymnastics **since** I was little.
(a specific time in the past)

2 ▶ ◀) 4.1 Watch or listen to people talking about sports. Match the speakers (1–9) with the sports they say they have done (A–H). You need to match some speakers with more than one sport.

- **A** swimming: .... , ... , ...
- **B** racquets: ....
- **C** skiing: ....
- **D** hockey: ....
- **E** netball: .... , ...
- **F** football: ....
- **G** dancing: ....
- **H** basketball: ....

3 ▶ ◀) 4.2 Watch or listen again and complete the sentences.

1. I .... netball for the last two years.
2. In hockey I .... for my region.
3. I .... with dolphins but I still .... a chance to surf yet.
4. We .... some tournaments.
5. I .... tennis but I would like to try because it seems fun.
6. I .... in the sea but I .... in a river or lake.

4 Work in pairs. Put these verbs in the past participle form and write sentences using them.

buy   cut   do   find   have   play   see   start   watch   win

5 Complete the conversations with the present perfect form of these verbs.

do   go   live   swim   win

1. **A:** .... (you) any sport today?
   B: No, I ....
2. **A:** .... (your friends/already) home?
   B: Yes, they ....
3. **A:** .... (you/ever) in a lake?
   B: No, I ....
4. **A:** .... (you) a competition?
   B: Yes, I ....
5. **A:** .... (your family/always) in this house?
   B: No, they ....

6 e Read the review and for each question, write the correct answer. Write one word for each gap.

My review of our NEW CLIMBING CENTRE

Our new local sports centre has just opened. There are some great activities I want ¹............................ tell you about. I had a really great day at the climbing wall. ²............................ you ever seen a climbing wall? If you haven't climbed one ³............................ and want to try it for the first time, come along! When you try climbing, you may find that you use parts of your body that you have ⁴............................ used in other sports, so it's great fitness training. I'm sure you ⁵............................ love it. Mr Bower, our instructor, has taught climbing ⁶............................ many years and is very helpful and friendly. They always put their customers first, so don't worry – you'll be safe!

Speak up

7 Work in pairs. Take turns to tell your partner about your experience of sports and activities. Use verbs from Ex 5.

> I've never taken a yoga class.

VOCABULARY

sport

1 Complete the notices (1–8) with these words.

> changing rooms   coach   court   locker   match   prize   race   track

2 Read the sentences and replace the words or phrases in bold with the correct form of these verbs.

> beat   compete   hit   kick   lose   score   train   win

1 Dan **struck** the ball hard with the racket. ....
2 My team **are the best** in every game. ....
3 How many goals did they **get** in the last game? ....
4 Our team **are the worst in** each match they play. ....
5 He tried to **put the ball in the net with his foot**. ....
6 Hundreds of students **try to win** against other teams. ....
7 My coach helps me **prepare** for competitions. ....
8 Germany **got more points than** Italy. They won 3–1. ....

explore **language**

noun and verb forms

Some nouns are the same as the verb.

score (v) – score (n)   kick (v) – kick (n)   race (v) – race (n)

Some nouns sound the same as the verb but the spelling is different.

practise (v) – practice (n)

3 e Read the language box and then the report. For each question, choose the correct answer.

PORTUGAL vs TURKEY

Here's a report on the big football ¹........ last night between Portugal and Turkey. It was very exciting and the final ²........ was 4–0 to Turkey. Many people wanted Portugal to ³........ because they were the favourite, but the fans were disappointed. The team needs to ⁴........ more because they aren't fast enough. The Turkish players work as a team and they're really fast – that's why they ⁵........ lots of goals. I don't think anyone can ⁶........ them at the moment.

1 A sport   B match   C play   D race
2 A goals   B points   C result   D game
3 A win   B beat   C lose   D train
4 A train   B think   C kick   D coach
5 A collect   B hit   C score   D make
6 A race   B beat   C France   D compete

4 🔊 4.3 Listen and check your answers.

1 Noah Armstrong won the 10 km .... on Sunday. He ran it in forty-five minutes. Well done, Noah!

2 Please put your bags and football boots in a .... and leave your key with the PE teacher, Mr Short.

3 Congratulations to Ellen Granger who won first .... in the junior judo competition!

4 Running club: every Thursday at the new .... in the park. Everyone welcome.

5 Football .... against Carston High School on Saturday at nine o'clock. The coaches leave at 7.45 p.m.

6 Tennis club rule: all players must wear tennis shoes on the ...., please.

7 The gym .... are closed today because of a problem with the showers.

8 Good at tennis? You could be a tennis .... in our summer club. Two hours every day. Call 01772 56311.

Speak up

5 Work in pairs. Tell your partner about a sports match you have watched. Explain:

- who was playing.
- why they were playing (e.g. school competition).
- how well each team played.
- who you wanted to win and why.
- who won.
- what the losing team need to do better.

> I watched the school tennis final …

game on

Work in pairs. Explain a word from this page without saying it. Can your partner guess what it is?

A: It's something you do in sport. You do it with your foot.
B: Kick!

In 1954, the world record for running a mile was four minutes. In 2018 it was 3.43 minutes.

4 Taking part

LISTENING

Power up

1 Look at the girls in the photo. Why do you think they look happy?

Listen up

2 🔊 4.4 Listen to an interview with a student talking about sport. Is she good at sports?

3 Read the exam tip and complete the task.

> **exam tip: multiple choice**
>
> Listen carefully to the interviewer's questions. They will use words that help you decide where to find the correct answer, even though different words are used in the options.
>
> Read question 1 in Ex 4. Which two words do you expect to hear so you know when to listen for the answer?

4 e 🔊 4.5 Listen again. For each question, choose the correct answer.

1. What does Elena say about running in competitions?
   A It can take several years to prepare for a race.
   B You need to run a lot every day before the race.
   C You can choose to run the same distance without competing.
2. What does Elena enjoy about running?
   A the opportunity to be outside
   B the chance to test herself
   C running with companions
3. Elena wanted to play rugby because
   A it's a faster game than netball.
   B it has a lot of physical contact.
   C the competitions are better.
4. What advice does Elena give to people who are bad at sports?
   A Keep going and you will improve.
   B Use it as a way of getting fit.
   C Try to enjoy whatever you are doing.
5. What does Elena like about team sports?
   A the feeling of being in a group
   B the fact you can work less hard
   C the way the group helps you
6. Elena suggests that if there is too much competition in a sport,
   A it's better to pick another sport.
   B you should try doing the sport with a friend.
   C you should choose to practise the sport privately.

5 Read the grammar box and complete the examples with the correct form of the verbs in brackets.

> **explore grammar** ➙ p132
>
> **past simple and present perfect**
>
> **past simple**
>
> We use the past simple for an action that happened at a definite time in the past.
>
> A few years ago you ¹............................ (not enjoy) sports.
> When I was younger, I ²............................ (want) to play rugby.
>
> **present perfect**
>
> We use the present perfect for a past action when we don't know exactly when it happened or when the time isn't important. We also use it for a state or situation that started in the past and is still true now.
>
> I ³............................ (start) enjoying sport.
> I ⁴............................ (be) a runner for years.

6 Complete the sentences with the present perfect or past simple form of the verbs in brackets.

1. This is a difficult race. .... (they/do) enough training for it?
2. Freerunning is very exciting. I .... (try) it last summer.
3. Lucy and Connor .... (start) a freerunning club. Shall we join?
4. Nicole's very fit. She .... (run) in a marathon at the weekend.
5. I hope Nick wins the race. He .... (train) really hard for it.
6. We .... (not win) the football match yesterday.
7. .... (you/watch) the game on TV last night?
8. I can't go cycling this afternoon because I .... (not finish) my homework yet.

Speak up

7 Work in pairs. Tell your partner about a competitive experience you have had. Then give more details about that experience.

> I've climbed several mountains. The first one was in Peru two years ago.

SPEAKING

Power up

1 Look at the photo. What can you see in it? Complete the notes.

> place/weather: at home, in a house, on the sofa
>
> people: ....
>
> objects/clothes: ....
>
> actions: ....
>
> feelings: ....

2 Match the questions (1–6) with the answers (A–F).

1. Who is in the photo?
2. Where are they?
3. What are they wearing?
4. What are they doing?
5. How are they feeling?
6. What do you think about this activity?

A They're in a lounge. I can see a sofa. There's a white wall behind the sofa. It's bright in the room.

B I don't watch sport with my friends very often because I prefer doing sport.

C They're all really happy. I think they're enjoying the match. Perhaps they're celebrating because their team has scored a goal.

D They're watching sport on TV. It might be a match because they are looking excited. They're eating popcorn.

E Most of them are wearing T-shirts and jeans. Three of them are wearing a red and white football shirt. The boy standing is wearing a blue T-shirt and the boy on the left is wearing a white T-shirt. One girl is wearing a dress.

F It's a group of friends.

3 🔊 4.6 Listen to a girl describing the photo. What five things does she NOT mention from the answers in Ex 2 (A–F)?

4 Read the exam tip and complete the task.

exam tip: describing a photo ➜ p147

Remember to talk about different things you can see in the photo.

Describe these things about the boy on the right in the photo.
- What is he wearing?
- What does he look like?
- What is he doing?
- How do you think he is feeling?

Speak up

5 Read the useful language. Which of these phrases could you use to describe the photo?

useful language
describing what you see

It's a photo of … / The photo shows …

On the left / On the right / At the back / At the front …

He/She/They look(s) / look(s) like …

when you aren't sure or don't know

It could/might be …

Perhaps/Maybe it's …

I can't remember what this is.

6 e Work in pairs. Student A, turn to page 157. Student B, turn to page 159. Follow the instructions.

7 Work in the same pairs. Use your notes from Ex 6 to tell your partner what you thought about his/her description. Did he/she use phrases from the useful language?

> You used lots of interesting words.

> You described their clothes well.

> You didn't know the word for 'wetsuit', but I understood what you meant.

Speaking extra

8 Work in pairs. Think of friends and people in your family. Do they prefer watching or playing sport? Why? Tell your partner about two people.

Watching your team play can give your brain the same feelings as when you're playing yourself.

4 Taking part

WRITING

Power up

1 Work in pairs. Look at the photos of different sports and activities (1–3). Discuss the questions.
1 What is happening in each photo?
2 Have you tried any of these activities?

2 Read the advert. What does it invite students to write? What is the prize?

SPORTS FANS

We want to know about a sport you have tried.

- Why were you doing this sport?
- What happened when you tried it?
- Did you enjoy it and have you continued doing it in your spare time?

We'll send some sports equipment to the writer of the best article!

3 Read Jessica's article. Match the ideas (A–C) with the paragraphs (1–3).

A details of what happened when Jessica tried the sport
B an explanation of why Jessica was doing the sport
C information about if Jessica enjoyed the sport and has continued doing it

A new sport
by Jessica, 16

Star article

1 I've done lots of different sports. Last summer my cousin suggested trying cricket together, so we joined the local cricket club.

2 We divided into teams and played against each other. As soon as I hit the ball for the first time, I realised it was quite hard to play. You spend a lot of time on your feet and you need to concentrate. Although I'm not sure I was very good at it, I had a great time playing!

3 I haven't played cricket since last summer but I did enjoy it, so now I'm watching videos to find out how to play better so that I can play again next summer!

4 Read the language box and find examples of the linking words and phrases in the article.

explore language

linking ideas

I'll come on **either** Tuesday **or** Wednesday.

I called him **as soon as** I heard the news.

Everyone wanted to go to the match **except** Callum.

I'm doing my homework now **so that** I can go out later.

She's a good gymnast **although** she doesn't practise very often.

5 Match the words and phrases in bold in the language box with the meanings (1–5).

1 shows a choice
2 used to mean 'immediately'
3 used to mean 'not including'
4 shows purpose/reason
5 used to mean 'but'

6 Complete the sentences with these words or phrases.

although	as soon as	because	either … or
	except	so that	

1 You can watch the match .... you finish eating your dinner.
2 Luke's trained really hard .... he wants to win the competition.
3 All of the football players were happy with the score .... Sandra. She was upset.
4 We're doing .... hockey .... volleyball today.
5 .... she hasn't had any formal training, she is one of the best players in the team.
6 You should drink lots of water .... your body is ready for the race.

Plan on

7 Read the advert in Ex 2 again. Decide which sport or activity you will write about. Complete the notes with your ideas.

name of sport and why I was doing it

shoulder wars   ....

what happened

fell of, got back up, won   ....

Did I enjoy, etc.?

Yes!   ....

8 Read the exam tip and complete the task.

exam tip: article → p152

Make sure you expand each point you write about.

When you write about the first point in Ex 7, which is the best plan, A or B?

A name of sport/activity → why I played it
B name of sport/activity → why I played it → where I was when I played it → who I played it with

9 Expand your notes from Ex 7. Add more information for each point.

bike chariot racing – very hard
I didn't like bike chariot racing because it was very hard.

Write on

10 **e** Write your article in about 100 words.

Improve it

11 Check your article. Look carefully at the content points in the task.

12 Work in pairs. Read your partner's article and make notes about these points. Then talk about how you can improve your article.
1 Did your partner write about all three content points?
2 Did he/she give extra information for each point?
3 Are the ideas connected with linking words/phrases?

Kite flying has been popular in Thailand for over 700 years. It is now a professional sport.

SWITCH ON

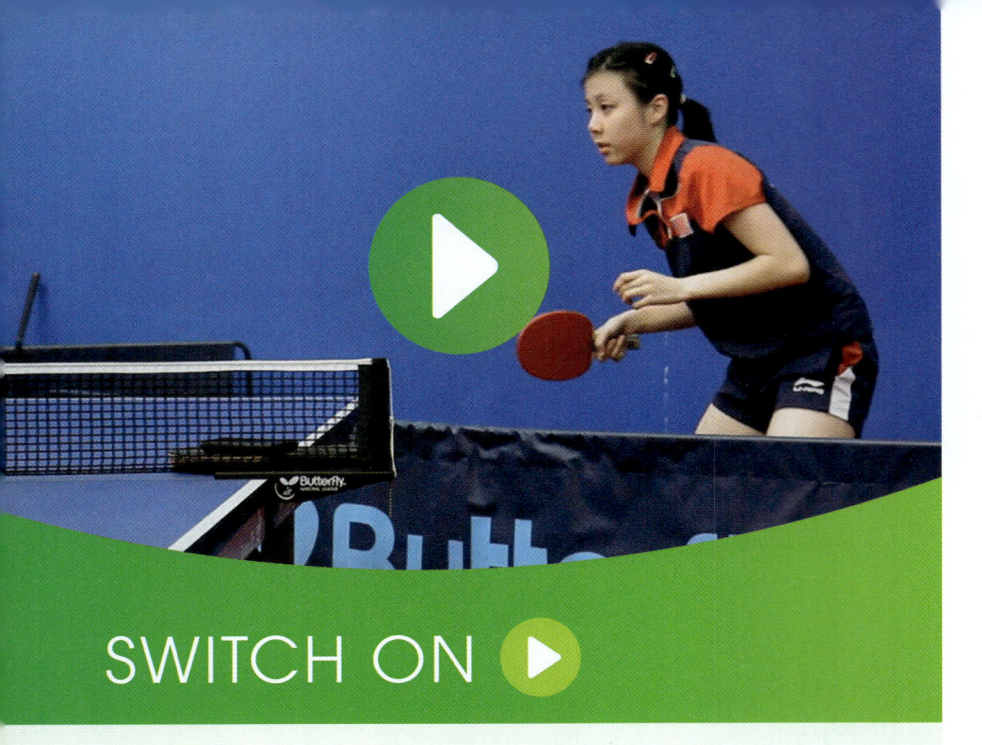

Top spin

1 Work in pairs and answer the questions.
1. What sports do you play? Why do you play them?
2. If you don't play sports, why not? Is it because you don't enjoy them or because you don't have the opportunity?

2 Watch the clip about young people who play a sport. What three adjectives are used to describe their sport?

3 Watch again. Are these sentences true (T) or false (F)?
1. Aerial's dad has quit his job to coach her full time. T / F
2. Lily doesn't have a social life – she only plays table tennis. T / F
3. Lily doesn't care about school. T / F
4. Michael studies from home. T / F
5. Chinese table tennis players train for fourteen hours a day. T / F

4 What are the advantages and disadvantages of practising and playing a sport at a professional level as a teenager?

Project

5 Work in small groups to plan a campaign for encouraging local sports clubs or organisations to motivate young people to be more physically active. Follow these steps
1. Research sports clubs, exercise classes and outdoor activities in your area.
2. Brainstorm ideas for how they could get more young people involved.
3. Plan how you will present your ideas to these clubs or organisations. Will you use an email, a flyer or a video?
4. Present your ideas to the class.
5. Which campaign do you think would be most effective? Why?

INDEPENDENT LEARNING

Grammar and vocabulary

1 Answer the questions about Unit 4. Check how much of the grammar and vocabulary you have used.
1. Did you use sports words in the main speaking activity (page 51, Ex 6)?
2. Did you use the present perfect and past simple in the main writing activity (page 53, Ex 10)?
3. How well do you think you used these?

2 Work in pairs. Compare your answers to Ex 1 and discuss these questions.
1. What can you do to make sure you use the grammar correctly?
2. What can you do if you don't remember vocabulary?

3 Work in new pairs. Can you think of any activities you can do at home to help you improve your grammar and vocabulary?

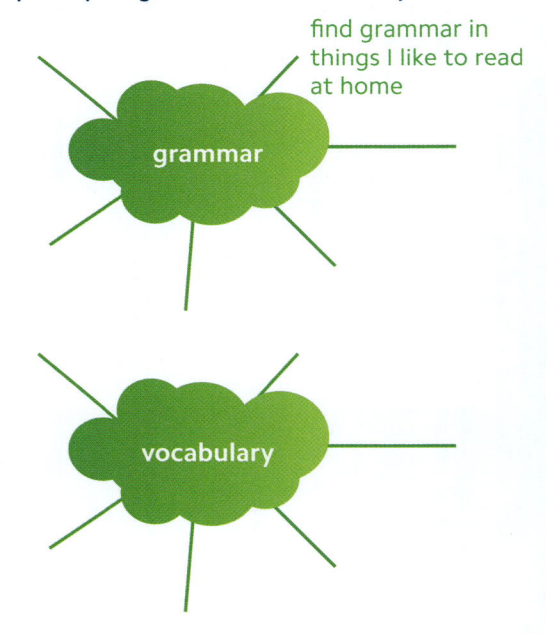

grammar — find grammar in things I like to read at home

vocabulary

4 Complete the sentences.
1. I'm going to try and practise .... new words every week by ....
2. I'm going to improve my grammar by ....

UNIT CHECK

Wordlist

Sports nouns
changing room
coach
court
kick
locker
match
practice
prize
race
score
track

Sports verbs
beat
catch
collect
compete
hit
kick
lose
practise
race
score
train
win

Sports equipment
goggles (n)
helmet (n)
net (n)
racket (n)
trainers (n)
wetsuit (n)

Competition
competitor (n)
goal (n)
player (n)
point (n)
record (n)
result (n)

Other
equipment (n)
event (n)
keep going (v)
knock down (phr v)
net (n)
run (v)
take part (phr)
take place (phr)
take something seriously (phr)

Extra
backhand (n)
capoeira (n)
field (n)
float (v)
forehand (n)
gymnastics (n)
individual (game) (adj)
inflatable (adj)
informal (adj)
juggle (v)
opponent (n)
professional (n)
shot (n)
teammate (n)
trampoline (n)
underwater (adj)
wrestling (n)

Vocabulary

1 Match the meanings with words from the *Sports nouns* section of the wordlist.

1 something the winner in a competition receives: ....
2 a place where you play tennis or basketball: ....
3 a place where people can put on or take off sports clothes: ....
4 a type of path or road that is usually in a ring shape: ....
5 a person who trains a team or athlete: ....
6 a game in which two people or teams play against each other: ....
7 a competition to find the fastest runner: ....
8 a small cupboard where you can leave your clothes: ....

2 Complete the sentences with verbs from the *Sports verbs* section of the wordlist in the correct form.

1 I can't .... the ball very hard. I've hurt my foot.
2 Ben always .... the most goals.
3 I hope our team .... the game!
4 Would you like to .... in the school gymnastics competition?
5 This is the most important match of the year. Our team mustn't .... it.
6 Emily is a great swimmer. She .... all the other girls in the competition last week.
7 Good footballers have to .... for hours every week.
8 The best tennis players can .... the ball very hard.

3 Complete the email with these words.

coach   compete   part   place
prize   record   train   win

From: **Megan**   To: **Katie**

Hi Katie,
I don't know what to do and I need your advice! I want to take [1]...........................
in the running competition. It's taking [2]........................... on Saturday and I want to [3]........................... in the 200 metres. I'd like to try and break the [4]........................... !
I usually [5]........................... , so I was really disappointed when I didn't get the [6]........................... for first place this year.
My [7]........................... says I need to [8]........................... more. But I haven't got any time! What do you think I should do?
Love,
Megan

UNIT CHECK

Review

1 🔊 **4.7** Listen to eight sentences. Write the past participle you hear in each sentence.

1 ....   5 ....
2 ....   6 ....
3 ....   7 ....
4 ....   8 ....

2 Complete the sentences with the past simple or present perfect form of the verbs in brackets.

1 Karen's excited about buying a skateboard. She .... (want) one for a long time.
2 Luke .... (have) a difficult time when he was at his old school.
3 I .... (not see) Sophie today at all. Do you know where she is?
4 James .... (annoy) Imogen and they're not talking to each other now.
5 We .... (be) bored yesterday because we didn't have anything to do.
6 I'm not going to enter the 100 m race. I .... (not do) enough training for it.
7 Unfortunately, they .... (not win) the game last week.
8 He .... (break) his leg, so he can't play next week.
9 Eric .... (be) in our team since January. He's one of our best players.
10 Amanda .... (come) third in the swimming competition on Saturday.

3 Put the words in the correct order to make sentences.

1 before / never / I / done / mud running / have
....
2 Mr Wilson / been / two years / our football coach / for / has
....
3 my friend Dan / you / have / met / ever?
....
4 the race / already / they / finished / have
....
5 my friend / told me / just / has / about the party
....
6 I was eleven / have / with this club / trained / since / I
....
7 never / my brother / tried / skiing / has
....
8 had / for / this wetsuit / I / four months / have
....

4 Complete the second sentence so that it has the same meaning as the first sentence.

1 This is the first time I've done kickboxing.
   I .... kickboxing before.
2 We arrived at the match a short time ago.
   We .... arrived at the match.
3 Patrick joined a different football club two years ago.
   Patrick has been in a different football club .... two years.
4 This isn't the first time I've tried mud running.
   I .... mud running before.
5 I will buy my new racket soon.
   I .... my new racket yet.
6 She became a swimming coach in July.
   She has been a swimming coach .... July.
7 He bought these goggles last week.
   He .... for a week.
8 Is this the first time you've played netball?
   Have .... netball before?
9 I met my teammates years ago, so we're good friends, too.
   I've known my teammates .... , so we're good friends, too.
10 This is the first time we've met a famous sportsperson.
   We .... a famous sportsperson before.

5 e Read the blog post and for each question, write the correct answer. Write one word for each gap.

Join the *fun!*

We had a really fun competition in our town the other day and I really recommend you come and watch next year! For our festival, the town decided to have some silly races. We **¹**.............................. done the competition **²**.............................. the last three years and more and more people do it every year. Anyone **³**.............................. take part because you don't need **⁴**.............................. train or have special skills. All the races are really silly, like chair racing or toe wrestling. I've **⁵**.............................. taken part myself but it looks like really good fun. At the end of **⁶**.............................. day we have a big party. We'd like more people to come, so check it out next year.

"I love to be on the stage."

Look at the photo and discuss the questions.
1. Who are your favourite entertainers? What do you like about them?
2. If you had to entertain an audience, what would you do (e.g. sing, dance, tell jokes)?
3. Do you think that it is good to work in the entertainment business? Why/Why not?

5

In the spotlight

READING
topic: growing up in the spotlight
skill: understanding what is being tested
task: signs and notices; multiple choice

GRAMMAR
zero, first and second conditionals
unless, in case, if I were you

VOCABULARY
entertainment

LISTENING
topic: music
skill: identifying agreement
task: multiple choice

SPEAKING
topic: live music
skill: dealing with unknown words
task: describing a photo

WRITING
topic: an evening of entertainment
skill: making positive comments, describing problems
task: article

SWITCH ON ▶
video: in search of fame
project: write a fact file

5 In the spotlight

READING

Power up

1 **If you had to choose, which of these people would you most or least prefer to have as a parent? Why?**

an actor   a sports star   a politician   a rock star

2 **Do you think that magazines and TV shows should tell stories about famous people's children? Why/Why not?**

Read on

3 **Read the exam tip and complete the task.**

> **exam tip: signs and notices**
>
> Think about what the questions are testing.
>
> Read texts 1 and 2 and the options in Ex 4. What is each one testing: understanding of grammar (e.g. modals or conditionals) or communicative functions (e.g. persuading or reminding)?

4 e **Read the texts again. For each question, choose the correct answer.**

1 Special offer!
Visit the cinema three times in one month and you could win two tickets for the opening night of Amy Trent's amazing new film – and a chance to meet the star's family!

- A If you see three films in four weeks, you might get free cinema tickets.
- B After you've seen three films, you get free cinema tickets.
- C You don't need to pay to see Will Smith's new film.

2 Jack Honick — 2 hours ago
Hi, guys. I've got spare tickets for Star Wars Night at the Odeon cinema – three films in one night for true fans! You can leave a comment below if you fancy coming along.

- A Jack is reminding some friends to meet him later.
- B Jack wants to persuade some friends to review his post.
- C Jack is inviting friends to join him for a special night at the cinema.

5 e **Read the article. For each question, choose the correct answer (A, B, C or D).**

1 In the first paragraph, the writer says that the children of famous parents
- A appear in the media too often.
- B find all the travelling a challenge.
- C are not properly understood by other people.
- D have little control over their private lives.

2 How did Willow feel about growing up with media attention?
- A upset that people rarely showed her good side
- B embarrassed by the negative attention she got
- C annoyed that her wishes were ignored
- D uncomfortable being photographed

3 What did the recent study find out about celebrity children?
- A They often find ways to succeed without their parents' help.
- B They are likely to be compared to their parents.
- C They benefit from having their parents' good looks.
- D They are good at persuading their parents' to help them.

4 How does Willow feel now she is older?
- A She is aware that she has done little to deserve her success.
- B She is relaxed now she has found new ways to stay private.
- C She is keen to try and benefit from her situation.
- D She is happy that many people want to help her.

5 What would be a good introduction to this article?
- A A famous name can open doors. In this article, famous children talk us through the ups and downs of the different periods of their lives.
- B Young people with rich parents have an easier life than the rest of us. We find out why.
- C For Willow Smith, nothing matters more than her family. She tells us why.
- D Having a famous parent creates a lifestyle with both advantages and disadvantages when growing up.

6 **Choose the best definition (A or B) for the phrases in bold in the article (1–7).**

1 A lose something because you were careless
  B be or have something you didn't expect
2 A had a good reason for doing (something)
  B were allowed to do (something)
3 A very worried about something
  B doing something to feel better about a situation
4 A when you make someone notice you
  B when a lot of people notice or talk about something bad
5 A they don't need this
  B this is the final point in a long list
6 A reject
  B return to
7 A expected to happen
  B because of

58   A UK survey showed 'social media and gaming' jobs to be the fourth most popular with children. (UCL)

Let me (and my family) entertain you

Famous families like the Kardashians, or the Beckhams appear in magazines every week, choosing to attend film openings or enjoying holidays in beautiful locations. Some famous children **¹end up with** a list of social media followers before they can even speak. But what is life like for celebrity children?

Willow Smith, the daughter of American actor Will Smith, spoke recently about her experiences growing up with photographers following her around. For Willow, it made her sad when people who didn't know her laughed at her or made comments about her, even though that didn't happen very often. She got particularly mad, though, when journalists felt they **²had the right** to know all about her life, after she'd asked them to leave her alone. Most teenagers would hate it if their private lives were so public.

A recent study has highlighted the many advantages for the children of celebrity parents. Top universities offer them places even when their grades aren't great and famous designers give them free clothes. But these kids are also **³under a lot of stress**. People expect them to be super-talented and super-attractive, just like their parents, and they are rude when the children aren't so talented or good-looking. If they didn't have rich and famous parents, they would never get all this **⁴negative attention**. Most of them are just ordinary kids exploring who they are, so **⁵the last thing they need is** to be told they'll never be as good as their mum or dad! If they could, perhaps many would prefer to **⁶turn their backs on** celebrity. Others decide to use their special contacts to try and become successful entertainers themselves.

Willow Smith chose the second option and in 2007 decided to become a singer. By 2010 she was the youngest artist on JayZ's record label 'Roc Nation'. However if she succeeds, some people will say that it's because of her family's contacts and not really **⁷due to** her musical talent. Willow has had to face a lot of hurtful comments and that hasn't always been easy, but she believes that to have real success, you have to work hard and that, eventually, people will recognise that, whoever your parents are.

> " Most teenagers would hate it if their private lives were so public. "

Sum up

7 Work in pairs and discuss the questions.
1 Did the study mentioned in the article agree with what Willow was saying? In what ways?
2 What did the article say might happen now Willow is making records?

> The study said that a lot of children felt stressed and …

Speak up

8 Work in pairs and discuss the questions.
1 Do you think any parent, famous or not, should be allowed to post photos of their children on social media without the children's permission?
2 Do children have the right to decide what information can be shared about them online? Why/Why not?

> In my opinion, many social media companies have a lot of private information about children these days. They know about their hobbies and interests through their parents' posts.

5 In the spotlight

GRAMMAR

1 Read the grammar box and complete the examples with the correct form of the verbs in brackets.

explore grammar → p134

zero, first and second conditionals

zero conditional

when/if + present simple, present simple – for things that are always true

If you **leave** a comment on the page, everyone **can see** it.

Top universities ¹_____ (offer) them places even when their grades ²_____ (not be) great.

first conditional

if + present simple, *will* + infinitive – for things that are possible or probable in the future

If she ³_____ (succeed), some people ⁴_____ (say) that …

My parents ⁵_____ (not let) me go to the festival **if** I ⁶_____ (fail) my exams.

second conditional

if + past simple, *would* + infinitive – for things that are unlikely or impossible now or in the future

If they ⁷_____ (can), perhaps many ⁸_____ (prefer) to turn their backs on celebrity.

If they ⁹_____ (not have) famous parents, they ¹⁰_____ (not get) all this negative attention.

Most teenagers **would hate** it **if** their private lives **were** so public.

2 Complete the first conditional sentences with the correct form of the verbs in brackets.

1 If Joe _____ (not have) his own piano, he won't be able to practise.
2 We'll go to the rock festival if we _____ (have) enough money for the tickets.
3 If my mum says it's OK, I _____ (join) a pop group.
4 We _____ (tell) Eve and Peter about the party if we see them tonight.
5 If I _____ (not have to) look after my baby sister, I'll go to the concert on Sunday.
6 You'll make new friends if you _____ (join) the school choir.
7 My brother _____ (be) very disappointed if he misses this year's festival.
8 If I _____ (get) you a ticket, will you come to the concert with us?

3 ▶ 🔊 5.1 Watch or listen to students using conditional forms. Which of the conditional forms in the grammar box do they NOT use?

4 ▶ 🔊 5.2 Watch or listen again and complete the zero and second conditional sentences.

1 If I _____ my friends after class, we usually _____ on social media or _____ to music.
2 If I _____ my friends after class, we usually _____ to the bus stop and on the way there we _____ get some food.
3 If I _____ my favourite actor, Emma Watson, I _____ her what age she started acting.
4 If my social media account _____ really popular, I _____ happy because I _____ loads of money.

5 Complete the emails with one word in each gap.

From: **Erin** To: **Laura** Re: **Festival**

Hi Laura,
Thanks for inviting me to the festival. I ¹_____ join you ²_____ I could, but I can't afford it this year. Why don't you email Sam? I'm sure he ³_____ say yes if you ask him. He loves festivals.
Erin

From: **Laura** To: **Erin** Re: **Festival**

Hi Erin,
Oh you can't miss this year's festival! ⁴_____ you come if I pay for your ticket? It'll be your birthday present – with love, from me to you! Please, please come! My mum says we can stay in a tepee! It won't ⁵_____ the same if you're not there. It's never fun when your best friend ⁶_____ not with you! And we can email Sam, too.
I'll book our tickets!
Love,
Laura

Speak up

6 Complete the sentences so they are true for you.

1 If I spoke perfect English, …
2 If my favourite band came to my school, …
3 I … if school closed early today.

If it talks like a duck, swims like a duck and quacks like a duck, it probably is a duck!

VOCABULARY
entertainment

1 Match these verbs with their meanings (1–8).

book   clap   entertain   film   interview   perform   record   review

1. write a report about something new, e.g. a book, a film, an album: ....
2. do something that other people find interesting or funny: ....
3. do something in front of an audience, e.g. act, sing, dance: ....
4. hit your hands together several times to show you liked something: ....
5. make a moving picture: ....
6. ask someone questions so that you can find out information: ....
7. put music, pictures, etc. on disk so people can listen to them or watch them: ....
8. arrange to have or do something at a time in the future: ....

explore language

related words

When you learn a new verb, find other words that go with it.
record a song / an album
interview an actor / a famous person
perform in a play / in a ballet / in a musical / on stage / in a TV show
book a ticket / a seat
film a documentary / a programme / a scene

2 🔊 5.3 Listen to five recordings. What is happening in each one? Use verbs from Ex 1 in your answers.

3 Match these words with 1–7 in the picture.

audience   choir   costume   exit   orchestra   row   stage

4 🔊 5.4 Listen to seven quiz questions. Answer each question with a word from Ex 3.

5 Choose the correct words to complete the text.

What's on?
Daily information on events in your area

- Tonight Jamie Crystal will **¹entertain / perform** songs from his new album. Tickets only cost £10, so **²book / record** early as this is going to be popular.

- Sara Borne is **³interviewing / reviewing** Ed Marler about his new book for the Teen Literature Festival. Admission is free.

- The rock group The Need are recording their new **⁴album / play** at Bassett Avenue Studio. Listen to them on Radio Sam FM at 6 p.m.

- Would you like to be on a TV programme? London studio is **⁵entertaining / filming** in Hammersmith this evening. Call this number: 08944 847 5764.

- The Urban Theatre School is looking for talented young people to perform in an exciting new **⁶show / stage**. Come and meet us from 4–6 p.m. this afternoon.

game on

Work in two teams. One person from each team should sit with their back to the board. Your teacher will write a word from the page on the board. You can describe the word, but you can't say it. Who will guess the word first?

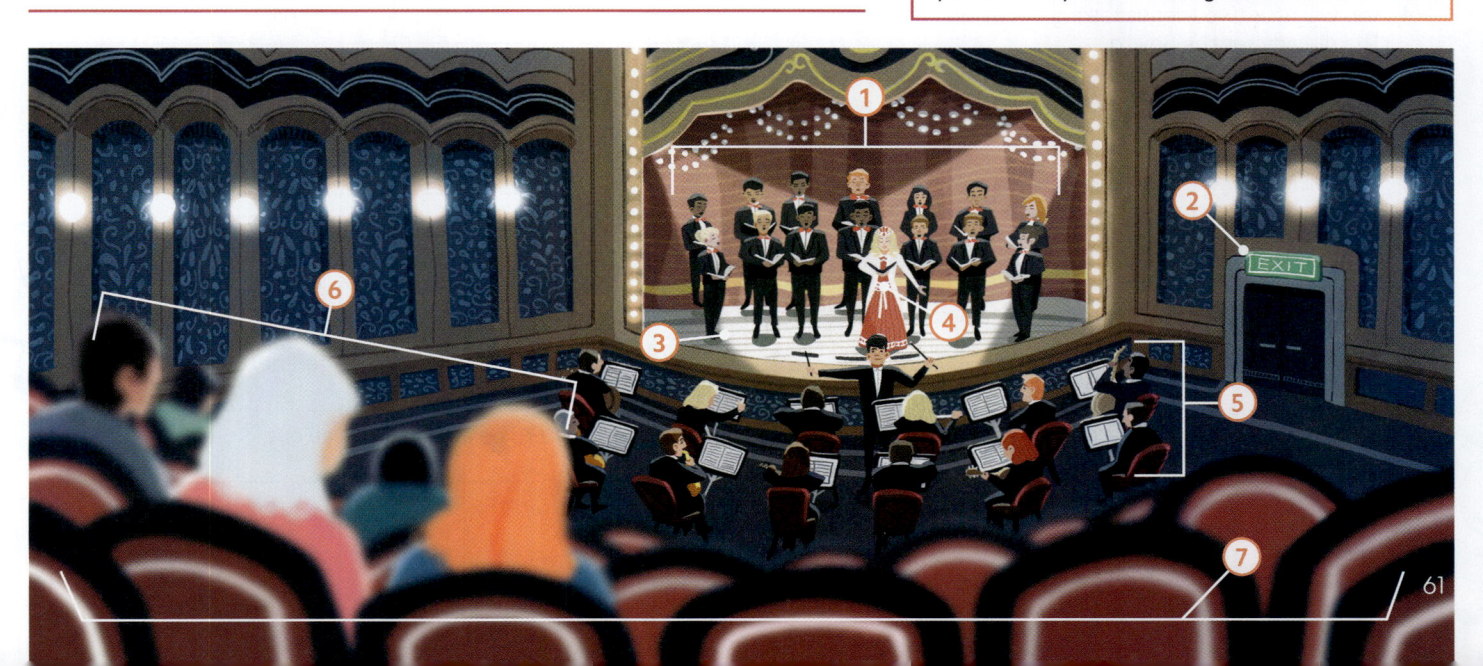

5 In the spotlight

LISTENING

Power up

1 Do you prefer to play music or listen to it? Why? Do you think all children should learn to play at least one instrument? Why/Why not?

Listen up

2 🔊 5.5 Read the exam tip and complete the task.

exam tip: multiple choice

With questions about agreement, make sure that both speakers say the same thing. If only one person has the idea or makes the statement, it's not agreement.

Listen to two friends talking about ways of finding out about new music. Which way do they both prefer?

3 e 🔊 5.6 Listen to six conversations. For each question, choose the correct answer.

1 You will hear a girl talking about her new music lessons. What does the girl say about her music lesson?
  A It is held near the school.
  B There are several people with her.
  C The lessons are cheap.

2 You will hear two friends talking about a band. The girl thinks that the band's songs
  A have funny words.
  B help her study.
  C make her feel relaxed.

3 You will hear a boy telling his friend about a rock concert he went to. How does the boy feel now?
  A hopeful of seeing them again
  B pleased that he had good seats
  C keen to share his photos of the event

4 You will hear two friends talking about singing on stage. The girl advises the boy to
  A practise every day.
  B sing often to his family.
  C watch other performances.

5 You will hear two friends talking about playing the guitar. They both agree that
  A it has a calming effect.
  B it makes a pleasant sound.
  C it can be played in different music styles.

6 You will hear two friends talking about a competition they entered. They agree that
  A the performances were good.
  B the judging seemed to be fair.
  C the location was the right size.

4 🔊 5.7 Listen to conversation 2 from Ex 3 again. Work in pairs and tell each other about a band you like. Give reasons.

5 Read the grammar box and complete the sentences (1–8) with 'unless', 'in case' or 'if I were you'.

explore grammar ➙ p134

unless, in case, if I were you

Use *unless* to mean 'if not'.
I could hardly see the stage unless I stood up.

Use *if I were you, I'd …* to give advice.
If I were you, I'd work on your body language.

Use (*just*) *in case* to say you want to be safe or prepared for something.
I pay attention just in case I hear a song I don't know.

1 .... you practise more, you won't improve your writing skills.
2 Take your guitar with you, ... they let you play.
3 .... , I'd enter a competition. You could win!
4 I'd be honest about your friend's singing ....
5 Let's call the concert hall, ... they still have tickets available.
6 I'll play the young man's part .... you want to.
7 I'd choose this song .... I'm sure everyone will love it.
8 You need to try harder. You won't win that competition .... you do your best!

6 Write some advice for each situation. Use 'if I were you' and these phrases.

go on a talent show   go to a pop concert
look online   join an orchestra
try another instrument   write lots of jokes

1 I love music and want to meet people.
....
2 I can't play the piano. It's too difficult.
....
3 I'm a good singer and I want to go on TV.
....
4 I don't know how to buy tickets for the festival.
....
5 I want to do something different tonight.
....
6 I'd like to be a comedian one day.
....

What's Beethoven's favourite fruit? Ba-na-na-naah! Ba-na-na-naah!

SPEAKING

Power up

1 What do you see in photos A–C? How are the photos the same or different?

Speak up

2 🔊 5.8 Listen to a conversation. In what order do the speakers mention photos A–C?

A ....   B ....   C ....

> **exam** tip: describing a photo → p147
>
> If you don't know the word for something or the name of a person, you can describe them. For exa`mple, talk about the size, colour and shape of an object or the clothes and appearance of a person.

3 🔊 5.9 Read the exam tip and complete the conversation with these phrases. Listen again and check your answers.

> it looks like   is made of metal   large, empty space
> red and black   thing that the boy is balancing on
> to do jumps and tricks   what kind of

A: Wow, you've got a lot of different photos on your phone! Isn't that your neighbour in the photo – playing in the street with that ¹... thing by his feet? It looks like a case for a musical instrument.

B: Yes, that's him! He's actually a really talented musician. That thing just behind his feet ²... and produces an amazing sound.

A: I guess the dog liked it too! I don't know ³... dog that is, but I think it's singing!

B: Well, it was trying.

A: So what's happening in this other photo? The one with the kids from school?

B: Yeah, they're filming something. It's a ⁴... – the kind you use for dancing. One is doing some sort of dancing. Another is doing something different – there's a ⁵... with wheels. You usually use it ⁶... outside.

A: I don't think he's going to dance on that!

B: The skateboard, you mean? No, that's my street dance group. The guy only uses that to get to class. He was just messing.

A: And what about this photo? This place looks great. ⁷... a festival of some sort.

B: Yeah, isn't it great? It was a family festival. It was really brilliant!

> **useful language:**
> **dealing with unknown words**
>
> It's a large empty space / long thing.
> It's made of metal/cardboard/wood/plastic.
> It's a thing which you use to/for …
> It looks like a festival / a kind of guitar.

4 🌐 Read the useful language box. Then work in pairs and turn to page 161. Practise describing everything in your photo in one minute. If you don't know a word, try to explain or describe it.

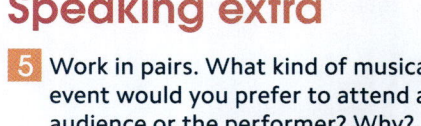

Speaking extra

5 Work in pairs. What kind of musical event would you prefer to attend as the audience or the performer? Why?

5 In the spotlight

WRITING

Power up

1 Match the comments (1–3) with the photos (A–C).

1 'One of the best films I've ever seen! Great music and fantastic costumes.'
2 'It's the best concert I've ever been to. Every song was brilliant.'
3 'An amazing TV show, with great singing and dancing, but mean judges.'

2 Work in pairs and discuss. How do you feel about these types of TV shows and films? Why?

comedy   documentary   historical drama   horror
romance   science fiction   soap opera   thriller

Plan on

3 Read the advert. What do you have to do?

An evening of entertainment!

Articles wanted!

Tell us about an evening of entertainment you have enjoyed. Maybe you went to see a film, a concert or you stayed in and watched a TV show.
- What was good about it?
- Was there anything that wasn't so good?
- How did you feel about the experience?

4 Read the article below. Put the questions in the order the student writes about them (1–3).

A What was good about the type of entertainment? ……..
B How did the person feel? ……..
C What was bad? ……..

Simply the best!

Last weekend lots of bands played a concert at a venue near me and I was lucky enough to go. If you want the best night ever, definitely go to a live concert!

The best thing about going to hear live music was listening to my favourite singer perform all my favourite tracks. She also wore a great costume for the show. Of course, going to a concert can be expensive, though, and it isn't something you can afford to do very often if you're a teenager.

The atmosphere was friendly and relaxed, and like the rest of the audience, I really enjoyed it, although it was a bit crowded and there wasn't much room to dance. It really was an unforgettable experience. You should go — you won't be disappointed!

5 Find words or phrases in the article that have these meanings.
1 a place where a public event happens: ....
2 songs from an album: ....
3 have enough money to buy something: ....
4 the feeling that an event or a place gives you: ....
5 when a place is full of people: ....
6 not happy because something wasn't as good as you wanted it to be:
....

6 Read the exam tip and complete the task. Then find more examples of positive and negative adjectives in the article.

exam tip: article ➜ p152

When you want to recommend something and are describing something positive, talk about the negative side too, to give balance.

Read the positive phrases (A). Complete the negative phrases (B) with the opposite of the highlighted adjective in each positive phrase.

1 A It's full of fast action.
  B The action seemed a bit ....
2 A There were strong main characters.
  B The main characters could be a bit .... at times.

7 Work in pairs. Read the comments below and discuss the questions.
1 Is the person referring to a TV show, a film or could it be both?
2 Are the opinions positive or negative?
3 Can you think of a film or TV show each phrase could describe?

A Unfortunately, you have to pay extra for the channel it's on.
B The scenery in it can be a bit disappointing.
C I think the special effects look better in 3D.
D It's perfect for a night in with friends.
E I really hope they make a second one.
F I felt quite sad when the series came to an end.
G Fans of the book won't feel disappointed by this.
H The ending seemed quite easy to predict.

8 Read the advert in Ex 3 again. Follow these steps to plan your article.
• Think of a title.
• Make notes for each question in the advert. Use Ex 4–7 to help you.
• Read the language box. Think about which key words or phrases you can use in your article.

explore language

making positive comments

The good thing about concerts/festivals is the atmosphere.

The best thing is the exciting storylines.

describing problems

The sound of live music can sometimes be poor.

The only bad thing about the show is the dull costumes.

Sitting in your comfortable pyjamas on the sofa is a lazy option, but I love it!

making a recommendation

If you watched/saw/tried this, you'd love it.

On the whole, I would/can recommend this concert/TV show/film.

Write on

9 e Write your article in about 100 words.

Improve it

10 Read your article. Did you:
1 answer all three questions in the advert?
2 include a range of adjectives?
3 use the language of entertainment? Look back at the vocabulary on page 61. Are there any words/phrases there that you could add to improve your article?

game on

Work in pairs. Take turns to describe the opening scene of your favourite film. Can your partner guess which film it is?

SWITCH ON

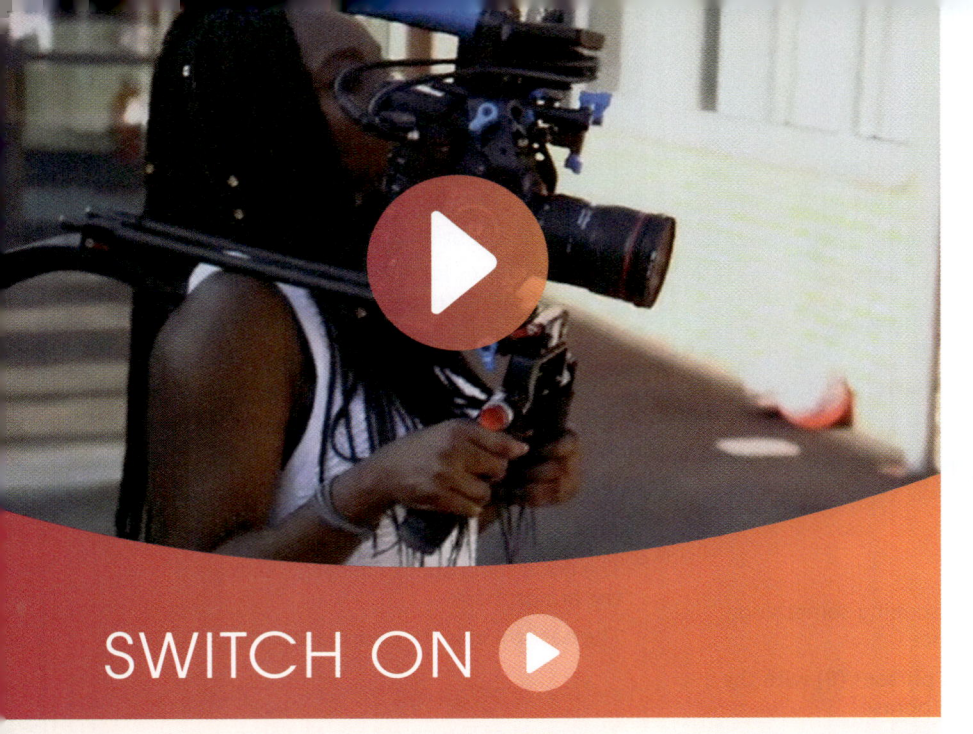

In search of fame

1 Work in pairs and discuss the questions.
1. Would you like to be famous? Why/Why not?
2. What would you like to be famous for?
3. Can you think of any negative sides to fame?

2 ▶ Watch the clip. What is Kyanne auditioning for? How does she feel about it?

3 ▶ Watch again and answer the questions.
1. There are lots of .... for young people to step into the spotlight.
2. But it's a .... – with lots of .... kids.
3. Auditions are .... for the performers and their parents.
4. Kyanne really .... Tyriek and she gets the job.

4 How do you think Kyanne's mother feels about her daughter wanting to be famous?

Project

5 Work in pairs to create a fact file about a 'child star' celebrity.
1. Research a famous person from your country or from another country. Think about these questions.
   - Do they come from a famous family? Did their parents push them 'into the spotlight'?
   - What are their skills? Acting? Singing? Dancing?
   - What was their first 'big break'?
   - What are they most famous for?
   - Was fame at a young age a positive or a negative experience?
2. Create your fact file. Add photos, video or drawings.
3. Share your fact file with the class.

INDEPENDENT LEARNING

Writing skills

1 Look at the article you wrote in this unit. Which statement best describes your goals in writing? Do you think you need a different goal?

1. I need to use better adjectives.
2. I need to use a wider range of language.
3. I want to organise my sentences in the best order.
4. I want to make it clear that I'm writing an article.

2 Match these tips (A–D) with the goals in Ex 1 (1–4).
- **A** Keep a list of the new grammar you have learnt. Can you introduce any of it into your writing?
- **B** Check your sentences. Do they all answer the questions?
- **C** Try to use three new words you've learnt that week in each writing task.
- **D** Make a checklist of do's and don'ts for writing articles and use it each time you write one.

3 Can you think of any other tips to give to students with these problems?

4 Set two goals for yourself in writing. Think about what you find difficult at the moment. How will you improve? How will you know that you have improved?

1. In writing, I want to ....
   I will do this by ....
2. I will know that I have done this when ....

UNIT CHECK

Wordlist

Entertainment
audience (n)
book (v)
choir (n)
clap (v)
costume (n)
entertain (v)
exit (n)
film (v)
interview (v)
orchestra (n)
perform (v)
record (v)
review (v)
row (n)
stage (n)

Celebrity
actor (n)
politician (n)
public (adj)
rock star (n)
sports star (n)

Types of show and film
comedy (n)
documentary (n)
historical drama (n)
horror (n)
romance (n)
science fiction (n)
soap opera (n)
thriller (n)

Other
(can) afford to (v)
be under a lot of stress (phr)
crowded (adj)
disappointed (adj)
due to (phr)
end up (with) (phr v)
have the right to (phr)
negative attention (phr)
the last thing I need (phr)
track (n)
turn your back on (phr)
venue (n)

Extra
atmosphere (n)
festival (n)
laugh at sb (v)
(pop) concert (n)
track (n)

Vocabulary

1 🔊 5.10 Listen to eight sentences. When you hear the beep, write the correct word from the *Entertainment* section of the wordlist.

1 ....   5 ....
2 ....   6 ....
3 ....   7 ....
4 ....   8 ....

2 🔊 5.11 Listen and check your answers.

3 Complete the sentences with words from the *Entertainment* and *Celebrity* sections of the wordlist in the correct form.

1 He's one of my favourite .... I've seen all of his films.
2 The .... in the film are beautiful – especially the dresses.
3 Lee is going to .... in the school play next year.
4 I prefer to sit in the .... and watch the acting or singing.
5 I remember being on .... dressed as a tree when I was six years old.
6 When the fire alarm went off, everyone rushed to the ....
7 I'd love to be a .... and sing in front of thousands of people!
8 She .... the school play on her smartphone and then posted it online.

4 Complete the article with words from the wordlist in the correct form.

The school play

Who doesn't have a photo at home somewhere of them dressed in a silly ¹........................... , standing on the ²........................... in the school hall? For me, my special moment came when I was seven years old, and I had a really important part in the school play – I was the third tomato! In a play about healthy eating, it was an important part to have.

Looking out behind a curtain, the room was very ³........................... . There were more ⁴........................... of chairs than I had ever seen before. There was a ⁵........................... of children that started singing as we walked on stage. Of course, all my family was in the ⁶........................... too – and I could see they were all really proud of me.

I think that all children enjoy hearing a room full of people who ⁷........................... and cheer for them. It gives them confidence and creates lifelong memories. It's important to ⁸........................... in school plays, even if you are just the third tomato on the left!

UNIT CHECK
Review

1 Choose the correct verb forms to complete the sentences.
1. If the concert **finishes / will finish** early, we **take / 'll take** the bus home.
2. I **help / 'll help** you if you **help / 'll help** me.
3. If the TV show **starts / will start**, I **call / 'll call** you.
4. When I **watch / 'll watch** 'Shrek', I **cry / 'll cry**.
5. If the costume **looks / 'll look** alright, I **let / 'll let** you know.
6. My brother **picks / 'll pick** us up after the show if we **ask / 'll ask** him.

2 Complete the first conditional sentences with the correct form of the verbs in brackets.
1. If I .... (not leave) now, I .... (be) late for my guitar class.
2. If you .... (speak) to John, ... (you/ask) him about the party?
3. I .... (not have) much money left if I .... (buy) those concert tickets.
4. .... (you/help) me if you .... (have) time later?
5. If we .... (win) the competition, we .... (appear) on local TV.
6. I .... (not buy) their new album unless it .... (be) better than the last one.

3 Complete the advice using these prompts.

ask / mum / let you in   go / shopping / something new
go / bed / earlier   look / grammar / again
practise / songs   speak / friend

1. My clothes are getting too small for me.
   If I were you, ...
2. I feel sad.
   If I were you, ...
3. I have a big test next week.
   If I were you, ...
4. I lost my keys.
   If I were you, ...
5. I need to sing on stage.
   If I were you, ...
6. I always feel tired in the morning.
   If I were you, ...

4 🔊 5.12 Listen to five people talking about video games. Have you played a video game similar to the ones described?

5 🔊 5.13 Complete the sentences with the correct form of these verbs. Listen again and check your answers.

be able to (x2)   drive   fall off   find   give   go
have   hit   make

What would happen if video games were real?

1. If you .... a building, you .... stand up again.
2. If you .... a sharp knife, you .... cut fruit in mid-air.
3. You .... diamonds if you .... a deep hole.
4. If you .... a mushroom, it .... you coins.
5. You .... at twice the speed if you .... over a special part of the track.

6 Choose the correct words to complete the article.

The attraction of singing competitions

People say that singing competitions have become so popular in recent years because we love to imagine being on stage. If we ¹**are / were** on the show waiting to perform, we would feel afraid and excited, just like the people on TV. Singing competitions are a kind of modern day fairy story. If someone is born poor, they ²**will / would** still become rich overnight if they practise enough. It's a nice idea, even if it's not really true. Most people ³**can / would** panic if they ever found themselves on stage. But because so many stars on television found fame through talent shows, it's very easy to believe that we could do the same. ⁴**When / If** we entered the competition, we could become rich and famous, too. Of course, in real life, ⁵**unless / so** you already sing like an angel, it's probably best to enjoy the show from the sofa. And if you do ever decide to actually enter a singing competition, remember to have a taxi waiting, just in ⁶**case / that** everything goes wrong.

7 Write three sentences of your own starting with:

If video games were real, …

> "We live in an **incredible world**."

Look at the photo and discuss the questions.
1 What can you see in the photo?
2 What other unusual natural places on Earth do you know about?
3 Which places on Earth do you think are the most beautiful? Why?

Down to Earth

6

READING
topic: our blue planet
skill: referencing in a text
task: gapped text

GRAMMAR
the passive: present simple and past simple
have/get something done

VOCABULARY
the natural world
order of adjectives

LISTENING
topic: young people who change the world
skill: avoiding distractors
task: multiple choice

SPEAKING
topic: being environmentally-friendly
skill: turn-taking
task: collaborative task

WRITING
topic: a place to visit
skill: thanking, inviting, accepting, refusing
task: email

SWITCH ON ▶
video: ocean culture
project: design a community

6 Down to Earth

READING

Power up

1 Look at photos A and B. Have you heard of these sea creatures before? What other sea creatures do you know about?

2 Read the blog post on page 71 quickly and answer the questions.
   1 What other sea creatures does the blog post talk about?
   2 Which facts did you find surprising?

Read on

3 Look at the pronouns in bold in the first paragraph of the blog post. What does each one refer to? Choose A or B.
   1 A the Earth's oceans
     B humans have explored five percent of oceans
   2 A the documentary series
     B the ocean
   3 A the ocean
     B the documentary series

4 Read the exam tip and complete the task.

> **exam tip: gapped text**
>
> Make sure that the subject/object pronouns or possessive adjectives in the sentences match the nouns before or after the gap.
>
> Read these sentences and decide if A or B best fits the gap. Use the words in bold to help you.
>
> I like **documentaries**. .... I learn a lot from **them**.
>
> A **It** teaches people things.
> B **They**'re interesting programmes.

5 Read these sentences. Five of them have been removed from the blog post. Find the pronouns in the sentences.

A They were quite dangerous.
B Eventually, it broke.
C I've since read this change isn't unusual for fish.
D But they then swam deep into the ocean.
E However, I definitely think it was worth the time.
F It's not an easy journey for them.
G It can swim as fast as sixty kilometres per hour.
H It's not only land creatures which are intelligent.

A green turtle

6 **e** Read the blog post again. For each question, choose the correct answer. There are three extra sentences which you do not need to use.

7 Find these words in the blog post. Match them with their meanings.

explore   incredible   planet   sight   survive   tiny creature

1 unbelievable: ....
2 continue to live in difficult conditions: ....
3 a large, round object in space that moves around the sun: ....
4 something you can see: ....
5 travel around to find out about a place: ....
6 a very small living thing that's not a plant: ....

Sum up

8 In your own words, explain what you have learnt about the sea creatures in the blog post.

Speak up

9 Work in pairs. Do you think you'd enjoy watching 'The Blue Planet'? Why/Why not? What would you like to watch a documentary about?

The Mariana Trench in the Pacific Ocean is deeper than five Eiffel Towers on top of each other.

Our blue planet

B kobudai fish

Did you know that humans have explored just five percent of the Earth's oceans? I find **¹that** surprising. Seventy percent of the Earth is covered with water, which means there's a lot we don't know about our planet. I recently watched a documentary series called 'The Blue Planet II'. **²It** was really interesting and taught its viewers about the ocean and life in **³it**.

For example, we saw the rather ugly adult kobudai fish turn from a female into a male. **1**............................ In fact, about 500 different types of fish experience it. Once the fish became male, he fought other male fish for the attention of the females.

There was also the tusk fish which used a rock as a kitchen tool. The fish put a shellfish in its mouth and then repeatedly hit the shell against a rock. **2**............................ The fish picked up what was inside the shell and ate it.

We discovered that baby green turtles must survive alone from the moment they hatch from eggs on the beach. They immediately travel several metres across the sand to the sea. **3**............................ They are sometimes caught and eaten by birds. Even if they reach the sea, they have to swim for many kilometres before they are safe.

The most surprising creature for me was the giant trevally fish. **4**............................ This ability helps it to follow a bird from under water and then jump out and catch it. It was a shocking sight.

These are just a few of the incredible animals we saw in the documentary series. It took film-makers four years to make. **5**............................ The photography was amazing and I was excited by what I saw. It made me realise just how little I know about our blue planet.

'Did you know that humans have explored just five percent of the Earth's oceans?'

6 Down to Earth

GRAMMAR

1 Read the example sentences (A–D) in the grammar box and answer these questions (1–3).
   1 Is each example sentence about the past or the present?
   2 Does it state who or what does/did the action?
   3 Does the information about who or what does/did the action appear before or after the verb?

2 Read the grammar box and check your ideas.

explore grammar → p136

the passive: present simple and past simple

A We use the passive when we want to focus on the action and not who/what did it.
   A rock **was used** to break open the shell.
   The series **was watched** all over the world.

B We also use the passive when we don't know who/what does the action or when it's obvious from the context.
   The documentary **was filmed** all over the world.
   The fish **was seen** on TV for the first time.

C If we want to say who or what does the action, we use *by*.
   The turtles are sometimes caught **by birds**.
   The shell is picked up **by the fish** and taken to a rock.

D **Note:** Always make sure **be** matches the subject.
   A baby green **turtle is** left to survive on its own.
   Thousands of **bottles** of water **are** found in the sea each day.

3 Choose the correct verb forms to complete the quiz questions.

How much do you know about our **planet?**

You've lived on Earth your whole life. But how much do you really know about it? Can you answer these five questions?

1 According to scientists, Earth **formed / was formed** how many billions of years ago?
2 The world's water **divides / is divided** into how many major oceans?
3 How many people **inhabit / are inhabited** the Earth?
4 What percentage of the Earth's surface **covers / is covered** in water?
5 The highest temperature on Earth **recorded / was recorded** in what country?

4 Work in pairs. Do the quiz in Ex 3.

5 🔊 6.1 Listen to people answering the quiz questions and check your answers. Do we generally know our planet well?

6 Work in pairs. Student A, turn to page 160. Student B, look at these sentences. Complete your sentences with the correct passive form of the verbs in brackets.
   1 Salt water .... (create) by rain hitting rocks.
   2 Around a quarter of living things .... (find) in the oceans.
   3 Around eight million tonnes of plastic .... (throw) into the sea last year.
   4 The longest range of mountains .... (locate) in South America.
   5 Ambergis (oil in a whale's stomach) .... (use) in some perfumes.
   6 Between 2014 and 2015, 381 new types of living things .... (discover) in the Amazon rainforest.

7 Work in the same pairs and share your sentences. Guess if they are true or false. Then check your answers. Student A, turn to page 162. Student B, turn to page 160.

Speak up

8 Work in pairs and discuss the questions about the facts in Ex 6.
   1 Which fact was the most surprising?
   2 Which fact was the most worrying?
   3 What other interesting facts do you know about our world?
   4 In what ways should we know our planet better?

VOCABULARY
the natural world

A: cloud, sunshine, rocks, snow

B: cliff, moon, star, sand, waves

C: storm, waterfall, fog, field, earth, path

1 Look at the pictures. Put the words in the correct group. Some words may go in more than one group.

sky and weather	forms of water	the ground

2 Complete the fact file with words from Ex 1.

Environment fact file

1 A .... is bad weather with rain, strong winds and sometimes thunder.
2 The outside layer of the Earth is made up of ....
3 Farmers need good .... , sunshine and rain to grow plants for food.
4 Rain is important. Without it, fields become deserts because dry earth becomes ....
5 Some .... are used to create hydroelectricity.
6 .... is created when warm, wet air rises up and meets cool air.
7 Stars create their own light, but light from the .... is reflected sunlight.
8 Some .... in the sea are created by the moon and the sun. Others are created by wind.

3 Read the language box and look at the examples. Can you think of any other opinion and fact adjectives?

explore language

adjective order

We usually put an opinion adjective before a fact adjective (opinion + fact + noun).

a **dangerous**, **icy** river   the **beautiful**, **blue** sea

When there are two fact adjectives, we put size or age before colour (fact (size or age) + fact (colour) + noun).

a **long**, **white** beach   the **large**, **brown** rocks

Note: We usually put a comma between the adjectives.

4 Decide which of these adjectives are fact adjectives (F) and which are opinion adjectives (O).

amazing   ancient   dangerous   flat   high   horrible
huge   incredible   low   narrow   pretty   scary

5 Put the words in brackets in the correct order to complete the sentences.

1 From our window, we could see the .... (snow, white, pretty).
2 Tom and his friend walked along the .... (path, long, narrow).
3 We found a .... and sat on it (flat, rock, black).
4 They stood on top of the .... (cliffs, huge, white).
5 There are some .... (strong, horrible, waves) in the sea today.
6 There are lots of .... (green, fields, big) here.
7 There's a really .... (beach, sandy, beautiful) over there.
8 There's a(n) .... (ancient, forest, incredible) near my house.

game on

Work in teams. Write a gapped sentence like the ones in Ex 5. Put the adjectives and noun in brackets, in the wrong order. Your teacher will read out the sentence to the other team(s). If they put the words in the correct order, they get a point. The team with the most points wins.

Speak up

6 Work in pairs. Have you ever experienced extreme weather conditions? Tell your partner about it.

What did the big tree say to the little tree? 'Leaf me alone!'

6 Down to Earth

LISTENING

Teens who have helped to change the world

Power up

1 Work in pairs. Read about the young people in the photos and answer the questions.
1. How has each one helped to change the world?
2. Why do you think they started their projects?
3. Do you know any similar people in your country?

Mary Grace Henry started making and selling headbands when she was eleven. The money has sent sixty-six girls in developing countries to school.

At the age of thirteen, Kelvin Doe built a generator out of waste so his village in Sierra Leone could have power. He uses it to run a radio station where he's known as DJ Focus.

Listen up

2 🔊 6.2 Listen to the beginning of a radio interview with a girl who created an app. What kind of app is it?

3 🔊 6.3 Read the exam tip and complete the task.

> **exam tip: multiple choice**
>
> Don't choose an option just because the speaker mentions it. All the answer options will be mentioned but only one will be correct. Listen carefully from beginning to end.
>
> Read question 1 in Ex 4. Listen again and choose the correct answer. Why are the other two options incorrect?

4 🔊 6.4 Listen to the full interview. Choose the correct answer for questions 2–6.
1. When did Holly's interest in recycling begin?
   A when she watched a documentary
   B when she attended a talk
   C when she read an article
2. People have told Holly they like the app because
   A they think it's fun to play.
   B it's easy for them to use.
   C it makes them feel good.
3. Holly thinks the most difficult thing about making the app was
   A advertising it to customers.
   B attracting someone to create it.
   C thinking of an idea for it.
4. Holly's main goal is to
   A make sure all plastic is recycled.
   B change the way people think.
   C reduce the use of plastic.
5. What does Holly do in her spare time?
   A She creates art.
   B She takes photographs.
   C She writes a blog for her website.
6. What are Holly's plans for the future?
   A to be employed by an environmental company
   B to start a computer company
   C to teach at a university

5 🔊 6.5 Listen again and check your answers.

6 Read the grammar box. What verb form is used after 'have' and 'get'?

> **explore grammar** ➔ p136
>
> *have/get something done*
>
> We use *have/get something done* when someone else does a job for us, e.g. a service that we pay for. We can use it in different tenses.
>
> My friends **get pizza delivered** every Friday.
> Sam**'s having his hair cut** at the moment.
> My sister**'s had her wedding dress** specially **made**.
>
> We use *by* to say exactly who does the job for us.
>
> I had my photo taken **by a well-known photographer**.

7 Complete the sentences with the correct form of 'have something done' and the verbs in brackets.
1. Louis .... his head .... (shave) at 10 a.m. later today, to collect money for charity.
2. Where can I .... my boots .... (mend)?
3. Gemma isn't here. She's gone to .... her photo .... (take) for the school magazine.
4. He usually .... his hair .... (cut) by the same hairdresser.
5. My parents .... a new sofa .... (deliver) to our house yesterday.

8 Work in pairs. Tell each other five things you 'have', 'had' or 'are going to have done' for you. Are they similar or different?

1 million plastic bottles are bought around the world every minute.

SPEAKING

Power up

1 Work in pairs. Why do people worry about each of these things? Think about money, health, living conditions and our planet.

carbon footprint   climate change   energy   loss of animal species   pollution   rubbish   transport

2 🔊 6.6 Listen to two students talking about the environment. What do you notice they do when talking? Do they find anything difficult?

3 🔊 6.7 Read the exam tip. Then listen to the same students again. What do they do to take turns this time?

> **exam tip: collaborative task**   ➔ p148
>
> Make sure you take turns to speak. Answer the questions but don't speak the whole time. If your partner is quiet, ask him/her questions to encourage him/her to say more.

4 🔊 6.8 Read the useful language. Listen again and complete the conversation. Then add four more phrases to the useful language.

> **useful language: taking turns**
>
> After you.   Carry on.   Do you agree?   What do you like?
>
> **A:** It's really important that we look after it. What do you ¹............................?
> **B:** I agree with you. It's …
> **A:** When we … Sorry, go ²............................ .
> **B:** It's the most important thing to worry about.
> **A:** ³............................ do you say that?
> **B:** … We need animals, plants and clean water to live.
> **A:** Yes, you're right. … I try to turn off lights when I leave a room. What do you ⁴............................ ?

5 Work in pairs. Choose any photo from this unit and talk about it and the topic it relates to. Use the phrases and questions from the useful language and Ex 4 to help you take turns.

Speak up

6 e Work in pairs. Read the exam tip, then turn to page 163 and complete the task. Use the useful language to help you.

7 Work in pairs and discuss the questions.
1 Which would you prefer: to spend time at the beach or in the mountains? Why?
2 Is it important for us to protect our environment? Why?
3 Do you think that children should have lessons at school about caring for the environment? Why?
4 What do you think you could do to be friendlier to the environment? Why?

Speaking extra

8 Work in groups. If you could create an eco-friendly charity, what would it be? Why? Make a list of ideas. Present them to the class.

> How about a project to encourage students to walk or cycle to school?

> Good idea! We can reduce pollution if we travel that way. What do you think?

> It is a good idea. But I'd prefer to start a charity for protecting animals.

6 Down to Earth

WRITING

Power up

1 Work in pairs and discuss the questions.
1. Have you ever participated in an exchange with another school? What happened?
2. If you could do a language exchange with a school in another country, which would you choose? Why?

Plan on

2 Read the email from Vincent, an exchange student who is going to visit Turkey soon. Answer the questions.
1. Is his email polite and formal or friendly and chatty?
2. What four points does Emad need to include in his reply?

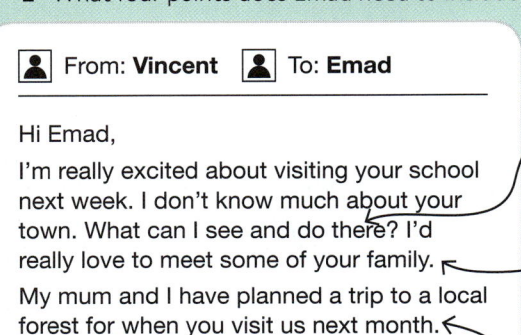

From: Vincent **To: Emad**

Hi Emad,

I'm really excited about visiting your school next week. I don't know much about your town. What can I see and do there? I'd really love to meet some of your family.

My mum and I have planned a trip to a local forest for when you visit us next month. It's really huge and I can take you mountain biking if you like. It's a lot of fun!

See you next week!
Vincent

say
invite to cousin's house
thank Vincent
yes!

3 Read Emad's reply and find one phrase for each of these functions.
1. inviting
2. thanking
3. accepting or refusing an invitation

From: Emad **To: Vincent**

Hi Vincent,

I'm glad you're excited about visiting my school. I'm really looking forward to it too.

Antalya's a big city by the sea. There are lovely beaches there and two water parks too. We could go there. There's also the popular Kursunlu Waterfall about 20 km away. It's really beautiful and I'm sure you'd like it. Oh yes, would you like to meet my cousins on Wednesday evening? My aunt and uncle are having a party and you're invited.

Thank you for organising a day trip during my visit next month. I'd love to go mountain biking! You can tell me more about it next week.

See you soon!
Emad

In the Rio Negro Valley, Columbia, students travel 800 metres by zip wire to get to school.

4 Put the words in the correct order to make sentences. Then match the sentences (A–D) with the functions in Ex 3 (1–3).

A ride / I / I'm afraid that / can't / a bike
....

B fantastic / forest trip / sounds / the
....

C for all / thanks / your help / so much
....

D having / how about / with my family / a picnic?
....

5 Read the exam tip and complete the task.

> **exam tip: email**   ↪ p150
>
> Learn phrases for different functions (e.g. thanking, inviting, accepting, refusing) and use them when you write. They'll help you sound natural.
>
> Complete the examples. Use one word in each gap.
>
> Thanks so ¹............................ for your advice.
> Would you ²............................ to go to a party?
> I'd love ³............................ meet your cousin.

6 Read an email from an exchange student coming to your school. What four things do you need to include in your reply?

(say)
(invite to youth club)

> **From: Megan**
>
> Hi!
> Next week is the big trip to your town. I'm looking forward to finally meeting you. What are some good places to visit? I'd like to hang out with some of your friends if I can.
> When you're here next month, we're going to spend the day in the mountains. My mum's bought us coach tickets. Would you like to go skiing or snowboarding? Let me know.
> See you next week!
> Megan

(thank Megan)
(tell Megan)

7 Work in pairs. Think about places in and around your area that Megan could visit. Discuss what students could see or do there and choose one or two to write about. Use these ideas or your own.

a beach   a lake   a museum   a palace   some mountains

8 Which phrases from Ex 5 could you use in your reply to Megan?

Write on

9 e Write your email in about 100 words.

Improve it

10 Read your email. Does it include all four points in Megan's email? Does it sound friendly?

11 Read your email again and answer the questions. Use your answers to help you improve it.

1 Have you used functional phrases to help you thank, invite, etc.?
2 Is your grammar accurate?
3 Is your use of vocabulary and punctuation correct?

SWITCH ON

Ocean culture

1 Work in pairs and discuss the questions.
1. If you could live in a remote place, where would you choose to live?
2. How would you use the natural resources of that place to survive?

2 ▶ Watch the clip. Name three ways Bajau people's lives are closely connected to the ocean.

3 ▶ Watch again and answer the questions.
1. Where do the Bajau people live?
2. How long can Jimmy hold his breath for?
3. What are Jimmy and his family eating for dinner today?
4. How does the Bajau way of life survive?

4 Would you like to live with the Bajau people? What would you like about living with them? What would you dislike?

Project

5 Work in small groups to design a community that depends on its natural surroundings. Follow these steps.
1. Think about these things to help you design your community.
   - how native peoples like the Bajau connect with nature.
   - the natural places in your area
   - the rural places near your area
2. Make an action plan: how will your community use its natural surroundings to survive?
3. Present your action plan to the class.
4. Listen to the other groups' presentations. Which ideas do you think would be most effective?

INDEPENDENT LEARNING

Reading skills

1 Complete the questionnaire. Think about the blog post on page 71 to help you.

My English reading skills

How much do you agree with these statements?
(5 = completely agree, 1 = completely disagree)

1. ☐ I can read and understand a text quickly.
2. ☐ I can understand the main points of a text.
3. ☐ I can understand detailed information in a text.
4. ☐ I have a big enough vocabulary to understand most of what I read.
5. ☐ When I don't know a word in a text, I work out the meaning or ignore it.
6. ☐ I find reading in English easy.
7. ☐ I enjoy reading in English.
8. ☐ Reading is my best skill in English.

2 Work in pairs and discuss your answers to Ex 1.

3 Match the goals (1–5) with the actions (A–E) that can help you achieve them.
1. I'll improve my reading speed. ....
2. I'll improve my vocabulary so I can understand a text better. ....
3. I'll read and understand a more challenging text. ....
4. I'll read more. ....
5. I'll understand more detailed information in a text. ....

A Read a text carefully and then write in your own words what it's about.
B Learn twenty new words about a topic and then read about that topic.
C Read three texts on a topic that you're interested in each week.
D Practise reading quickly without stopping to reread information.
E Choose a text from a B2 book and see if the level is challenging but not too hard.

4 How would you like to improve your reading skills? Set yourself a goal and decide how you are going to achieve it. Use Ex 3 to help you.

UNIT CHECK

Wordlist

The natural world
cliff (n)
cloud (n)
earth (n)
field (n)
fog (n)
ground (n)
moon (n)
path (n)
rock (n)
sand (n)
sky (n)
snow (n)
star (n)
storm (n)
sunshine (n)
waterfall (n)
wave (n)
weather (n)

Adjectives
amazing
ancient
dangerous
flat
high
horrible
huge
incredible
low
narrow
pretty
scary
tiny

The environment
animal species (n)
carbon footprint (n)
climate change (n)
energy (n)
plastic (n)
pollution (n)
recycle (v)
recycling (n)
rubbish (n)

Other
creature (n)
explore (v)
planet (n)
sight (n)
survive (v)
transport (n)

Extra
documentary (n)
sunlight (n)
thunder (n)
wind (n)

Vocabulary

1 🔊 **6.9** Listen to eight sentences. When you hear the beep, write the correct word from the wordlist.

1 .... 5 ....
2 .... 6 ....
3 .... 7 ....
4 .... 8 ....

2 🔊 **6.10** Listen and check your answers.

3 Choose the correct words to complete the sentences.

1 We can't cycle down that path. It's too **narrow / flat**.
2 I wonder how old these rocks are? I bet that they're **ancient / high**.
3 Experienced surfers usually want to surf a **huge / low** wave.
4 The land around here is really **flat / narrow**. There's not a hill in sight.
5 That was a really **horrible / low** storm. I thought I was going to die!
6 It's definitely not the best waterfall I've seen but it's **incredible / pretty**.
7 The view from the top of the cliff was **incredible / high**.
8 We spent the whole day in the mountains and had an **ancient / amazing** time.
9 The bird was so **low / tiny** it could fit in my hand.
10 Swimming with sharks? No, thank you – that's way too **scary / flat** for me!

4 Match the meanings with words from the *The natural world* and *The environment* sections of the wordlist.

1 the planet that we live on: ....
2 bottles and shopping bags are often made from this material: ....
3 the sun, moon and stars are in this: ....
4 when the air, water or land are dirty: ....
5 things you no longer need and throw away: ....
6 you can walk along this, e.g. on a mountain or through a forest: ....

5 Complete the article with words from *The environment* and *Other* sections of the wordlist in the correct form.

THE environment

¹........................... Earth is amazing. It's full of living ²........................... and plants. Some of them can ³........................... in very hot or cold temperatures. We still don't know exactly how many different species of plants or animals live on Earth. Every year scientists ⁴........................... new parts of the world and find new ones. That's why people are worried about the effect of ⁵........................... on the world. As temperatures go up, it affects our world. People try to protect the environment by ⁶........................... rubbish and using less ⁷........................... – for example, to light their house. They might use public ⁸........................... too, to reduce air pollution.

Review

1 Choose the correct verb forms to complete the signs. Then choose the correct answer, A, B or C.

① Visitors **is / are** asked to use the right bins for recycling.

What must visitors do?
A   recycle rubbish correctly
B   use their own recycling bins
C   ask about recycling

② **TURTLE BEACH**
This beach is **use / used** by nesting turtles. Please do not put sun umbrellas or other objects in the sand.

What mustn't visitors do?
A   leave their sun umbrellas
B   walk or sit near the turtle nests
C   put things in the sand

③ **Clearwater Beach**
This beach **are clean / is cleaned** each evening. Any lost property is taken to the hotel reception.

Who will clean the beach?
A   visitors
B   the receptionist
C   we don't know

2 Complete the text with the correct passive form of the verbs in brackets.

I went on a school camping trip last summer. We ¹............ (take) to a valley in the middle of nowhere in a coach. Tents ².............. (put up) for us as soon as we arrived, so that was good. Breakfast and dinner ³.............. (cook) on the campsite but lunch ⁴.............. (bring) in from a local café. Dinner ⁵.............. (eat) round a camp fire. Every year students ⁶.............. (drive) to a small mountain where they ⁷.............. (teach) how to climb. This year, we couldn't. Instead, we ⁸.............. (take) to a lake where we ⁹.............. (give) fishing equipment. A grand total of one fish ¹⁰.............. (caught) between us!

3 🔊 6.11 Listen and check your answers.

4 e Read the article and for each question, write the correct answer. Write one word for each gap.

Are we losing touch with nature?

In 2015 dozens of nature words were removed from a children's dictionary and replaced by technology words like 'blog' and 'chat room'. This news ¹.............. reported by the media and many people complained to the publisher. The publisher explained that, because ².............. is limited space in a dictionary, old words have to go when new ones are added.

In my view, it's important that the dictionary includes words which ³.............. used by children today. Technology is a major part ⁴.............. our lives, so children need technology vocabulary. Because most young people grow up in towns and cities these days, we don't really need to know ⁵.............. names of trees and plants like our great-grandparents did.

On the other hand, without the natural world, we cannot live. If we are ⁶.............. connected to it, we won't be able to survive in future. Perhaps learning the words for the things around us is the first step to building a connection.

5 Complete the sentences with the correct form of 'have something done' or 'get something done' and the verbs in brackets.

1   My sister.............. her hair.............. (cut) once a year.
2   We.............. pizza.............. (deliver) every Saturday evening.
3   I.............. my nails.............. (do) yesterday.
4   I need to.............. my eyes.............. (check) soon. I think I need glasses.
5   Last week we.............. our house.............. (tidy up) by a cleaner.
6   I always.............. my clothes.............. (iron) by my dad.
7   We.............. our swimming pool.............. (clean) last weekend.
8   My dad.............. the house.............. (paint) every three years.

6 Write a paragraph about things that you 'have done' or 'get done' for you. Who does them?

I have a lot of things done. For example, I have my clothes cleaned. I throw them on a chair in my room and the next day they're in my drawer all nice and clean!

"It's all about getting there."

Look at the photo and discuss the questions.
1 Do you prefer to visit places that are similar or different to your home? Why?
2 How much do you enjoy the journey when you travel to new places? Why?
3 What's the best journey you have ever been on? Why?

Travellers' tales

7

READING
topic: ways of travelling
skill: matching details
task: multiple matching

GRAMMAR
defining relative clauses
modals of obligation, prohibition and necessity

VOCABULARY
travel
verb and noun forms

LISTENING
topic: travelling the world
skill: identifying the type of information missing
task: sentence completion

SPEAKING
topic: travel problems
skill: referring back to what someone said
task: discussion

WRITING
topic: holiday tips
skill: creating interest
task: article

SWITCH ON ▶
video: surf around the world
project: prepare a research-based presentation

7 Travellers' tales

READING

Power up

1 What things are important to you when you go on holiday? Why? Put these factors in order of importance (1 = most important).
- activities
- people
- place
- journey
- weather
- accommodation

Read on

2 Work in pairs. Look at the photo on page 83 and discuss the questions.
1 What kind of transport is this?
2 Which do you think is the most convenient way to get around a big city?
3 Which types of transport have you tried?

3 The young people below are visiting a city for the day. Read what each one says about their day. Who has visited the city before?

4 Read the article on page 83 quickly. Which tour would you like to go on?

5 Read the exam tip and complete the task.

> **exam tip: multiple matching**
> If two texts seem to be a good match for a person, keep reading until you find something which means that one is not correct.
>
> Read description 1 in Ex 3 again about Mala. What does she want? Find three things that are important for her. Which is the only city tour text which matches all three things?

6 e Read the article again. Decide which city tour (A–H) would be the most suitable for the people in Ex 3 (1–5).

7 Find phrasal verbs in the texts that have these meanings.
1 get on (text D): ....
2 get off (text D): ....
3 visit for a short time (text F): ....
4 book (text G): ....
5 travel around (text H): ....

Sum up

8 Work in pairs. Decide on one advantage and one disadvantage of each tour.

Speak up

9 Work in groups and do a survey. Follow these steps.
1 Find out which type of travel the other students in your group would like to use in a city and why.
2 Organise the results of your survey.
3 Look at your results. Which type of travel is the most popular in your group? Why?
4 Compare the results of your survey with other groups.

A day in London

1 Mala is excited about her first trip to the city but she wants to know how people live there. She likes visiting places and discovering things on her own and in her own time.

2 Dan and Sophie are going round Britain. They have only a day in the city, so they want to go to as many places as possible and would like someone well qualified to show them round.

3 Christa has been to the city before, so she's seen the centre. She's interested in history and would like to get a wider view of the city in a way that is modern and different.

4 Carlos has never been to the city before but he would like to see it slowly and get an unusual view of it. He also wants to see what the city looks like after dark.

5 Roopa wants to get to know the centre of the city slowly and to see the real life as she goes along as well as having some time to explore the things she's interested in.

EIGHT CITY TOURS

A Tony's Tours

Join one of these tours and you'll get to see some amazing views of the city and the river. You'll travel on a cable car which has all the latest entertainment technology, including music and information videos. Allow about half an hour as we take you slowly across the river to see the oldest parts of the city and the sea.

B ABC Travel

If you want to see the real streets, then try our pedicab tours. Our driver will take you around on our special bicycles that have seats on the back. It's a gentle way to get to know the very heart of the city. And you can stop off where you want and sightsee. We will wait for you!

C Best Tours Ltd

The metro is huge and covers a very wide area of the city and even areas outside. Our tours include a guide who is very experienced and can take you to parts of the city where tourists don't normally go. Our price includes your ticket for one day and the opportunity to visit three different places.

D AboutTownTours.com

Our tour tickets use the famous city buses. The big advantage is that you can see all the sights as you travel. You choose your own tour for one day or a week. And remember: you can jump on and jump off where you want and simply catch the next bus.

E Smith & Co Tours

Our river bus is the oldest form of transport in the city. It's not the quickest way to travel but it is unique and very relaxed and you can get some of the best views in the city without the traffic. We have a café on board with drinks and refreshments and you can also see the city by night!

F First Class Travel

Our tours allow you to hire a cycle and we give you small interactive maps and an App guide for the main sights. You can go at your own pace and stop off where you want. It's a great way to visit the parks or ride along by the river as long as you are comfortable cycling in the traffic.

G Zebedee Sights

Why not tour the city like a resident? Walking means you avoid the traffic and get to know the city really well! Sign up and you'll get our special map and an App gives you all the information you need. You listen to the information about the sights on your phone, so it's like having a private tour guide.

H Sharp's Tours

If you're feeling fit, you might want to try a Segway. You can hire these individually but you can also join a tour group with a guide to take you round the city. It's a great way to get about if you have enough time – we do ask you do a short training course with us.

7 Travellers' tales

GRAMMAR

1 Read the grammar box and choose the correct words to complete the examples.

explore grammar → p138

defining relative clauses

Defining relative clauses tell us exactly which people, things or animals we are talking about. We use *who* for people, *which* for things and animals and *where* for places.

You'll travel on a cable car ¹**which / where** has all the latest entertainment technology.

Our guide can take you to parts of the city ²**where / that** tourists don't normally go.

Our tours include a guide ³**who / which** is very experienced.

We can also use *that* instead of *who* or *which*.

Our driver will ride you around on our special bicycles ⁴**that / who** have seats on the back.

You can get weekly passes ⁵**who / that** make it more economical.

We can leave out *which*, *who* or *that* when it is the object of the verb, especially in speech and informal writing.

Our special map gives you all the information (that) you need.

2 🔊 7.1 Listen to two students doing a quiz. What are they answering questions about?

3 🔊 7.2 Listen again and complete the quiz questions with 'who', 'which' or 'where'. Then answer the questions. Choose from these words.

a pilot   Captain Scott   Chile   London
Matthew Henson   the bullet

1 What is the very fast train .... runs in Japan?
2 Who is the famous explorer .... went to the Arctic circle?
3 Which is the country .... is furthest south?
4 What is the name of the city .... you can take the Underground?
5 What do we call the person .... flies a plane?
6 Who was the man .... went to the South Pole?

4 Join the sentences using relative clauses. Use 'that'.

1 Rome is a beautiful city. It's very popular with tourists.
2 Do you know the student? He spoke to you.
3 They enjoyed sightseeing at the old castle. It's in the mountains.
4 We're going to see our cousins. They live near the lake.
5 I love travelling on trains. I like the ones that go fast.

5 🔊 7.3 Listen and check your answers.

6 Complete the sentences with relative pronouns. Write '–' if a pronoun is not necessary.

1 Let's go back to the place .... we saw yesterday.
2 The flight .... we were waiting for was late.
3 We met some tourists .... recommended a good restaurant in the city centre.
4 Snorkelling is a holiday activity .... many tourists enjoy.
5 We loved the beach near Patara .... has sea turtles.

7 Complete the article with relative pronouns. Write '–' if a pronoun is not necessary.

A BIG ADVENTURE!

Flying is something ¹.................. Kimberley Anyadike loves. Kimberley is a teenager ².................. comes from California in the USA. When she was fifteen years old, Kimberley flew a small plane across the USA. She took off in California and landed in Virginia and then flew back home. The flight ³.................. she made took thirteen days.

Kimberley learnt to fly when she was twelve. Her family isn't rich and the plane ⁴.................. she flew across the USA in isn't her own. It belongs to a plane museum ⁵.................. helps young pilots to learn about flying.

Kimberley found it hard to be in places ⁶.................. she couldn't see her family. Another problem was the weather ⁷.................. was sometimes very stormy! So why did she do it? 'I wanted to inspire other kids to really believe in themselves,' she said.

Speak up

8 Complete the sentences about things that are important to you.

1 .... is a friend who ....
2 .... is a place where ....
3 .... is a sport which ....

84   In the USA, if people forget their luggage at the airport, it is sold for charity after ninety days.

VOCABULARY

travel

1 🔊 **7.4** Listen to the words and their definitions. What part of speech is each word: a noun (n), a verb (v) or an adverb (adv)?

1 destination ....
2 flight ....
3 land ....
4 motorway ....
5 abroad ....
6 border ....
7 check in ....
8 delay ....
9 passport ....
10 sightseeing ....
11 take off ....
12 traffic jam ....

2 Put the words in Ex 1 in the correct group.

air travel	either air or road travel	road travel

3 Read the dictionary definitions. Then choose the correct words to complete the sentences below.

A **travel** (v): make a journey

B **travel** (n, uncountable): the action of travelling

C **journey** (n, usually singular): the time when you are travelling from one place to another

D **trip** (n): a short visit to a place, usually to go there and return home

1 My friend Sam is going to **travel / trip** to Australia next year.
2 There was a long delay on the **journey / trip** back home.
3 Our **journey / travel** to Amsterdam took eight hours.
4 We had a brilliant **travel / trip** to Turkey.
5 I love **travel / travels**. I'd like to go around the world
6 My mum is away on a business **journey / trip** to Madrid.

explore language

verb and noun forms

Some nouns are almost the same as verbs. Some are identical.

verb	noun
delay / be delayed	delay
travel	travel
take off	take-off
check in	check-in

4 Read the language box. Complete the sentences with words from the box in the correct form.

1 When we got to the airport, there was a long queue at the c.......... .
2 Fasten your seat belts for t.......... and landing.
3 Our friends c.......... to the hotel yesterday.
4 I was looking out of the window when the plane started t.......... .
5 I hate t.......... by plane. I prefer trains.
6 The traffic jam on the motorway d.......... us for about an hour.

5 🇪 Read the story. For each question, choose the correct answer.

I **almost** didn't get there!

A lot of people use their holidays to visit their family in other countries. My family is no different and this summer we went on a trip to Turkey to visit my mum's family. Our ¹...... was Kusadasi, which is on the coast. It was my first trip ²......, and I was very excited. At the airport, we checked ³...... our luggage. Mum gave our passports to the woman at the ⁴......, but mine wasn't there. We searched for ages. I took everything out of my luggage and then I found it inside a magazine in my bag! Luckily, we didn't miss our ⁵...... because there was a two-hour ⁶...... . Next time I know I need to put my passport somewhere safe!

1	A place	B destination	C end	D location
2	A outside	B foreign	C abroad	D external
3	A in	B out	C into	D for
4	A reception	B table	C office	D desk
5	A voyage	B flight	C tour	D journey
6	A pause	B gap	C delay	D hold

game on

Work in pairs and answer the questions. You have two minutes.

Can you name:

1 a capital city abroad?
2 a country or sea that is on the border of your country?
3 two popular tourist destinations near you?
4 a place to go sightseeing in your town?
5 two reasons why people like/hate take-off and landing?
6 two things that can cause a travel delay?

Compare your ideas with the rest of the class. You get one point for each new idea.

7 Travellers' tales

LISTENING

Power up

1 Work in pairs and discuss the questions.
1 What kind of things do you think you can learn when you travel to new places?
2 Do you think you can learn the same things better in school? Why/Why not?

Listen up

2 🔊 **7.5** Listen to a girl talking about how she and her family are travelling the world. Answer the questions.
1 Has she enjoyed travelling? Why/Why not?
2 Where does she go to school?

3 🔊 **7.6** Read the exam tip and complete the task.

> **exam tip: gap fill**
> Look carefully at the words before the gap. For example, an article is followed by a noun; a number may be followed by a plural noun. Also check how many words you think might be missing.
>
> Look at gap 1 in Ex 4. What are you listening for? How do you know? There are two possible answers in the recording. Listen and decide which one is correct. Why is the other option incorrect?

4 e 🔊 **7.7** Listen again and complete the sentences. Write one or two words or a number or a date or a time.

Learn while you travel

Sarah is home-schooled but travels a lot.
She first started travelling at the age of ¹............................ .
She travelled around Australia and then visited the south of ²............................ .
She has only visited places which are ³............................ .
She likes to read ⁴............................ about places she has visited.
She has had the opportunity to go walking and ⁵............................ in beautiful places.
The most important part for Sarah is making ⁶............................ .

5 Read the grammar box and complete the examples with modal verbs.

> **explore grammar** ➔ p138
>
> **modals of obligation, prohibition and necessity**
>
> **must/mustn't**
> We use *must* when we think it is important to do something. We use *mustn't* to mean, 'Don't do this!'
> My parents said we ¹............................ just study from books.
> We ²............................ learn subjects like geography and history.
>
> **have to / don't have to**
> We use *have to / don't have to* when something is/isn't necessary.
> We don't have a traditional lifestyle because we ³............................ go to school.
>
> **had to**
> *Had to* is the past tense of both *must* and *have to*. *Must* has no past form.
> We ⁴............................ sell our house before we could go overseas.
>
> **will have to**
> *Will have to* is the future form of both *must* and *have to*.
> Soon we ⁵............................ go home.
>
> **need to / don't need to**
> We use *need to / don't need to* when we think something is/isn't necessary but not an obligation.
> We ⁶............................ get out and travel.

6 Choose the correct modal verbs to complete the sentences.
1 We **must / mustn't** change some money today. We've only got ten euros left.
2 You **don't have to / mustn't** come with me to the airport. I know how to get there.
3 Your suitcase is full. You **must / mustn't** buy any more souvenirs.
4 I **mustn't / won't have to** buy any sandals. I've already got some.
5 Tanya and Sarah **had to / need to** get up early yesterday to catch their flight.

7 Complete the second sentence so that it has the same meaning as the first sentence.
1 It was necessary to wait at the train station.
   We .... wait at the train station.
2 Planning is important if you want a good holiday.
   You .... make a good plan if you want a good holiday.
3 It's important not to forget your passport.
   You .... forget your passport.
4 It isn't necessary to take lots of luggage.
   You .... take lots of luggage.

Ross Island in Antarctica is the driest place on Earth.

SPEAKING

Power up

1 What kind of problems might someone have when they travel? How bad are these problems? Give each one a number: 1 = not too bad, 2 = annoying, 3 = a disaster!

1. You lose all your money. ....
2. You buy a great souvenir but it breaks on the way home. ....
3. Your phone battery dies. ....
4. You can't find your family in a busy market. ....
5. You forget your ticket. ....
6. You have to share a bedroom with your cousins. ....

2 🔊 7.8 Listen to two students answering one of these questions. Which question is it?

1. What do you think is the best way to prepare for going on a trip?
2. Has something surprising ever happened to you while you were travelling?
3. What would you do if you lost something at an airport or a train station?
4. How do you make sure all your things are safe when you travel?

3 🔊 7.9 Read the useful language and listen again. Which phrase does the girl use to start her answer? Why?

> **useful language: referring back to what someone said**
>
> As (Jack) said, …
> I've never done that. / That's never happened to me.
> I'd do the same as (Jack). / I wouldn't do the same as (Jack).
> I'm not sure I agree with (Jack).
> Like (Molly), I (keep everything in a bag).
> Unlike Molly, I (keep everything in my pockets).

4 Which phrases from the useful language could you use to start your answer to the other three questions in Ex 2? More than one answer might be possible.

5 Work in pairs. Do you believe the boy's story? Why/Why not?

Speak up

6 Read the exam tip. Why is it a good idea to refer back to what your partner said?

> **exam tip: discussion** → p149
>
> If the examiner asks you both the same question and your partner answers first, try to refer back to what they said, e.g. say if you agree, have had the same experience or like the same thing. It shows you were listening to your partner and understood his/her answer.

7 🅔 Work in pairs and discuss the questions in Ex 2. Take turns to answer first and second. When you answer second, refer back to your partner's answer.

Speaking extra

8 Work in pairs. Take turns to tell your partner a travel story. Choose one set of words (1–3) to use in your story. Your partner will ask follow-up questions as you are speaking.

1. amazing   strange   wrong   bag
2. disaster   funny   late
3. new   weird   expensive   lost

7 Travellers' tales

WRITING

Power up

1 Work in pairs. Look at the holiday photos and answer the questions.
1. Where did the people take these photos?
2. What are they doing in the photos?
3. Do you think it was easy or difficult to take these photos?

2 Why do people take photos like these? Have you got any similar photos?

Plan on

3 Read the advert below and answer the questions.
1. Who might read the article? Why?
2. What must writers include in their article?
3. Can they give their own opinion in the article?

We want your top tip for travelling!

Do you have a good travel tip you can share with our readers?

What is your tip and how does it help you when you are travelling?

Write an article answering these questions. We will publish the most interesting ones on our site. Only 100 words, please!

4 Read Gabriel's article below and find these things.
1. an invitation for the reader to give their opinion
2. a travel tip
3. the title
4. how the tip can help the reader
5. a question to get reader's interest

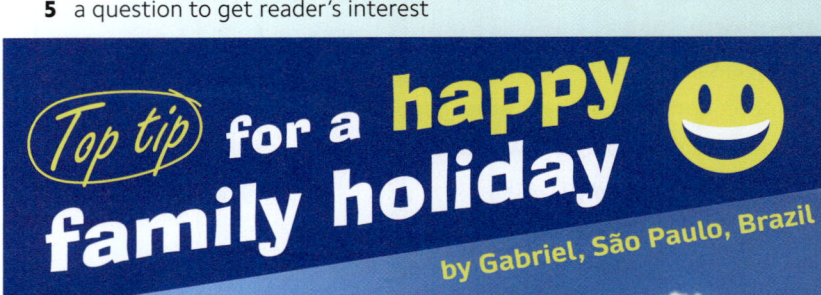

Top tip for a happy family holiday
by Gabriel, São Paulo, Brazil

How important is it for you to have photos of your holiday?

My parents love taking photos of tourist attractions and scenery. Last year, we went to São Salvador, which we all loved. But every day Mum and Dad had their cameras ready and said things like, 'Stand here!', 'Don't move!' and 'Smile!' When we got home, we had lots of photos but my sister and I looked bored in every single one.

So what's my top tip? Grab the camera or use your mobile and take some funny or unusual photos.

What do you think of my suggestion? Would you do this?

Elsie Wright and Frances Griffiths fooled the public with their fake photos of the 'Cottingley Fairies' in 1917.

5 Work in pairs. Think of tips for each of these travel problems.

1. crying baby on a bus or plane
2. getting travel sick
3. dropping your camera in the sea
4. not getting to sleep on the bus or plane

6 Read the exam tip and the language box. Write an opening question and a closing question for each problem in Ex 5. Use phrases from the language box.

exam tip: an article ➙ p152

Use questions in your article to address your reader and get their interest. Then invite comments from them.

explore language

opening questions to your readers

Have you ever … ?
Do you like … ?
How important is it for you to … ?

inviting other people to give their opinions

Do you think that … ?
What do you think of this photo/idea/plan?
Let me know what you think.
Have you got any suggestions/good ideas?

7 Read the advert in Ex 3 again and look at the ideas in Ex 5. Choose the problem and tip you want to write about.

8 Think of a title and the first question you want to ask your readers.

Write on

9 e Write your article in about 100 words.

Improve it

10 Check your article. Have you included all the content points in the task?

11 Work in pairs. Read your partner's article and make notes about these points. Then talk about how you can improve your article.

1. Has the article got a title?
2. Is there an opening question for the reader?
3. Are all the content points included?
4. Does the article invite the reader to give an opinion?

SWITCH ON

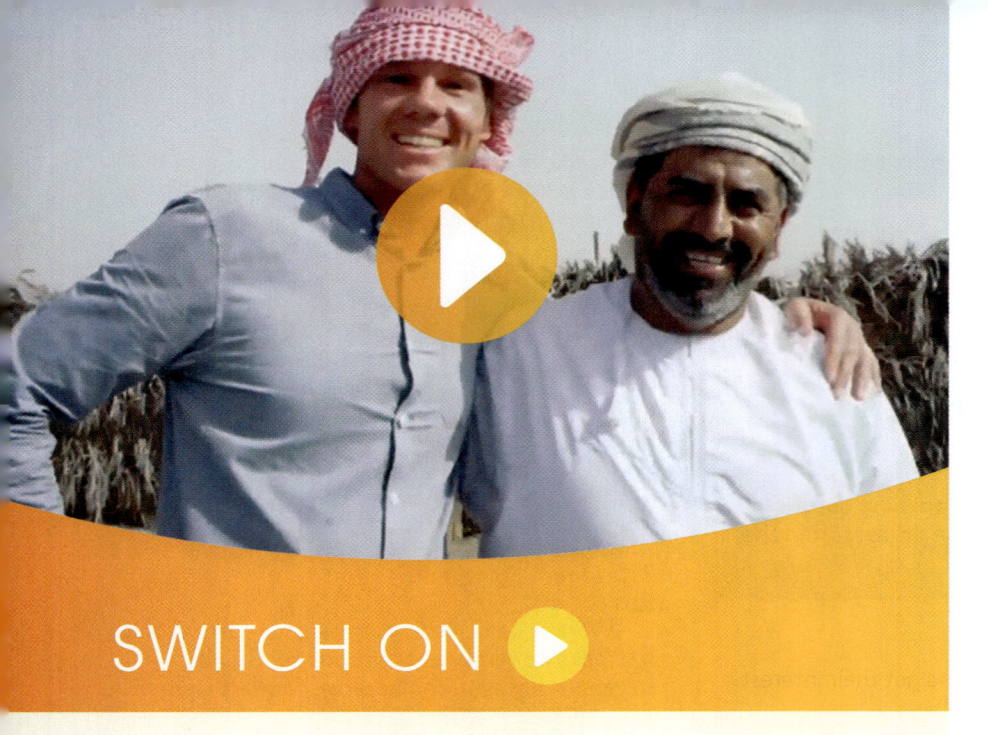

Surf around the world

1. Work as a class. Make a list of all the countries you have visited. Talk about your favourites and the culture in those countries.

2. ▶ Watch the clip and complete the sentences.
   1. Sam Bleakley is a European champion ....
   2. Sam isn't only interested in surfing; he is also interested in the local people, their .... and their ....
   3. Joshua is a keen Ghanaian style ....
   4. Oman is very hot and has vast areas of ....

3. ▶ Watch again. Are these sentences true (T) or false (F)?
   1. Surfing is just as popular in Ghana as it is in America and Australia. T / F
   2. Joshua's dancing abilities help make him a good surfer. T / F
   3. Local people have only just started surfing in Oman. T / F
   4. Bedouin people are traditionally nomadic and move around a lot. T / F

4. If you could visit the culture and introduce an activity or hobby that you enjoy, like Sam takes surfing to Ghana and Oman, what would that activity be? And why?

Project

5. Work in pairs to research and write a presentation about another culture. Follow these steps.
   1. Choose a culture and research it. Think about these things.
      - what they eat and drink
      - what they wear
      - what their jobs are
      - what they do for fun
   2. Find or draw pictures to add to your presentation.
   3. Present your ideas to the class.

INDEPENDENT LEARNING

Speaking skills

1. Think about the Speaking lesson of this unit. Answer the questions.
   1. Did you feel confident when you were doing the main speaking task? Why/Why not?
      ....
   2. Did you stay focused on the task?
      ....
   3. How did you refer back to your partner's answer?
      ....

2. Work in pairs. Compare your answers to Ex 1 and look back at the speaking exam tips you have seen so far. Which ones did you find useful? Why?

3. Work in new pairs. Imagine you are going to give advice to someone else who is learning English. Make a list of things they can do at home to help them improve and practise their pronunciation and speaking skills.

	activities
speaking skills	practise recording myself speaking and listen back to it
pronunciation	

4. Complete the sentences.

   1. I'm going to improve my pronunciation by
      ....
      ....

   2. I'm going to improve my speaking by
      ....
      ....

UNIT CHECK

Wordlist

Travel
abroad (adv)
air travel (n)
be delayed (phr)
border (n)
check in (phr v)
check-in (n)
delay (n, v)
destination (n)
flight (n)
journey (n)
land (v)
motorway (n)
passport (n)
road travel (n)
sightsee (v)
sightseeing (n, adj)
take off (phr v)
take-off (n)
traffic jam (n)
travel (n, v)
trip (n)

Phrasal verbs
get about
jump off
jump on
sign up
stop off

Other
hold (n)
location (n)
place (n)
reception (n)

tour (n)
travel sick (adj)
voyage (n)

Extra
cable car (n)
foreign (adj)
metro (n)
pedicab (n)
river boat (n)
Segway (n)
souvenir (n)
(the) Underground (n)

Vocabulary

1 Choose the correct words to complete the sentences.

1 This year Anna's going **abroad / sightseeing** for the first time. She's never visited another country before.
2 They wouldn't let Luca travel because his **flight / passport** was out of date.
3 They walked over the **border / check-in** between Italy and Switzerland during the night.
4 After the plane **landed / took off**, the flight attendant brought round food and a drink, and we watched a film.
5 We heard about the **flight / traffic jam** on the radio, so we chose a different road into town.
6 The students enjoyed the ski **journey / trip**, and didn't want to come home.
7 We had a two-hour **delay / flight** because there was a problem with the plane.
8 The train journey was terrible and it took five hours for us to reach our **destination / motorway**.

2 Choose the correct answers to complete the sentences.

1 What time does the ...... to Rome leave?
   A journey   B flight   C motorway
2 I had a fantastic holiday but the ...... home was long and very boring.
   A trip   B journey   C travel
3 They couldn't ...... their bags when they arrived because it was too early.
   A take off   B delay   C check in
4 The planes couldn't ...... because it was too foggy.
   A take off   B check in   C land

3 Complete the leaflet with these words.

check in   delay   destination   flight   passport
sightseeing   take-off   travelling

Welcome to Jolly Airlines!

- Please ¹............ at the airport at least two hours before your ²............ .
- Have your ³............ and ticket with you at all times.
- If there is a ⁴............ of more than three hours, all passengers will receive a free meal.
- Please turn off your mobile phone, laptop or tablet before ⁵............ .
- Jolly Airlines can help you before you arrive at your ⁶............ . If you would like to book theatre tickets or a ⁷............ trip, please ask for details.

Thank you for ⁸............ with Jolly Airlines!

UNIT CHECK

Review

1 Complete the sentences with 'who' or 'which'.
1. The pilot .... flew our plane is my dad's cousin.
2. The flight .... has just landed is from Ankara, Turkey.
3. Will the passenger .... has lost a passport please go to the check-in desk?
4. There's a meeting after school for all the students .... are going on the ski trip.
5. The train .... goes to Seville is on platform ten.

2 Choose the correct words to complete the sentences.
1. I heard a loud noise **who / which** my dad did not hear.
2. She wants to visit the town **that / where** her grandad was born.
3. Is that the boy **whose / that** guitar broke during the concert?
4. I think Erin and Martin were the people **who / whose** performed best.
5. Where's the ticket **that / where** was right here on my desk this morning?
6. They're looking for a place **there / where** they can practise for the concert.
7. The girl **that's / whose** talking to Sarah is Lee's sister.
8. The student **who's / whose** poem got first prize won 100 euros.

3 Complete the sentences with the correct form of 'must' or 'have to' and the verbs in brackets.
1. You .... (buy) your tickets now. You can get them at the station.
2. The passengers were tired because they .... (sleep) in the airport last night.
3. It's a fantastic theatre. We .... (go) there one day.
4. The motorway will be closed this evening, so we .... (use) the smaller roads.
5. We .... (forget) our cameras when we go away at the weekend.
6. Louise's in a choir and she .... (practise) three times a week.
7. You can look at my costume for the play, but you .... (laugh) at it.
8. Linda wanted to go sightseeing, but first she .... (unpack) her bags.

4 e Read the article. For each question, choose the correct answer.

Harry Styles, from the pop group One Direction, is a singer ¹....... has everything: millions of fans, lots of money and a close family. It's a life ²....... lots of talented teenagers would like to have. ³....... really happens when a young teen suddenly become famous? For a start, they often ⁴....... to travel a lot, and that can be difficult. School life also changes. Some teen pop stars ⁵....... to go to school because they haven't got time. Perhaps that sounds fun, but ⁶....... teaches them? Even pop stars know that they ⁷....... get an education, so many of them travel around the world with a tutor. It isn't easy, but most of these young stars are people ⁸....... wouldn't change a thing.

	A	B	C	D
1	that	who	which	where
2	that	what	who	then
3	Why	Who	What	How
4	had	will	must	have
5	don't have	didn't have	doesn't have	mustn't
6	what	when	where	who
7	need	needn't	mustn't	must
8	which	who	where	what

5 e Read the blog post and for each question, write the correct answer. Write one word for each gap.

My last holiday

I'm from New Zealand and last summer I went to Australia ¹.................... my parents. We all enjoy sightseeing a lot but we don't often go abroad ².................... I get travel sick. And my mum hates flying! This means that when we do go away, we like to stay ³.................... nice with plenty of sunshine. So last year my dad persuaded us to go to Australia. He told the travel agent we needed ⁴.................... go to a place that was sunny! I was worried about the dangerous snakes and spiders ⁵.................... live there. But instead, we saw kangaroos jumping around and koalas with their cute babies. We went swimming in the sea and saw Sydney, so in the end, we ⁶.................... a lovely time.

"Do more of what makes you happy."

Look at the photo and discuss the questions.
1 What is the girl in the photo doing?
2 What hobbies were popular with your parents' generation? Which ones are still popular today?
3 How do you think young people's use of free time has changed over time?

Time out

8

READING
topic: developing patience
skill: finding synonyms
task: multiple choice

GRAMMAR
reported speech
indirect questions

VOCABULARY
hobbies and interests

LISTENING
topic: unusual hobbies
skill: avoiding distraction
task: multiple choice (pictures)

SPEAKING
topic: talent shows
skill: making and responding to suggestions
task: collaborative task and discussion

WRITING
topic: celebrity hobbies
skill: paragraph openers
task: article

SWITCH ON
video: domino art
project: write a video script

8 Time out

READING

Power up

1 Work in pairs. Look at the activities in group A. What qualities from group B do you think are needed for these hobbies? Why?

A	3D printing art chess coding collecting action figures drama listening to music making documentaries photography writing short stories
B	creative intelligent optimistic passionate patient self-confident self-controlled sociable

2 Do you think that young people today are more impatient than in the past? Why/Why not?

3 Work in pairs. Look at the photos of situations where you need to be patient. Which situation would you find the hardest? Why?

4 Work in pairs. Student A, turn to page 160. Student B, turn to page 162. Follow the instructions and then check your answers together. Then look at Ex 1 and find two words to describe the children who get two marshmallows.

Read on

5 Read the exam tip and complete the task.

> **exam** tip: **multiple choice**
>
> Use key words in the questions to find the answer. Then look for synonyms of the key words in the options.
>
> Look at question 1 in Ex 7 and the first paragraph of the article. Find synonyms in the paragraph for the highlighted words in the options.

6 Find the key words in questions 2–5 in Ex 7.

7 e Read the article and each question, choose the answer.

1 The writer says many adults think that teens
  A spend too much time on computers.
  B are bad at spending time on their goals.
  C have more things to interest them today than in the past.
  D are able to concentrate better now than in the past.

2 What does the writer tell us about the marshmallow test in the 1960s?
  A It predicted later success in life.
  B It worked with very young children.
  C It produced the same results for a long time.
  D It became popular with professionals.

3 Protzko believes his test showed that
  A it is important to look at several different skills.
  B child experts understand young people better than anyone else.
  C young people today are more patient.
  D teenagers are getting taking more chances.

4 What complaint has been made of Protzko's work?
  A He persuaded the children to wait longer.
  B Different kinds of children were tested.
  C The results may be affected by social changes.
  D The children had help from their parents.

5 What was the writer's purpose in writing this article?
  A to recommend the Marshmallow test for everyone
  B to make the reader think about how we change as we get older
  C to suggest activities that encourage greater patience
  D to show that ideas about this generation are not fair

Are modern children really less patient?

How many times have you heard older people complaining that today's kids need to be entertained all the time and move constantly from one activity to another? They say that technology has changed today's children – they now demand everything immediately and they won't work to earn rewards.

An American psychologist, John Protzko, decided it was time to test these opinions. His idea was to repeat a test that was first used in the 1960s, and then compare the results for those children, with children today. The Marshmallow Test was part of an experiment to see if children could control their own behaviour. Interestingly, among that first group of children, the ones who did well in the test, showing good self-control, ended up doing better in adult life than those who did badly. The test is still used today to understand child **development**.

Before comparing the results of children taking the test in the 1960s and 2010s, Protzko asked 260 child experts what they thought he would learn from the exercise. Interestingly, only sixteen percent of them said that they thought children would get better at the test over time. The rest said that they believed the test would show children's self-control has **decreased**.

In fact, Protzko found performance has **improved** over the last fifty years, which is the opposite of popular opinion. Children's ability to wait for rewards has actually **increased** over time. Perhaps this shouldn't be so surprising. Research shows **progress** in other areas, too. Exam results for teenagers have **continuously** improved, and teenagers put themselves in fewer dangerous situations than their parents' generation did. This is a sign that they're becoming more responsible.

However, not all experts are convinced by Protzko's results. Some have questioned if these results really show that today's children have greater self-control, and suggested other explanations. For example, some experts said that they thought children's attitudes to sweets may be different now to in the past, particularly as sweets are available everywhere. Most parents today frequently tell their children that sugar is bad for them, which may also influence children's attitude to eating sweets. It's an interesting argument, but still, all the signs suggest young people are, it seems, becoming more patient.

> *Interestingly, among that first group of children, the ones who did well in the test ended up doing better in adult life than those who did badly.*

8 Match the words in bold in the article with the words in bold in these sentences.

1. Scientists believed that the level of patience would **go down**. ....
2. Academic results have **gone up**. ....
3. This **process of getting better** has surprised many people. ....
4. The test results have **got better** in all subjects. ....
5. The **growth** of children is an important field of study. ....
6. People misjudge teenagers **all the time**. ....

Sum up

9 Work in pairs. Talk about these things.

1. how young people are better than their parents when they were at the same age; give examples
2. the problems with comparing the two groups

> Young people are more patient these days because …

Speak up

10 Do you think you and your friends have good self-control? Do you find it easy to wait for something you want? How about your parents or grandparents?

'The best fighter is never angry.' (Lao Tzu, Chinese philosopher)

8 Time out

GRAMMAR

1 Read the grammar box and choose the correct verb forms to complete the examples.

explore grammar → p140

reported speech

reported statements

The main verb usually goes back one tense into the past.

'It**'s** time to test these opinions,' said American psychologist John Protzko.

An American psychologist, John Protzko, said it **¹is / was** time to test these opinions.

reported questions

For *yes/no* questions, we use positive sentence word order, change the tense and add *if*.

'**Do** the results really **show** greater self-control?' some people asked.

Some people asked **if** the test results really **²show / showed** greater self-control.

For *wh-* questions, we use positive sentence word order and change the tense.

'What **will** I **learn** from the exercise?' Protzko asked 260 experts.

Protzko asked 260 experts **³if / what** he **⁴will / would** learn from the exercise.

pronouns in reported speech

We change first and second person pronouns to third person pronouns.

'Sugar is bad for **you**!' parents told their children.

Parents told their children that sugar was bad for **⁵them / you**.

2 8.1 Watch or listen to people reporting statements and questions. Match four of the speakers (1–8) with the questions they asked (A–D).

- **A** Can I borrow a pen?
  Speaker ....
- **B** What time are you going to arrive in the village?
  Speaker ....
- **C** Can you drop me into town?
  Speaker ....
- **D** Can I borrow your phone charger?
  Speaker ....

3 8.2 Watch or listen again and complete the sentences.

1 This morning I asked my brother .... his phone charger.
2 The last time I asked a question was when I asked my friend .... a pen.
3 I last asked a question to my mum. I asked her .... me into town.
4 The last time I asked someone a question was yesterday, when I asked my uncle .... going to arrive in my village.
5 The last person I spoke to was my cousin and she said .... leave at two o'clock to come and see my family.

4 Martin has invited friends from his drama group to his house after school. They have left messages on his phone. Rewrite the messages into reported speech.

1 Jane: I can come after eight o'clock.
2 Ed: I'll bring some snacks.
3 Chris: I can't come because I'm sick.
4 Melanie: I love rehearsing after school!
5 Simon: I'm going to be late. I haven't left the house yet.
6 Lizzie: I really want to try on the new costumes!

5 8.3 Listen and check your answers.

6 Read Fatima's post. Rewrite her questions in reported speech.

> Hi, guys. Can anyone help me? Does anyone know about the Denver Film Academy? Is it near the school? What are the teachers like? What time does the group meet? And finally, what are the short films like? Are they any good?
>
> Thank you so much!

Write on

7 Work in pairs. Follow these steps.

1 Write three sentences about what you did last weekend, drawing emojis in place of words where possible.
2 Swap sentences. Can you work out your partner's story?
3 Work in new pairs. Tell the story to your new partner. Use reported speech.

VOCABULARY
hobbies and interests

1 Match the comments (1–9) with the activities (A–I).

1 I get together with my friends at weekends and we build and paint whole sci-fi battle scenes.
2 I practise with a band on Friday evenings.
3 I often play against my cousins, but my wi-fi's poor at the moment.
4 My favourites are nature scenes, particularly wildlife.
5 I'm really into kickboxing. It's a fun way to exercise.
6 I make rings and necklaces with plastic.
7 This year we're doing a musical. You can join in if you want.
8 I have over 5,000 trading cards, and some of them date back to the 1990s.
9 My speciality is cookies. I just love the smell while they're in the oven.

A collecting things
B cooking
C doing drama
D keeping fit
E making jewellery
F making models
G online gaming
H practising a musical instrument
I taking photos

2 🔊 8.4 Listen. Which activities from Ex 1 do you hear?

3 Match these words with their meanings.

battery glue ingredients paintbrush recipe zoom lens

1 a long, thin brush that you use to add colour to something: ....
2 things that you use to make a particular type of food: ....
3 an object that provides power for a machine or piece of equipment: ....
4 a piece of curved glass or plastic that makes things look bigger: ....
5 instructions for how to cook something: ....
6 something that you use to join things together: ....

4 Match the words in Ex 3 with the hobbies (A–C).

A cooking: .... / ....
B photography: .... / ....
C making models: .... / ....

explore language

talking about your hobbies and interests

be into photography / making models
be mad about cooking / keeping fit
chill out with friends / at home / at the beach
hang out with friends / other football fans / my cousins
join in the dancing / the fun

5 e Read the language box and the blog post. For each question, choose the correct answer.

THE HOBBYIST

Are you looking for a new hobby or do you just want to hang out ¹....... friends who have the same interests? Perhaps you like ²....... old comics or you're ³....... designing your own jewellery. We've got something for everyone at The Hobbyist. This month Kylie Rigg is going to write on our blog. Kylie's ⁴....... about building models and she's going to share her designs for some cool 3D models of animals. Why don't you ⁵....... in the fun? All you need is some cardboard and a few ⁶....... . What are you waiting for?

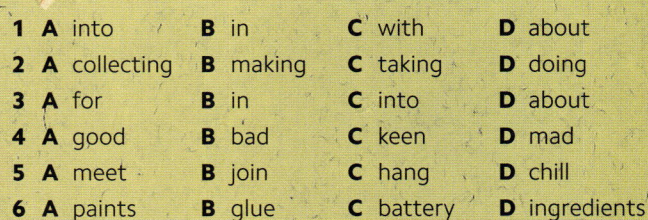

1 A into   B in   C with   D about
2 A collecting B making   C taking   D doing
3 A for   B in   C into   D about
4 A good   B bad   C keen   D mad
5 A meet   B join   C hang   D chill
6 A paints   B glue   C battery   D ingredients

Speak up

6 Work in pairs. What could you write on a hobby blog? What do you like about that hobby?

game on
Ask ten questions!

Work in pairs. Think of a hobby each. Your partner has to guess what the hobby is. He/She can ask up to ten yes/no questions. Make sure you only answer 'yes' or 'no'.

8 Time out

LISTENING

Power up

1 🔊 **8.5** Listen and match the speakers (1–8) with the options (A–H). Then work in pairs. Check your answers and share true sentences using some of the numbers.

A	1.5	C	21/01/19	E	£4.57	G	12,500
B	12,500,000	D	999	F	70%	H	€4.57

Listen up

2 🔊 **8.6** Listen and for each question, choose the correct answer.

1 What does the boy still need for his course?
 A   B   C

2 What did the man spend so long trying to make?
 A   B   C

3 Which activity does the boy do?
 A   B   C

4 Where does the girl keep her huge 'Star Wars' collection?
 A   B   C

5 What did the girl use to make the necklace?
 A   B   C

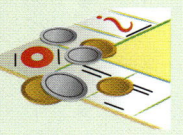

6 What did the boy make for the competition?
 A   B   C

7 What part did the girl get in the play?
 A   B   C

exam tip:
multiple choice (pictures)
Use the second listening to check your answers. Listen carefully, even when you are sure you have the right answer.

3 🔊 **8.7** Read the exam tip. Listen again and check your answers.

4 🔊 **8.8** Listen again. What do these numbers refer to?

6   2010   13,000   9.5   4.45

explore **grammar** ➔ p140

indirect questions

For *yes/no* questions, we use *if* + positive sentence word order.

Do you know if he made them from gum?

For *wh-* questions, use a *wh-* word + positive sentence word order.

Can you tell me what kind you need?

5 Put the words in the correct order to make indirect questions.

1 why / can I ask / never come / you / cycling with us?
2 open today / do you know / the music centre / is / if?
3 cost / could you tell me / how much / your photography course?
4 whether / the new game / available yet / is / can you tell me?
5 studied drama / you / have / can I ask / how long?

6 Complete the indirect questions. Work in pairs and ask and answer the questions.

1 What is your hobby?
 Can you tell ....?
2 Is it expensive?
 Can I ask ....?
3 How did you learn to do it?
 Could ....?
4 Is there any online help for your hobby?
 Do you ....?

7 Do a class survey. Interview three different people. Ask them the questions in Ex 6.

Making jewellery out of human hair was one of the most popular hobbies in Ancient Egypt.

98

SPEAKING

Power up

1 Work in pairs. Read the advert. Which act would you suggest? Why? Tell the class.

THE BEST TALENT SHOW ACT EVER

What is the best act of all time from TV talent shows in recent years? Tell us below!

Speak up

2 🔊 8.9 Complete the conversation with these phrases. Listen and check your answers.

> agreed   how about   I don't think it'd be easy
> I'd prefer to   I'm really not sure about that   let's look   shall I
> that's a great   would you like   yes, OK

A: OK, so we have to do an act for the talent show. ¹_____ training my dog to do a few tricks?

B: I like the idea. Your dog is so cute, but ²_____ to train her in such a short time. We've only got a couple of weeks.

A: I guess not. ³_____ to do a song, then? We can use a recording with some backing music.

B: ⁴_____ . I know you sing in a choir, but I can't sing very well, and there are some other really good singers in our school. ⁵_____ do something really different, like rapping.

A: I love it! ⁶_____ idea! I can rap, I'm sure. ⁷_____ start looking online for a good poem?

B: ⁸_____ . That sounds like a good place to start. I know: ⁹_____ together. Why don't we meet up tonight after classes?

A: ¹⁰_____ !

exam tip: → p148, p149
collaborative task and discussion

If you want to reject a suggestion, try to give a reason and make an alternative suggestion to sound more polite.

3 🔊 8.10 Read the exam tip and the useful language. Listen again and find one example for each function (1–3).
1. a response accepting a suggestion
2. a response rejecting a suggestion
3. a reason for rejecting a suggestion

useful language: making and responding to suggestions

Why don't we recommend … ?	That's a good idea!
Shall we suggest … ?	That sounds great!
Would you like to start … ?	I don't think so.
Let's look at the first …	I'm not sure about that.
What/How about suggesting … ?	I'd rather / I'd prefer to choose …

4 Work in pairs. Turn to page 164 and complete the task.

5 Work in pairs. Take turns to ask and answer the questions.
1. Would you like to enter a talent show? What would you do? / Why not?
2. What do people need to do to prepare for a talent show? Why?
3. What kind of acts are the most popular on talent shows in your country? Why do you think that is?
4. Which types of acts do you prefer to watch? Do other people you know find them interesting too?
5. Which do you think is the most relaxing talent to learn? Why?

Speaking extra

6 What is the strangest act you've seen on a talent show or on the internet? Would you like to try it? Why/Why not?

8 Time out

WRITING

Power up

1 What do you know about hobbies from the past? Read the quiz and decide which sentences are true (T) or false (F).

2 Do you know anyone who has a hobby or a pastime that you wouldn't expect them to have? Share your answers with the class.

3 Read the useful language. Then read this article about a celebrity with an unusual hobby. Find at least two adjectives and two adverbs.

True or False?

1 Snake wrestling was a hobby the Romans really enjoyed practising. — T / F
2 The competitors in the Olympic Games in Ancient Greece were people who just did sports for fun. — T / F
3 Pole sitting, a game where contestants sat on a seat on top of a flag pole for as long as possible, became a popular pastime in 1920's America. — T / F
4 The Victorians had a keen interest in plants and often had seaweed collections. — T / F
5 The British invented football in the eighteenth century and that is why it is the UK's national sport. — T / F
6 'Grass balling', or rolling a ball of grass to make a decoration, has long been a pastime in Japan, particularly with children and young people. — T / F

WHAT DO THE STARS DO WHEN THE PARTY'S OVER?

We all need a hobby, and even celebrities need a way to relax. Have you heard about the benefits of doing creative crafts? If so, you won't be surprised to learn that Taylor Swift is keen on making snow globes in her free time.

Taylor is a fantastic singer and songwriter. She's written a huge number of successful hits. She once said that this busy lifestyle brought many challenges. Making snow globes for close friends and family gave her a chance to do something completely different.

I think a hobby is extremely important because it helps you to forget about work or studies and relax. I would love to try this hobby and share the results with my friends.

useful language: adjectives and adverbs

You might be **surprised** / **amused** / **amazed** to learn that …
I think a **good** / **interesting** / **weird** hobby is …
X's hobby is **great** / **fantastic** / **helpful** because it's …
She **once** / **famously** / **publicly** said that …

Some people list strange hobbies on their CVs, including time travel, hacking, sleeping and being awesome.

Plan on

4 Read the article again. In which paragraph does the writer do these things?

1. introduce the hobby ....
2. say why the person likes the hobby ....
3. introduce the person with the hobby ....
4. say why this hobby is good ....

5 Find one example of reported speech in the article.

6 Read the advert. What do you need to write? What should it be about?

Articles for 'Activity News'

Do you know someone with an interesting or unusual hobby? Why do you think they do that hobby?

Explain whether you'd like to do this hobby or not.

Write an article for our magazine. We'll put the best ones in next week's issue.

exam tip: article ➡ p152

You can start an article with a question. This makes your reader interested from the beginning.

7 Think of a person you know with an interesting hobby. Use these ideas or your own. Read the exam tip and make notes using the points (1–4) in Ex 4.

collecting things   creating songs
designing their own clothes   making videos
writing a blog

8 Look at your notes from Ex 7. What adjectives and adverbs can you use to describe:

1. the person? *very funny, really interesting*
2. the hobby? *quite exciting*

Write on

9 e Write your article in about 100 words.

Improve it

10 Read your article again. Did you:

1. give it a title?
2. cover all the points in the advert?
3. include all the things in Ex 4?
4. make the hobby sound interesting with adjectives and adverbs?
5. start with a question?

101

SWITCH ON

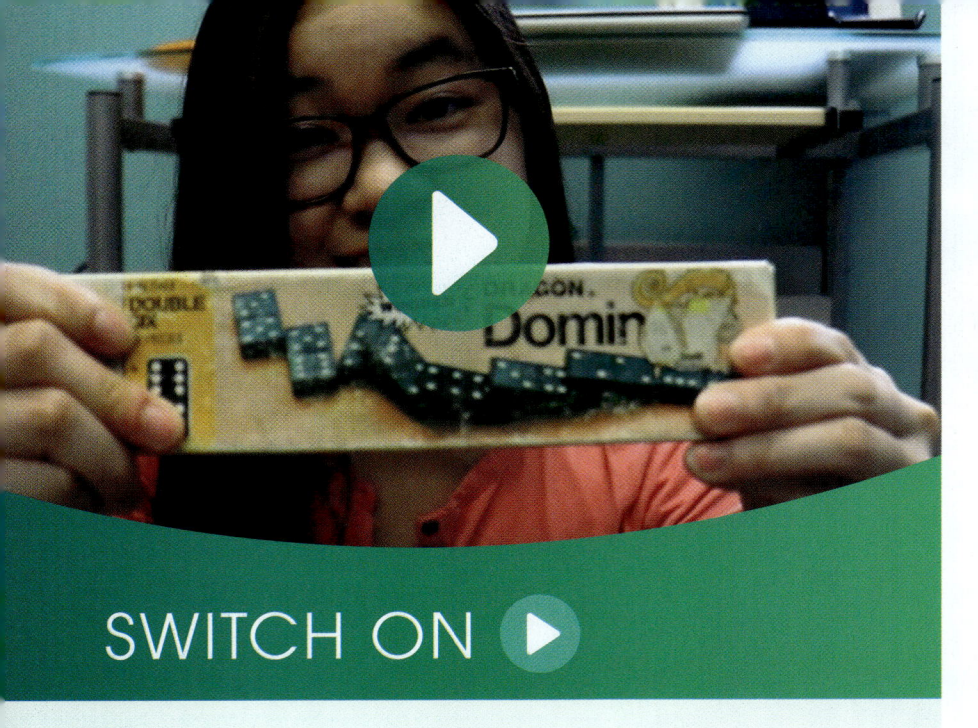

Domino art

1 Work in pairs and discuss.
- Do you watch YouTube videos? If so, what kind?
- Would you like to be a YouTuber? Why/Why not?

2 ▶ Watch the clip. Match the information (1–6) with the numbers (A–F).

1	number of views of Lily's videos	A	500 million
2	number of subscribers to Lily's channel	B	10
3	number of dominos in the largest tower	C	70,000
4	age when Lily started her hobby	D	2 million
5	pieces in Lily's first set	E	3,000
6	dominoes Lily has now	F	28

3 ▶ Watch again and answer the questions
1 What's the best part of a domino trick for Lily?
2 What does Lily want people to understand about her tricks?

Project

4 Work in small groups to write a script for an introductory YouTube video about one of your hobbies. Follow these steps.
1 Watch 1–2 videos from famous YouTubers to get some ideas. Make notes.
2 Decide what hobby you want to share with people. How will you make it seem interesting?
3 Assign roles for your video and write the script.
4 Film or plan your video and share it with the class.
5 Share your plans or videos with the class. Which hobby would you be most interested in taking up? Why?

INDEPENDENT LEARNING

Listening skills

1 Think about your listening skills. Are any of these statements true for you?
1 'I can understand the audio scripts when I read them, but I just can't hear what people say when they talk.'
2 'They use too many new words and I can't understand.'
3 'I find people speak too fast for me to keep up.'
4 'I get lost easily and find it hard to understand when the conversation changes direction.'

2 What do you think might cause each of the problems in Ex 1? Match the problems (1–4) with these possible reasons (A–D).
A limited vocabulary
B little experience listening to English speakers
C poor understanding of linking words
D problems with pronunciation

3 Work in pairs. Brainstorm ideas to help each student in Ex 1. Then choose your two favourite suggestions and tell the class.

4 How will each of the students in Ex 1 know if they have improved? Match the students (1–4) with these suggestions (A–D).

I will:
A create a list of five new functional phrases from the internet and learn when to use them.
B practise five vowel sounds, and will know the difference between similar sounds.
C watch five short videos online and will try to keep up with the ideas.
D practise all of the words from this unit.

5 Choose one of the suggestions from Ex 4 for yourself or create a new one.

UNIT CHECK

Wordlist

Hobbies and interests
3D printing (n)
art (n)
battery (n)
chess (n)
coding (n)
collecting (action figures/toys/things) (phr)
cooking (n)
documentary (n)
drama (n)
glue (n)
ingredient (n)
keeping fit (n)
listening to music (phr)
making jewellery/models (phr)
online gaming (phr)
paintbrush (n)
paper flower making (phr)
photography (n)
practising a musical instrument (phr)
recipe (n)
taking photos (phr)
writing short stories (phr)
zoom lens (n)

Phrases to talk about hobbies and interests
be into sth
be mad about sth

chill out (with sb/at a place)
hang out (with sb)
join in (sth)

Personal qualities
creative (adj)
intelligent (adj)
optimistic (adj)
passionate (adj)
patient (adj)
self-confident (adj)
self-controlled (adj)
sociable (adj)

Other
amazed (adj)
amused (adj)
continuously (adv)
decrease (v)
development (n)
famously (adv)
helpful (adj)
improve (v)
increase (v)
progress (n)
publicly (adv)
weird (adj)

Extra
ability (n)
adult (n)
behaviour (n)
patience (n)

Vocabulary

1 Complete the sentences with words from the *Hobbies and interests* and *Phrases to talk about hobbies and interests* sections of the wordlist. Put the words in the correct form.

1 Do you like these biscuits? I got the .... online.
2 Oh no! My camera won't work. I think the .... is dead.
3 I just love .... In fact, I made the necklace I'm wearing today.
4 I love tennis. I used to watch my brother play and decided to .... one day.
5 I forgot to clean my .... yesterday after I finished that picture.
6 I'm going to .... with my friends at band practice later.
7 I have always been into .... things. I have over 100 toy action figures.
8 My little sister is .... about online gaming. She plays for hours.

2 🔊 8.11 Listen and check your answers.

3 Choose the correct words to complete the sentences.

1 Jane makes incredible paintings. She's very **creative / sociable**.
2 Jack studies hard and gets top marks. He's very **intelligent / passionate**.
3 Nicola is **optimistic / passionate** about boxing and trains every day before class.
4 Rebecca is very **intelligent / sociable** and is great at organising parties.
5 Daniel has a competition next week and he's **optimistic / self-controlled** about winning.
6 Max always does his homework as soon as it's set. He's very **creative / self-controlled**.
7 Amanda keeps trying until she gets it right. She's very **patient / sociable**.
8 Liam believes in himself. He's very **self-confident / creative**.

4 Complete the sentences with words from the *Other* section of the wordlist in the correct form.

1 If you keep practising the language, your marks will ....
2 The number of students learning Italian in my school has .... Last year there were twenty-five students and this year there are only fifteen.
3 The shop assistant was very .... He showed me some good cameras and helped me choose the one that was right for me.
4 We were all .... to learn that he had won first prize!
5 A really .... thing happened yesterday: a stranger called and said he had something he wanted to give my dad.
6 Joe has been working hard and he is making good .... His marks are much better this term.
7 We were all .... by her story. It was interesting and really, really funny!
8 It has rained .... for five days this week.
9 Unfortunately, the number of students joining our club has .... since last year. There are only five of us this year.
10 The star refused to talk about the matter .... He said it was between him and his family.

103

UNIT CHECK
Review

1 Put the phrases in bold in the correct order to complete the sentences.
1. Jack said that **help / would / he** me later.
   ....
2. My friend said that **did / she / yoga**.
   ....
3. My cooking instructor **said / the recipe / needed / I / to follow**.
   ....
4. My best friend **me / was / worried / she / told**.
   ....
5. One of my followers **I / if / Halo / liked / me / asked**.
   ....
6. My team mates **doing / asked / what / was / I** later.
   ....

2 Complete the reported statements with the correct form of the verbs in brackets.
1. He told Jo that .... (he/need) to see her.
2. My friend said that .... (she/want) to start a new hobby.
3. His guitar teacher told .... (him/have to) practise more often.
4. Adam said that .... (he/have) something important to tell me.
5. My parents said that .... (I/can) go to the concert.
6. Mike told me that .... (he/not like) the new game.
7. I told Katie that .... (I/cannot) wait for her because I was busy.
8. Mike told me that .... (he/not have to) go to school that day.

3 Rewrite the questions in reported speech.
1. 'Are you free later?' asked Max.
   ....
2. 'Are you going?' asked Ahmad.
   ....
3. My food technology teacher said, 'Can you put the salt and pepper in next?'
   ....
4. 'What are you doing?' asked John.
   ....
5. 'Which necklace did you make?' asked my mum.
   ....
6. 'Where will you be?' asked my friend.
   ....
7. 'Can you help us?' they asked me.
   ....
8. 'Where do you live?' the boy asked her.
   ....

4 Complete the indirect questions.
1. Do you have a hobby?
   Can you tell me .... ?
2. How long have you done this hobby?
   Could you tell me .... ?
3. What is the best thing about your hobby?
   Can I ask .... ?
4. Do other people have this hobby?
   Do you know .... ?
5. What are you going to do next?
   Can you tell me .... ?

5 **e** Read the blog post and for each question, write the correct answer. Write one word for each gap.

The Denver Film Academy

When I first spoke to the head of the Denver Film Academy, I knew this was going to be a special experience. She said that they had schools in 120 countries and all their students **1** .... the opportunity to create films for their local audience. From the start, they told us that we **2** .... not get the same boring old acting classes that other schools offer. Unlike many other drama schools, they prepare students for film, not the theatre. When I asked **3** .... they thought this made a difference, they told me they believed that it **4** .... , as cameras really show all the details that an audience wouldn't normally see. I also spoke to some of the students in the year above, and they said that they **5** .... looking forward to graduating and starting work. I asked them **6** .... the best thing was about the school, and they said that a lot of TV companies looked for talent in the school. It was a real opportunity.

6 Who is your favourite YouTuber? Write three questions you would you ask him/her. Use indirect questions to sound polite.

"Life is all about the experiences you have."

Look at the photo and discuss the questions.
1. What is the most interesting experience you have ever had?
2. Has an experience ever made you think or feel differently?

Life experiences

9

READING
topic: summer bucket list
skill: identifying linking
task: gapped text

GRAMMAR
past perfect
used to

VOCABULARY
feelings
-ed and -ing adjectives

LISTENING
topic: experiences
skill: listening for advice
task: multiple choice

SPEAKING
topic: living on a desert island
skill: describing likes and dislikes
task: discussion

WRITING
topic: a day out
skill: ordering events
task: story

SWITCH ON ▶
video: finding your voice
project: debate a topic

9 Life experiences

READING

Power up

1 Read the survey and answer the questions.

2 Work in pairs. Compare your answers in Ex 1. Explain why you chose these activities. Are your answers similar or different? How?

My top three summer holidays

If you could do anything during a summer holiday, what would it be? What activity would you choose? Answer the questions in our survey and then send them to us. We'll post the most popular suggestions online at the end of the month!

1. What would you like to do and why?
2. Where would you do it?
3. Who would you do it with?
4. What would you have to plan to be able to do that activity?

Read on

3 Read the introduction to Sophie's blog post. What is a 'bucket list'?

> Last summer I wrote a bucket list for the summer holidays. Bucket lists have become really popular between my friends and me. They're a list of things you want to do in your life or, in this case, during the summer holidays. ¹...........................
>
> I think a bucket list is a good idea because it helps you set goals. ²........................... After you do that, you feel really good about yourself. I'm really glad I created one. ³...........................

4 Read the exam tip and complete the task.

exam tip: gapped text

Make sure that linkers and tenses in the missing sentences match the information before and after the gap in the text. Missing sentences might give examples of things just mentioned.

Choose from the sentences (A–C) the one which fits each gap (1–3) in the text in Ex 3.

A It also pushes you to achieve your aims.
B It was a lot of fun, too.
C These can be experiences or achievements.

5 Check your answers to Ex 4. Which of the sentences you chose:

1. adds another idea? ....
2. gives examples? ....
3. is the only one which matches the tense of the sentence before the gap? ....

6 e Read the rest of Sophie's blog post about her summer bucket list. Five sentences have been removed. For each question, choose the corect answer. There are three extra sentences which you do not need to use.

A Later, we went inside.
B They included both indoor and outdoor activities.
C It also stopped me getting bored.
D After we'd done that, we built a huge sandcastle.
E I wasn't very happy at all.
F It will be difficult to find the time for that.
G I saw six in total.
H I didn't win a single one.

7 Find words or phrases in the blog post that have these meanings.

1 prepare or produce (para 1): ....
2 a lot of (para 3): ....
3 make someone remember something in the past (para 3): ....
4 admired by a lot of people for a long time (para 4): ....
5 existing or happening first (para 4): ....
6 pleased about something you've done (para 5): ....

Sum up

8 Work in pairs and answer the questions.

1 What activities were on Sophie's summer bucket list?
2 How did she feel about having a bucket list?

Speak up

9 Work in pairs and discuss the questions.

1 Do you think a summer bucket list is a good idea? Why/Why not?
2 Which of the activities on Sophie's bucket list would you like to do?
3 What other activities would you put on your summer bucket list?

My summer bucket list

by Sophie Forrester

First, I read an article about summer bucket lists. I thought it was a cool idea so I decided to give it a try. I searched online for some different ideas. I then put together a list of my top twenty things to do. **1** .... Here are a few of the ones I did.

I had a picnic at the beach with some friends. As a small child, I'd done it with my family but this was different. We ate sandwiches and snacks that we'd taken with us, then we swam in the sea. **2** .... I hadn't made one for a long time. It was fun.

My friends and I also went camping … in my back garden! In the evening we had a water fight – also on my list. We got really wet but it was funny. Then we got into the tent and played loads of old board games which my dad had found in the attic. **3** .... But playing them reminded me of being younger.

Another thing I did was have a movie marathon. I watched films all day in my bedroom, one after the other. **4** .... They were all classic films. My parents had recommended them, or rather, told me to watch them! Some were better than others but a couple of them were brilliant. I finally saw the original *Star Wars* film too.

I'd done all twenty things on my list before I went back to school. I'd also done things that I hadn't planned. I felt proud of myself. The list helped me to make the most of my summer holidays. **5** .... I'll definitely make a list again next year.

By the way, the final thing on my list was to start this blog! 😃

A 'bucket list' was originally a list of things you wanted to do before you 'kicked the bucket', or died.

9 Life experiences

GRAMMAR

1 Find two actions in each sentence. Which one happened first? Read the grammar box and check your answers.
1. We ate sandwiches and snacks that we'd taken with us.
2. I watched films all day in my bedroom. My parents had recommended them.
3. I'd done all twenty things on my list before I went back to school.

explore grammar ➜ p142

past perfect

We use the past perfect (had + past participle) to talk about an action that happened at an earlier point in the past.
I had a picnic at the beach with some friends. As a child, I'd done it with my family.

past perfect and past simple

We use the past perfect and the past simple in the same sentence to show that one action happened before another.
We **played** some old board games which my dad **had found** in the attic.

past — 1 ——————— 2 — now
dad had found games | we played games

We often use these adverbs of time and time linkers with the past perfect: *before, once, when, just, never, ever.*
After we'd swum in the sea, we built a huge sandcastle.

2 🔊 9.1 Listen to Max talking about a summer holiday experience. What did he do? Do you think he enjoyed it? Why/Why not?

3 Choose the correct verb forms to complete the sentences.
1. A few summers ago I **saw / had seen** a TV programme about orienteering.
2. I **didn't hear / hadn't heard** of it before but I thought it looked exciting.
3. I really wanted to try it because I **spent / had spent** a lot of time at the park as a child.
4. She **recently ran / 'd recently run** a half-marathon, so I knew she was the right teammate.
5. After we'd put our boots and stuff in the car, we **drove / had driven** to a nearby forest.
6. Once we **worked / 'd worked** out the quickest way, we ran faster.
7. We **were / had been** pleased when we got to the finish line.
8. When they announced the winners, we found out that we **won / had won**!

4 🔊 9.2 Listen again and check your answers.

5 Complete the blog post with the past simple or past perfect form of the verbs in brackets.

Our first festival

My friends and I ¹_____ (decide) to go to Latitude after we'd read a review about it. We wanted to do something different and we ²_____ (not go) a festival before. We booked our tickets online and downloaded a list of things to take that the organisers ³_____ (put) on the website. My backpack ⁴_____ (be) really heavy because my mum had given me lots of food! We travelled with hundreds of other teenagers who ⁵_____ (buy) tickets for the festival. At the campsite, it took ages to put up our tent because we ⁶_____ (not pack) the instructions. It was exhausting! At last, we were ready. There were poetry classes, art exhibitions, dance demonstrations and lots more. Finally, we ⁷_____ (arrive) at the stage where my favourite singer ⁸_____ (just/start) his performance. He was amazing!

Speak up

6 Think of something special or unusual you did during a summer holiday. Think about these questions.
1. Where and when was it?
2. Who were you with?
3. Had you done it before?
4. What had happened before that?
5. How did you feel?

7 Work in pairs. Tell each other about your summer holiday experiences. Think carefully about which tenses you use.

> I wanted to go camping because I'd only done it once before.

Where do sharks go for their summer holiday? To Finland!

VOCABULARY

feelings

1 Which of these adjectives describe the people in the pictures (A–D)?

amazed   annoyed   calm   confident   disappointed   embarrassed   frightened   guilty   jealous   nervous   relaxed   worried

2 Work in pairs. Are the adjectives in Ex 1 positive (P), negative (N) or can they be both (B)?

3 Work in pairs. How might you feel in these situations?
1 before an exam when you haven't prepared for it
2 when the book you read is not as good as you expected
3 when you have nothing to worry about at all
4 when someone has something you want
5 when you do something wrong and feel bad about it
6 after you fall over in front of people
7 when you want to do something but your parents won't let you
8 before a presentation that you've prepared really well for

4 Work in pairs. Choose six adjectives from Ex 1. Talk about when you last felt that way and why.

> I felt guilty last week because I promised to call my grandma and then forgot.

> I felt embarrassed yesterday when I spilt food all over my clothes.

5 Read the language box. Choose the correct adjectives to complete the examples.

explore language

-ed and -ing adjectives

Some adjectives have both an *-ed* and an *-ing* ending. The *-ed* adjective ending describes a person's feelings. The *-ing* adjective describes an action/thing/situation.

I was ¹**worried / worrying** because I hadn't heard from Sara.

The film was really ²**depressed / depressing**. It made me feel sad.

6 Turn to page 165 and choose the correct words to complete the quiz. Work in pairs and do the quiz. Do you agree with your result? Why/Why not?

7 Read the text. For each question, choose the correct answer.

What a feeling!

According to scientists, there are twenty-seven groups of feelings. I think I felt all twenty-seven of them yesterday! Firstly, I sat on my glasses and broke them. I was really ¹...... with myself. On the way to school, I thought I saw a bear. I screamed and everyone ²...... at me. Of course, there are no bears here – it was just a dog, but I couldn't see without my glasses. I was really ³...... by the whole situation. In the afternoon, I received my maths test results. I was disappointed by the low score because I'd ⁴...... better. In the evening, things improved. My parents had ⁵...... my bedroom in a pretty purple colour and got me all new furniture, too. It looks great and now my brother is ⁶...... of me because there's enough space for my friends to stay.

1 A disappointing	B worried	C annoyed	D guilty
2 A studied	B looked	C noticed	D saw
3 A miserable	B nervous	C brave	D embarrassed
4 A hoped	B expected	C thought	D planned
5 A cleaned	B tidied	C decorated	D changed
6 A upset	B anxious	C unhappy	D jealous

game on

Work in teams. Complete the sentences as creatively as possible. Vote on which team's sentences are the funniest. (You can't choose your own team!)

Will was excited because he'd …

Emily was frightened because she'd …

Dan was amazed because he'd …

9 Life experiences

LISTENING

Power up

1 Match the phrasal verbs and verb phrases in bold in the questions (1–5) with their meanings (A–E). Then work in pairs and discuss the questions.

1 Which of your friends do you **hang out** with the most?
2 Are you good at **dealing with** lots of things at the same time?
3 What kind of job do you think you'll **go for** in the future?
4 What are you **looking forward to** doing at the weekend?
5 What event would you like to **take part in** in the future?

A be involved in
B choose
C take necessary action, especially to solve a problem
D spend a lot of time (with)
E be excited about a future event

Listen up

2 🔊 9.3 Listen to a conversation between two friends about work experience. Which of these phrases for giving advice do you hear?

> Why don't you … ?   You could …
> You ought to …   You should …

3 🔊 9.4 Read the exam tip and complete the task. Then listen again.

> **exam tip: multiple choice**
>
> When you have to listen for the advice someone gives, listen for phrases such as *you should* or *you ought to*. Often, phrases like *I won't bother telling you to* or *I won't suggest* introduce the ideas in the incorrect answers.
>
> Listen again. What advice does the girl give the boy?

4 e 🔊 9.5 Listen to all six conversations. For each question, choose the correct answer.

1 You will hear two friends talking about work experience. The girl advises the boy to
  A choose something easy.
  B do something he'll enjoy.
  C pick something useful.

2 You will hear two friends talking about going climbing. Why does the boy advise the girl to join him?
  A She'll really enjoy it.
  B She'll feel proud.
  C She'll love the feeling of danger.

3 You will hear a boy telling a friend about a summer holiday experience. How did he feel about it?
  A He was bored by the games he tried while he was there.
  B He was sad that none of his favourite characters were there.
  C He was disappointed there were so many people there.

4 You will hear two friends talking about a school trip. What do they agree was the best thing about it?
  A doing something new
  B being away from home
  C researching the area

5 You will hear a girl telling a friend about an embarrassing situation. What do they agree was the worst thing about it?
  A She made the same error twice.
  B She got a family member's name wrong.
  C She typed something by accident.

6 You will two friends talking about helping other people. They agree that the experience
  A is useful for the future.
  B teaches you some new skills.
  C makes them feel satisfied.

5 🔊 9.6 Listen again and check your answers.

6 Read the grammar box. What verb form follows 'used to'?

> **explore grammar** ➜ p142
>
> **used to**
>
> We use *used to* for actions that happened regularly in the past but do not happen now.
> I **used to help out** at a home for elderly people.
> I **didn't use to like** speaking to new people.
> **Did** you **use to do** it every weekend?

Speak up

7 Work in pairs and talk about things you used to / didn't use to do when you were younger. Are any of them similar?

'You used to be much muchier. You've lost your muchness!' (The Mad Hatter, Alice in Wonderland)

SPEAKING

Power up

1 What stories do you know about desert islands? Why do you think people are interested in them?

Speak up

2 e Work in pairs. A group of friends are going to spend a month on a desert island for a TV show. The picture on the right shows some items they can take with them. Talk about each object and decide which one would be the most useful.

3 Share your decision from Ex 2 with the class. Is there anything else that you would take?

4 Match the questions (1–6) with the answer beginnings (A–F).
1 Why do you think people like having adventures?
2 Do you prefer to do the same things or try new things?
3 Is it important to try new things?
4 What do you think is the best way to spend your summer holidays?
5 What activities do people your age like doing?
6 What skill would you like to learn in the future?

A They usually enjoy …
B Yes, it is because …
C I prefer to … because …
D I think the best thing to do is …
E I'd love to …
F I'd say it's because …

5 🔊 9.7 Listen to two students discussing question 2 from Ex 4. Do they both like trying new things?

6 🔊 9.8 Listen again and complete the sentences from the conversation.

A: I ¹_____ love trying new things.
   I can't ²_____ doing the same things all the time.
   I'd ³_____ to do more of it.
B: I'm not ⁴_____ on going to big events.
   I don't ⁵_____ trying new things with a few friends.

7 Read the language box. Can you think of any other phrases for each group?

explore language

likes: I really/quite like …   I'm really into … at the moment.
dislikes: I don't like … very much / at all.   I hate …
preferences: I prefer to …
wants: I'd like to …

8 Read the exam tip and complete the task.

exam tip: discussion → p149

Don't just use *I like* to talk about likes and dislikes. Use a range of language.

I've always **loved** computer games but these days **I'm** also **really into** manga comics.

Work in pairs. Take turns to tell your partner about things you like doing in your free time. Use a range of language to express your ideas.

9 e Work in pairs and discuss the questions in Ex 4. Use phrases from Ex 4 and the language box.

Speaking extra

10 Work in pairs. Choose a topic set to talk about. Take turns and talk for one minute each. Get five points for speaking for one minute. Take away one point for every pause or repetition of information. The person with the most points wins.

	Student A	Student B
Topic set 1	school	music
Topic set 2	films	holidays
Topic set 3	family	sports
Topic set 4	hobbies	future plans

9 Life experiences

WRITING

Power up

1 Read the magazine survey. Choose the answers that are true for you.

My perfect day

1 I wake up at
  A 7 a.m. (I like to start things early.)
  B 9 a.m. (It's later than a school day.)
  C lunchtime. (I need to sleep!)

2 The weather is
  A sunny. (Yeah! Let's go out!)
  B cloudy. (Good, it isn't too hot.)
  C wet and cold. (Brilliant! I can stay in and watch a film.)

3 I spend the day
  A with friends. (Of course!)
  B with family and friends. (I love being with lots of people.)
  C on my own. (I can do what I want!)

4 I get a nice surprise and it's
  A a present. (a big one)
  B a big cake. (chocolate!)
  C an invitation. (for something fun)

5 The day ends with
  A a book and bed.
  B a good film and a pizza.
  C a party that finishes very late!

2 Compare your results with the rest of the class. Which answers are the most popular?

3 You are going to read a story that starts with the phrase below. Look at the photo. What do you think happened?

It was a frightening experience for Dennis and his friends.

4 Read the story quickly and check your ideas.

A It was a frightening experience for Dennis and his friends. They had taken a chairlift to the top of a huge hill. 'The lift closes in thirty minutes,' an employee had warned them.

B ¹.........................., they looked at the amazing views of the city. ².........................., they took some selfies. ³.........................., they went back to the chairlift. The employee had gone but they jumped on. ⁴.........................., without warning, the chairlift stopped. Oh no! The park had closed.

C 'Help!' Dennis and his friends shouted. No one replied. They couldn't get a phone signal. All they could do was wait. A few hours ⁵.........................., the chairlift came back on. The employee had remembered the friends were still on the hill and returned to rescue them. They were very pleased to see him!

5 Complete the story in Ex 4 with these time words and phrases. How do they help you to understand the story?

after that   eventually   first   later   suddenly

6 Match the events (1–5) with the paragraphs in the story (A–C).

1 how they dealt with the frightening thing ....
2 what frightening thing happened ....
3 what they did before the frightening thing happened ....
4 what happened in the end ....
5 background information about the trip ....

112

Plan on

7 Work in pairs. You are going to write a story beginning with this sentence. What kind of day out could it be? Make a list of ideas.

> Florence and her friends were really excited about their day out. ...

8 Choose one of your ideas from Ex 7. Read the questions and make notes.

- Where did Florence and her friends go and why?
- How did they get there?
- What did they do there first?
- What surprising/funny/exciting etc. thing happened next?
- How did they feel?
- What happened in the end?

Story

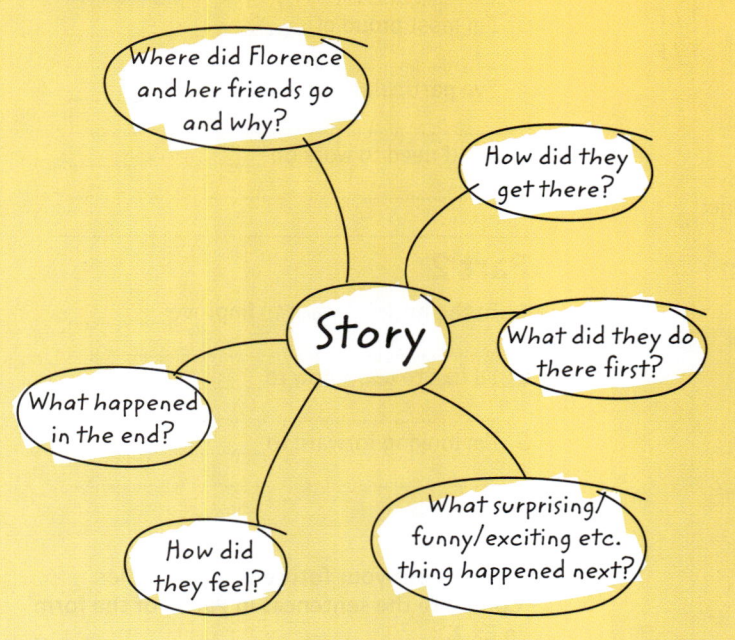

9 Read the language box. Use the words and phrases in the box to write sentences you could use in your story. You can change their order.

explore language

ordering actions in a story

First, (they) …
After that / Then / Next, …
When (we) had finished, …
Suddenly, …
Eventually, …
Finally, …
After a (long/tiring/brilliant) day, …

10 Read the exam tip and answer the question.

exam tip: a story → p154

Make sure your story has a clear beginning, middle and end. Use time expressions and past tenses to show the order of events.

How could you organise the information in Ex 8 into a clear beginning, middle and end using phrases from the language box?

Write on

11 e Write your story in about 100 words.

Improve it

12 Read your story and answer the questions. Use your answers to improve your story.
1. Is there a clear beginning, middle and end?
2. Are the past tense verbs correct?
3. Have you used time linkers to order events?

Great stories include 'The Arctic Ocean' by I.C. Waters and 'Over the Cliff' by Hugo First.

113

SWITCH ON

Finding your voice

1 Work in pairs. Think about a time when you felt nervous. What were you doing? How did you cope with the situation?

2 ▶ Watch the clip. How would you describe Ellis's experience? Do his feelings change?

3 ▶ Watch again. Are these sentences true (T) or false (F)?
   1 The students already had debating experience. T / F
   2 Monica improves Ellis's self-esteem by encouraging him to speak quietly. T / F
   3 Ellis's speech is a great success. T / F
   4 Learning to debate has been a negative experience for Ellis. T / F

4 Work in pairs and discuss the questions.
   1 Do you think there should be a debating class at your school? Why / Why not?
   2 Do you think learning to debate would change you like it changed Ellis? Why / Why not?
   3 How do you think taking part in a debate would make you feel?

Project

5 Debate an issue that is important to you. Follow these steps.
   1 Work as a class. Choose a topic for your debate. Use these ideas or your own.
      • things that happen in your community
      • issues related to school life
      • changes you would like to see in your country
   2 Create a statement for the debate.
   3 Work in small groups and think about your arguments for or against the statement.
   4 Hold the debate in your groups.

INDEPENDENT LEARNING

Study skills

1 Think about what you have learnt during this course. Work in pairs and make a list of some of the language and skills you have studied.

language	skills

2 Think about your language skills at the beginning of the course and now. Complete the sentences in Part 1 of the form.

Course reflections

Part 1
1 I've really improved in ....
2 My .... has/have also got better.
3 I'm most proud of ....
4 I've particularly enjoyed ....
5 I still need to work on ....

Part 2
1 In the future, I want to improve ....
2 I'd like to learn how to ....
3 I'm looking forward to ....

3 Think about your future English studies. Complete the sentences in Part 2 of the form in Ex 2.

4 Work in pairs. Talk about your sentences in Ex 3. Give each other advice on how to reach those goals. Can any of the exam tips from Units 1–9 help you?

UNIT CHECK

Wordlist

Adjectives to describe feelings
amazed
annoyed
anxious
bored
calm
confident
depressed
disappointed
embarrassed
excited
frightened
guilty
jealous
miserable
nervous
relaxed
satisfied
unhappy
upset
worried

Adjectives to describe actions/situations/things
amazing
annoying
boring
depressing
disappointing
embarrassing
exciting
frightening
relaxing
satisfying
worrying

Phrasal verbs and verb phrases
deal with (phr v)
go for (phr v)
hang out (with) (phr v)
look forward to (phr v)
put together (phr v)
remind (someone of) (v)
take part in (phr)

Time expressions
after that (phr)
eventually (adv)
finally (adv)
first (adv)
later (adv)
next (adv)
suddenly (adv)
then (adv)

Other
classic (adj)
loads of (adv)
original (adj)
proud (adj)

Vocabulary

1 9.9 Listen to eight speakers. What feeling is each person describing? Write the correct word from the *Adjectives to describe feelings* section of the wordlist.

1 ....
2 ....
3 ....
4 ....
5 ....
6 ....
7 ....
8 ....

2 Choose the correct adjectives to complete the sentences.

1 I had to sing on my own in front of everyone. It was so **embarrassed / embarrassing**!
2 We're all really **excited / exciting** about the party.
3 The team was **satisfied / satisfying** with the 1–1 score after losing five matches.
4 Are you sure you're comfortable in that chair? You don't look very **relaxed / relaxing**.
5 The old films that my parents like are **bored / boring**.
6 I've never seen such a **frightened / frightening** film.
7 We were all **annoyed / annoying** with Pete for being late for practice.
8 It was a good book, but it was a bit **depressed / depressing** at the end.

3 Complete the blog post with words from the wordlist in the correct form.

Becoming a unicyclist!

Last month I decided that I wanted to learn how to ride a unicycle. ¹............................, I watched ²............................ of online videos about how to do it. Then I borrowed my aunt's unicycle and gave it a try. It wasn't easy. I fell off a lot but ³............................, after several days of practice, I could cycle a few metres. I was really ⁴............................ of myself for doing it. A few weeks later, I ⁵............................ a circle skills course at the local college. I learnt how to cycle better and juggle at the same time!

UNIT CHECK

Review

1 Complete the sentences with the past perfect form of the verbs in brackets.

1. Louisa realised that she .... (not see) her cousin for over a year.
2. Ben got lost because he .... (not ask) for directions before he left.
3. Everyone had to leave the area because the storm .... (cause) a lot of damage.
4. I couldn't believe what I .... (just/hear) on the news report.
5. After they .... (finish) their picnic, they picked up all their rubbish and went home.
6. Alex couldn't call his mum because he .... (forget) to charge his mobile.

2 Complete the article with the past simple or past perfect form of the verbs in brackets.

Being a tourist in my own town

Last weekend my mum and I decided to be tourists in our own town because we ¹........................... (not visit) any of the tourist attractions in the area before. We read some reviews to find out what places visitors ²........................... (enjoy) the most. We then put together a list of things to do. On the first day, we ³........................... (go) to the biggest art gallery in the area. Before we got there, we ⁴........................... (not realise) how many amazing paintings we'd see there! We really enjoyed it.

The next morning, we ⁵........................... (take) a guided tour of the city. The guide knew a lot about the different buildings because he ⁶........................... (be) an architect when he was younger. I didn't think I'd like it but I did. In the afternoon, we walked around the park and ⁷........................... (look) at the amazing sculptures there – I ⁸........................... (never/notice) them before. I think that's why it's good to be a tourist in your own town for a weekend. You see things you didn't know were there.

3 🔊 9.10 Listen and check your answers.

4 Complete the sentences with the correct form of 'used to' and these verbs.

be   do   have   love   not get on   not live   not wear   play

1. When I was little, I .... an imaginary friend called Fred.
2. My sister and I .... well when we were young but we do now.
3. My parents .... in this area. They moved here ten years ago.
4. Did you .... all your homework in primary school? I didn't!
5. I don't like pop music now but I .... it when I was younger.
6. Where did you .... volleyball? I'd like to join a club after school.
7. My mum .... glasses when she was my age.
8. Joanne's grandad .... a teacher – he taught history at our school.

5 🅔 Read the article and for each question, write the correct answer. Write one word for each gap.

A different life

When I was eight, my family and I lived in Japan for one year because my dad had a job there. I ¹........................... been abroad before but it was still a big adventure for me. We had a small apartment where we slept on a very low bed on the floor and we sat on the floor to eat meals too. We had Japanese food like sushi. I had ²........................... tried it before I lived there, so it was new to me. I went to an international school with people ³........................... all over the world. The school days were longer ⁴........................... they are in Britain, but we studied similar subjects. After school, my friends and I used ⁵........................... do the same things most children do. We went to the playground, ate ice cream and watched TV. In the summer holidays, my dad used to take ⁶........................... all to Disneyland. We loved that!

6 Write a paragraph about the activities you used to do when you were younger.

> "Every summer has its own story."

Look at the photo and discuss the questions.
1 What do you enjoy most about the school holidays?
2 How is your life different during the summer holidays?
3 If you were going to earn money in the holidays, what kind of work would you choose to do? Why?

Summertime!

10

READING
topic: holiday jobs
task: multiple choice, open cloze, multiple choice cloze

LISTENING
topic: work experience
task: notes completion; multiple choice

SPEAKING
topic: various
task: talking about yourself, describing a photo, collaborative task, discussion

WRITING
topic: various
task: email, article, story

10 Summertime!

READING

Power up

1 Do you think it is important to go to school? Does it do enough to prepare students for life after school?

2 Read the article quickly. Does it mention any of your ideas from Ex 1?

Read on

3 Read the article again. For each question, choose the correct answer.

1 The writer says that today's schools are
 - A organised in the right way.
 - B different in other countries.
 - C useful for modern life.
 - D the same as in the past.

2 According to the writer, what is the most important skill that schools teach?
 - A how to achieve your goals
 - B how to talk to people
 - C how to use your brain
 - D how to work in a team

3 What does the writer suggest about learning real-life skills at school?
 - A They are less important than school subjects.
 - B Students can learn them in higher education.
 - C Schools should teach more of them.
 - D Schools are unlikely to teach them in future.

4 What does the writer say about parents and real-life skills?
 - A They are unhappy about teaching their children real-life skills.
 - B It is easier for parents to teach children real-life skills than schools.
 - C Some rely on grandparents to teach children real-life skills.
 - D They will do more to teach children real-life skills in the future.

5 What would be a good introduction to the article?
 - A Student Amy Smith argues that schools need to make big changes to how they work.
 - B Amy Smith describes her experiences learning real-life skills at school.
 - C Do schools help to prepare students for real life? Student Amy Smith discusses this question.
 - D Student Amy Smith suggests that schools have never taught real-life skills.

Speak up

4 Work in pairs. What could schools do to better help students prepare for life in the real world?

Life after school

Schools haven't changed much over the last 150 years. Students are divided into classes. Lessons are divided into subjects. Teachers teach. Students take tests. It's a system you can see all over the world. But some people are asking whether this system works for the twenty-first century and if it helps students to get ready for life after full-time education.

Schools teach us a variety of skills. Firstly, they teach us to think. They also help us to develop skills such as communicating and working with our classmates, and getting things done by a certain date. Above all, we learn to set aims and achieve them by working hard at school. This is something we need to be able to do in every single area of our lives – at work and at home.

There are, of course, many real-world skills that we don't always learn at school. We don't learn how to sew a button onto a shirt, change a tyre or pay an electricity bill. We do learn maths that only a few of us will actually use in the outside world. Is it therefore a good idea for us to develop more everyday abilities while still in education and leave some of the advanced subjects to university later in life? I think it is.

Families are responsible for teaching real-world skills, too. In fact, our parents have a lot more opportunities to teach us everyday skills around the home than schools do. We might not always be glad of this, but our parents can teach us things that they learnt from their own parents. I've learnt how to cook some simple dishes, for example. I'm not sure I can say the same for all my friends but there's still time yet.

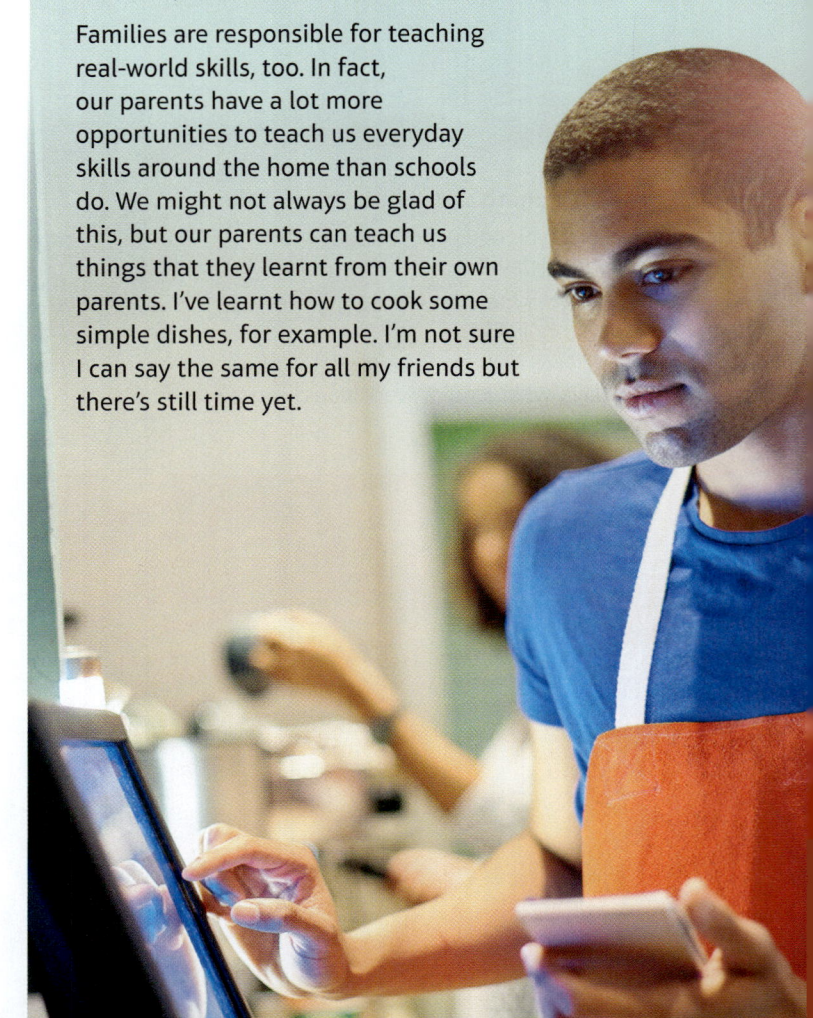

Power up

5 Read the first paragraph of the article. What two things is it going to discuss? What do you think are the advantages of each one?

All work and no play?

School's out. The holidays are here! So, is it time for us young people to relax and have fun or should we think about a holiday job?

There are **1**...... to both. A holiday job can help you learn all kinds of things. You'll learn useful **2**...... , such as problem solving and how to **3**...... with people of all ages. You'll meet new and interesting people, too.

You can also earn money from a holiday job which can help you become more **4**...... from your parents. You can learn how to **5**...... your money.

Of course, it's not all positive. When you work, you can't do as many fun things during the holidays or see your friends as often. But I believe you make a bigger **6**...... to enjoy the free time you do have and so you never get bored.

Read on

6 Read the article. For each question, choose the correct answer.

	A	B	C	D
1	offers	pleasures	qualities	advantages
2	skills	training	experiences	talents
3	say	communicate	tell	inform
4	independent	free	confident	alone
5	prepare	order	arrange	manage
6	energy	try	effort	push

7 Work in pairs. Would you like to have a part-time summer job? Why/Why not?

8 Read the title of the article. What do you think the article will say?

Why fewer teenagers have jobs these days

For decades, teenagers in the UK have had part-time jobs to earn money but in recent years, the number of young people with jobs **1**.................. dropped. Some people suggest this is because young people today are lazier than they were in the past. However, this is **2**.................. very fair. A more likely reason is that young people are encouraged to concentrate more on their studies these days. Exam results are becoming more important as people compete **3**.................. university places and jobs.

Another reason is that there aren't **4**.................. many jobs available for teenagers as there once were. They are taken by more experienced adult workers **5**.................. don't want to retire yet or are happy to have lower-paid jobs. One final reason is that some typical teenage jobs are disappearing. People don't have their newspapers delivered any more, **6**.................. teenagers aren't needed to do it.

9 Read the article quickly. Does it mention any of your ideas from Ex 8?

10 Read the article again and for each question, write the correct answer. Write one word for each gap.

Speak up

11 Work in pairs and discuss the questions.

1. Is it common for teenagers to have a part-time or holiday job in your country? Why/Why not?
2. Do you agree that it's hard for young people to find holiday work these days? Why/Why not?

10 Summertime!

LISTENING

Power up

1 Work in pairs. Discuss what skills and experience you need to do these holiday jobs.
- gardener
- lifeguard
- make-up artist
- shop assistant
- sports coach
- waiter

Listen up

2 10.1 You will hear a student talking about her job as a lifeguard in the summer holidays. Listen and complete the notes. Write one or two words or a number or a date or a time.

> Being a lifeguard
>
> Minimum age before you can apply: [1] ....
>
> What you need to find a job: [2] .... to hand in to employers
>
> How often each guard has to clean the pool: every [3] ....
>
> Main responsibility: the safety of the [4] .... at the pool
>
> Two advantages:
> - can teach you how to be a [5] ....
> - you use skills you have from your [6] ....

3 10.2 Listen again and check your answers.

4 You will hear a radio interview with a young make-up artist called Kat Sparkes. Read the questions in Ex 5 and find the key words that will help you answer each question.

5 10.3 Listen to the interview. For each question, choose the correct answer.

1 What does Kat like about her job as a make-up artist?
 A working with paint
 B helping people to look good
 C creating interesting designs
2 What did Kat do to practise her skills?
 A She tried out different designs on her family.
 B She did lots of painting when she was a child.
 C She learnt how to create new hairstyles.
3 While she was at college, Kat found it helpful to
 A learn from different people.
 B use paintings to get ideas.
 C copy work by other artists.
4 In Kat's opinion, what is one of the good things about her job?
 A Make-up artists often become rich.
 B Make-up artists usually work short days.
 C Make-up artists sometimes work with celebrities.
5 Kat doesn't mind working for no money at the moment because
 A she will be able to get work more easily in future.
 B she gets to work with many different companies.
 C her friends are in the same situation.
6 What does Kat advise young students to do?
 A start to practise on their own at home
 B try to work for a short time with someone who does good work
 C do a lot of research about the job they are interested in

6 10.4 Listen again and check your answers.

Speak up

7 Work in pairs and discuss the questions.
1 Which of the two jobs you heard about would you like to try? Why?
2 Would you be happy to work for free to get some experience?
3 What kind of work experience would you like to have? Why?

SPEAKING

Power up

1 Work in pairs. What are some important things to remember when taking a speaking test? Make a list of ideas.

Speak up

2 e Work in pairs. Take turns to ask and answer the questions. Remember to give more information each time.

Student A
1. What is a place you like?
2. Which season do you prefer, summer or winter? Why?
3. If you could learn another language, which would you choose? Why?

Student B
1. How often do you read?
2. What activities do you enjoy doing with your friends?
3. Which do you like best, staying in or going out during the summer holidays?

3 e Work in pairs. Follow the instructions to complete the speaking tasks.

Task 1

A Student A, photo A shows young people at a campsite. Tell Student B what you can see in the photo. Talk for one minute.

B Student B, listen to Student A and note down your answers to these questions.
1. Does your partner speak fluently without a lot of pauses?
2. Does your partner use a range of vocabulary or just simple words?
3. Does your partner speak with clear pronunciation? Could you understand him/her?

Task 2

A Student B, photo B shows young people in a café. Tell Student A what you can see in the photo. Talk for one minute.

B Student A, listen to Student B and note down your answers to questions 1–3 in Task 1 above.

4 Work in pairs. Discuss the speaking tasks you did and compare the notes you made in Ex 3.

5 e Work in pairs. Turn to page 166 and follow the instructions.

6 Work in pairs and discuss the questions about Ex 5.
1. Did you listen to your partner and respond to his/her answers?
2. Did you give reasons for your ideas?
3. Did you use accurate language?

7 e Work in pairs and discuss the questions.
1. Do you prefer to go away for your summer holidays or to stay at home? Why?
2. What do you need to have a fun summer holiday? Why?
3. What do you think is the best summer holiday activity? Why?
4. Would you like to go abroad for the summer? Why? Where? / Why not?
5. Which do you think is more interesting: doing sport or making something? Why?

8 Work in pairs and discuss the questions about Ex 7.
1. Did you give reasons and/or examples to extend your answers?
2. Did you organise your ideas clearly? Did you connect them using linkers?

10 Summertime!

WRITING

Power up

1 Work in pairs and discuss the questions.
1. What kind of writing do you do every day? Why?
2. What kind of writing do you find the easiest? The most difficult? Why?

Plan on

2 Read the writing task below and decide which of these points you need to include.
1. what I've been doing
2. thank Joss for the invitation
3. accept the invitation
4. explain which week I can do the course
5. ask how Joss's family is
6. give Joss information about which sport I prefer and say why
7. suggest an activity for the weekend before
8. ask Joss to visit me

Read this email from your English-speaking friend Joss, and the notes.

Write your **email**, using all the notes. Write your answer in about **100 words**.

3 Read Chris's answer. Which points from Ex 2 does he include?

From: **Chris**   To: **Joss**

Hi Joss,

Really nice to hear from you. You're right, the holidays are quite long! I think it would be a great idea to do something together.

A sports course sounds good. If the course is one week, I need to come in the middle of August because I'm away with my family after that. I've never done a sports course before. I'd prefer to go swimming as I think it's easier! Also, it would be great if I could come the weekend before we start. We could go to the festival in your town and meet your friends.

I'm really looking forward to it!
Chris

4 What would you say in a reply to Joss? Make notes for each point. Then work in pairs and compare your notes. Can you expand or improve on your ideas?

Write on

5 e Write your email for the task in Ex 2 in about 100 words.

From: **Joss**

Hi,
How are you? We've got the long summer holidays coming up! I think it'd be nice to do something together. Can you come to visit me? *great!*

What about doing a sports course for a week? I've found out about some and they look brilliant. We can do an outdoor sport or go swimming or to the gym – which do you prefer? *yes! say when* *tell Joss*

You could come to stay with me the weekend before the course and we can have fun doing something else. *suggest activity*

Let me know,
Joss

Plan on

6 Read the two writing tasks. You only need to choose one. Which task would you choose? Why?

Task 1

You see this notice in an online English-language magazine. Write your **article** in about **100 words**.

ARTICLES WANTED!
Unusual holiday jobs

Have you or someone you know had a really fun or strange holiday job? What was it? Why was it different? Would you recommend it?

Write an article answering these questions and we will publish the most interesting articles on our website.

Task 2

Your English teacher has asked you to write a story. Your story must begin with this sentence:

'Anna and Maria were babysitting one night when there was a knock at the door.'

Write your **story** in about **100 words**.

7 Look at the table. Then read two students' answers to Tasks 1 and 2 from Ex 6. Match the language in the table with the answers (1, 2 or both).

grammar	vocabulary	purpose
narrative tenses	words for activities	to entertain
descriptions	adjectives for feelings	to give an opinion
modals	exciting adjectives	
questions	action verbs	
	connecting words/phrases	

①

An unusual holiday job

Have you ever wanted to be a prince or princess? Well, a friend of mine got a great summer job as a party princess!

She worked for an agency that organised characters for children's parties. She had to dress up as Cinderella or Elsa and the boys had to be Gaston or a pirate. You go to the birthday party and behave as your character and entertain the children.

It's not a typical working day but you make the children really happy. It's a good job if you're interested in acting. And, in the future, you may be able to get a job at a theme park and earn real money!

What do you think?

②

Anna and Maria were babysitting one night when there was a knock at the door. They looked at each other because they weren't expecting anyone. They knew they shouldn't answer the door to strangers. The children were asleep upstairs.

Then there was another knock and this time it was louder. Maria went to the door and looked through the glass. She could see a dark figure. 'I'm scared,' said Anna. 'Who is it?' Suddenly, the letterbox flew open. 'Hi, it's me,' said a voice. Maria and Anna sighed. It was the children's mother. 'I forgot my keys!' Anna and Maria opened the door and hugged her. They were very happy.

8 Work in pairs. Compare your answers to Ex 7 and discuss these questions.
1 What language from the table do you feel most confident about using?
2 Which task would you choose now? Why?
3 Is it the same task you chose in Ex 6? Why/Why not?

9 Make notes for the task you have chosen.

Write on

10 e Write your answer to Task 1 or Task 2 in about 100 words.

11 Check your work. Use the table to help you.

assessment criteria	my work	✓ / ✗
content	Have I written about all the points in the task?	
communicative achievement	Have I used the right language style (formal/informal)?	
organisation	Have I organised all the points well?	
	Have I used linking words?	
language	Is my grammar and vocabulary accurate?	
	Have I used a range of appropriate language?	

GRAMMAR FILE

GRAMMAR FILE STARTER UNIT

REFERENCE

articles

We use the indefinite article (*a/an*):
- before single countable nouns that we are talking about for the first time.
  I've got **an** umbrella – here you are.
- before a noun that is one of many.
  Is there **a train station** near here?

We use the definite article (*the*):
- before single countable nouns that we have talked about before.
  We saw **a film**. **The film** was about a boy and girl.
- with uncountable nouns or plural nouns, when we are talking about a specific object or group.
  The children stayed at home.
  Could you pass **the water**, please?
- when there is only one of something.
  I went on **the Internet** last night.

  We don't use an article:
- before uncountable and abstract nouns.
  Do you want **sugar** in your coffee?
  Life is amazing sometimes.
- before plural nouns, when we are talking about something in general.
  Cats are wonderful **pets**.

past simple

We use the past simple to talk about:
- an action that started and finished in the past.
  I **visited** my grandparents.
- two or more past actions that happened one after the other.
  I **made** the salad and then helped my mum **set** the table.

For more information on the past simple, see page 128.

comparative and superlative structures

We use *as* + adjective + *as* to compare two people or things that are equal.
Jane is **as tall as** her sister now.

We use *not as* + adjective + *as* to compare two people or things that are not equal.
Tennis is**n't as dangerous as** rugby.

We can also use comparatives (adjective + *-er* + *than* or *more* + adjective + *than*) to compare two people or things that are not equal.
My brother's room is **bigger than** mine.
I was **more upset than** you were about the results.

To compare three or more things, we use superlatives (*the* + adjective + *-est* or *the most* + adjective).
Yesterday was **the coldest** day of the year so far.
This is **the most beautiful** beach I've ever seen.

type of adjective	comparative/superlative
most one syllable	+ *-er* → fast**er**
	+ *-est* → fast**est**
one syllable ending in *-e*	+ *-r* → nice**r**
	+ *-st* → the nice**st**
one syllable ending in one vowel and one consonant	double the consonant + *-er* → bi**gger**
	double the consonant + *-est* → bi**ggest**
one or two syllables ending in *-y*	change *-y* to *-i* + *-er* → happ**ier**
	change *-y* to *-i* + *-est* → happ**iest**
two or more syllables	*more* + adjective → **more beautiful**
	the most + adjective → **the most beautiful**
irregular	good → better → best
	bad → worse → the worst
	far → further/farther → the furthest/the farthest

PRACTICE

articles

1 Choose the correct words to complete the sentences.
1. I've got **a / the** new video game at home.
2. Is there **a / the** supermarket near your home?
3. I bought **a / the** book last week.
4. **A / The** book was about **a / the** sports star.
5. My dog doesn't like **a / the** moon.
6. My grandfather had **a / an** amazing life.
7. There's **a / an** university near my home.
8. Do you want **– / the** milk in your coffee?
9. **– / The** books are still popular.
10. I think **– / the** beauty is over-valued.

2 Complete the text with 'a/an', 'the' or no article (–).

I was on holiday last summer, and me and my brother were at ¹.................... river near our house. We wanted to go swimming, so we had ².................... towels and ³.................... stuff with us. We left our ⁴.................... jeans on the ⁵.................... ground and jumped into ⁶.................... water. It was freezing! While we were swimming, we heard ⁷.................... loud cry. We looked around and there was ⁸.................... enormous crocodile swimming past us. We were terrified!

past simple

3 Complete the sentences with the past simple form of the verbs in brackets.
1. I .... (help) my sister with her homework.
2. .... (you/arrive) in time for the film?
3. My brother .... (not finish) his project yesterday.
4. The chef on TV .... (use) a whole bar of chocolate for the cake.
5. .... (the shops/open) early last weekend?
6. My friend .... (not like) his holiday.
7. We .... (watch) a great movie last night.
8. .... (you/check) your last exercise?

4 Complete the sentences with the past simple form of these verbs.

bring   come   fall   go   send   sing   swim   think

1. Jo .... with me to the park at the weekend.
2. My mum .... in a band when she was younger.
3. I .... that the book was absolutely brilliant.
4. John .... cookies to our meeting yesterday.
5. My parents .... to Paris without me this year.
6. I .... and broke my arm over the summer.
7. We all .... in the pool at the end of the day.
8. My friend .... me an email last night.

comparative and superlative structures

5 Complete the sentences with the comparative or superlative form of the adjectives in brackets.
1. My sister is so much .... (short) than me.
2. That was the .... (kind) thing anyone ever did for me.
3. My last holiday was much .... (nice) than this one.
4. My old phone was much .... (large) than my new one.
5. That was the .... (happy) day of my life.
6. Fish is much .... (smelly) than most other meals.
7. The coffee is .... (expensive) that shop than one near home.
8. The TV documentary was the .... (interesting) thing on TV last night.

6 Complete the second sentence so that it means the same as the first sentence. Use the words in brackets.
1. That tree is the same size as our house. (as)
   That tree .... our house.
2. My bag is stronger than Sam's bag. (not as)
   Sam's bag is .... mine.
3. I've never seen a bigger cat. (the)
   It's .... I've ever seen.
4. London isn't as near to my home as Manchester. (far)
   London is .... away from my home than Manchester.
5. Me and my best friend as the same age.
   I'm .... my best friend. (as)
6. Documentaries are more interesting than soap operas. (not)
   Soap operas .... documentaries.

GRAMMAR FILE UNIT 1

REFERENCE

talking about the present

present simple

positive

I/We/You/They	dance.
He/She/It	dance**s**.

negative

I/We/You/They	**don't** dance.
He/She/It	**doesn't** dance.

questions

Do	I/we/you/they	dance?
Does	he/she/it	

short answers

Yes,	I/we/you/they	**do**.
	he/she/it	**does**.
No,	I/we/you/they	**don't**.
	he/she/it	**doesn't**.

We use the present simple to talk about:
- permanent states.
  She **lives** in Spain.
- habits or repeated actions
  He **sees** his friends most weekends.

present continuous

positive

I	**'m (am)**	
He/She/It	**'s (is)**	work**ing**.
We/You/They	**'re (are)**	

negative

I	**'m not (am not)**	
He/She/It	**isn't (is not)**	work**ing**.
We/You/They	**aren't (are not)**	

questions

Am	I	
Is	he/she/it	work**ing**?
Are	we/you/they	

short answers

Yes,	I	**am**.
	he/she/it	**is**.
	we/you/they	**are**.
No,	I	**'m not**.
	he/she/it	**isn't**.
	we/you/they	**aren't**.

We use the present continuous to talk about:
- actions that are happening now.
  She**'s talking** to the teacher.
- actions that are happening around now.
  We**'re studying** ancient Greece at school.

Note: Look at the spelling changes:

put – put**t**ing   tak**e** – tak**ing**

present simple and present continuous

We can contrast permanent activities (present simple) with activities happening now or around now (present continuous).

I**'m studying** French this summer but in school I **do** German.

stative verbs

Stative verbs describe states, not actions. Some common stative verbs are:
- verbs of being and owning, e.g. *be*, *have*, *own*.
- verbs of feeling or wanting, e.g. *hate*, *like*, *love*, *need*, *prefer*, *wish*.
- verbs of thinking, e.g. *believe*, *know*, *remember*, *think*, *understand*.
- verbs that describe the senses, e.g. *feel*, *hear*, *smell*, *see*, *taste*.
- verbs that describe appearance and qualities, e.g. *appear*, *look* (= seem), *seem*, *sound*
- other verbs, e.g. *cost*, *mean*.

Note: We also use some stative verbs in the continuous form when we describe actions.

We**'re having** lunch at the moment. (having = eating)

I**'m thinking** about my answer. (thinking = considering)

adverbs of frequency, time phrases

We use adverbs of frequency to say how often something happens. Some common adverbs of frequency are: *always*, *usually*, *frequently*, *often*, *sometimes*, *occasionally*, *rarely*, *hardly ever*, *never*.

Adverbs of frequency come:

I **never go** swimming in the winter.

Mark **is always** happy.

You **must never** open this door.

Other time expressions usually go at the end of a sentence.

We go to the cinema **twice a month**.

PRACTICE

present simple and present continuous

1 Choose the correct words to complete the sentences.
1 Carla **sends / is sending** a lot of text messages, so she's always on her phone.
2 Our football team **is practising / practises** hard for the competition on Saturday.
3 **Are you chatting / Do you chat** on the phone? I need your help.
4 We **don't have / aren't having** any lessons when it's the festival.
5 Look! She **runs / 's running** really quickly.
6 They **stay / are staying** at home because they are ill.

2 Complete the text with the present simple or present continuous form of the verbs in brackets.

Hi. I'm Brian and I **¹**............................ (be) from California. At the moment I **²**............................ (stay) with my grandparents because my parents **³**............................ (work) in Hong Kong. I **⁴**............................ (study) hard at school because I **⁵**............................ (try) to get good results in my exams. I really **⁶**............................ (love) playing volleyball with my friends and I think I'm quite good at it. I **⁷**............................ (practise) hard now because we **⁸**............................ (want) to do a competition with another school.

3 Make questions using the present simple or present continuous. Then complete the answers.
1 where / you / live?
   A: ....
   B: .... in Paris.
2 who / you / live / with?
   A: ....
   B: .... my brothers.
3 how / usually / you / get / to school?
   A: ....
   B: .... by bus.
4 you / like / school?
   A: ....
   B: Yes, ...
5 what / you / study / at the moment?
   A: ....
   B: .... science.
6 what / you / do / now?
   A: ....
   B: .... TV.

4 Choose the correct verb forms to complete the email.

Hi Nico,
Thanks for your email. Now I can tell you about myself.
At the moment I **¹sit / 'm sitting** in my bedroom in my flat. I **²live / 'm living** here with my grandparents.
I've got lots of friends but they **³aren't coming / don't come** to the flat very often. We usually **⁴meet / are meeting** in town. Today it **⁵snows / 's snowing** outside, so I **⁶stay / 'm staying** at home.
What about you? **⁷Does it snow / Is it snowing** in New York at the moment too? What **⁸do you do / are you doing** when it snows?
Speak soon,
Jack

stative verbs

5 Choose the correct words to complete the sentences.
1 **Do you think / Are you thinking** about your holiday?
2 My mother **doesn't like / isn't liking** using a laptop.
3 **Are you understanding / Do you understand** this lesson?
4 I **don't need / 'm not needing** any help right now, thanks.
5 We **have / 're having** dinner. Do you want to join us?

adverbs of frequency, time phrases

6 Write these words and phrases in the correct place in the table.

at the moment   every day   never   now   often   on Tuesdays
once a month   this week   today   usually

present simple	present continuous

7 Complete the sentences with the present simple or present continuous form of these verbs.

come round   cook   go   go out   make   talk

1 At the moment I .... the dog for a walk.
2 She .... now, so she can't talk to you.
3 Every Friday we .... for a pizza.
4 Once a week I .... to visit my grandparents.
5 She often .... to my house after school.
6 I .... my bed every day except Sundays.

8 Choose six words/phrases from Exercise 6. Use them to write true sentences about you.

127

GRAMMAR FILE UNIT 2

REFERENCE

talking about the past

past simple

positive

I/He/She/It/We/You/They	**helped** at the event.
I/He/She/It/We/You/They	**went** to the event.

negative

I/He/She/It/We/You/They	**didn't help** at the event.
I/He/She/It/We/You/They	**didn't go** to the event.

questions

Did	I/he/she/it/we/you/they	**help** at the event?
Did	I/he/she/it/we/you/they	**go** to the event?

short answers

Yes,	I/he/she/it/we/you/they	**did**.
No,	I/he/she/it/we/you/they	**didn't**.

We use the past simple to talk about:
- an action that started and finished in the past.
  David **finished** his maths homework.
- one completed past action after another.
  I **got** home and **sat** down.
- a past habit or regular past event.
  Maria and Eva **visited** the lake everyday on their holiday.

Note: Look at the spelling changes:

help – help**ed** practise – practis**ed**
study – stud**ied** chop – cho**pped**

past continuous

positive

I/He/She/It	**was**	wait**ing**.
We/You/They	**were**	

negative

I/He/She/It	**wasn't**	wait**ing**.
We/You/They	**weren't**	

questions

Was	I/he/she/it	wait**ing**?
Were	we/you/they	

short answers

Yes,	I/he/she/it	**was**.
	we/you/they	**were**.
No,	I/he/she/it	**wasn't**.
	we/you/they	**weren't**.

We use the past continuous to:
- talk about an action in progress in the past.
  I **was playing** video games.
  We **were eating** breakfast.
- set the scene in a story.
  The sun **was shining**.
  My dad and brother **were watching** TV.

We use the past simple for an action that interrupts or happens during another action in progress in the past. For the action in progress, we use the past continuous.

Claudette **was studying** in Pisa when she **met** Katerina.

We can use *while* instead of *when*, but we put *while* before the past continuous verb.

Dan **heard** the news **while** he was reading through his social media account.

When Dan **heard** the news, he was reading through his social media account.

stative verbs

We don't usually use stative verbs in the past continuous form. See page 126 for more information on stative verbs.

-*ing* form

We use the -*ing* form:
- as the subject or object of a sentence.
  Eating vegetables is good for you.
  I really love **surfing**!
- after prepositions.
  I always end **up leaving** my keys at home.
  I went home **after finishing** my game.
- after some verbs: *begin, continue, enjoy, finish, hate, like, love, imagine, practise, remember, start, stop, suggest*.
  I **remember stopping** at the shop on the way home.
  I **continued playing** in the rain.

PRACTICE

past simple

1 Complete the sentences with the past simple form of the verbs in brackets.

1. I .... (see) my friend last night.
2. I .... (enjoy) the book more than the film.
3. The lesson .... (not end) on time.
4. We .... (speak) Italian when we were on holiday.
5. Where .... (you/be) last night?
6. I .... (not want) the night to end.

2 Read the sentences and complete the questions.

1. I saw Connor yesterday morning.
   Who .... ?
2. The concert ended really early.
   When .... ?
3. They left the party at about 11 p.m.
   What time .... ?
4. The teacher gave us a lot of homework.
   How much .... ?
5. The old man told them a story.
   What .... ?

past continuous

3 Complete the sentences with the past continuous form of the verbs in brackets.

1. What .... (you/do) at this time last week?
2. I .... (not consider) entering the competition.
3. .... (your sister/play) tennis in the park on Saturday?
4. The internet .... (not work) at home, so I couldn't go online.
5. .... (it/rain) on your way home yesterday?
6. I had the TV switched on, but I .... (not pay) attention to it.

4 Complete the sentences with the past simple or past continuous form of the verbs in brackets.

1. I .... (do) the washing-up while I was listening to the song.
2. When I .... (come) in, my friends were waiting for me.
3. I .... (tidy) my room when the phone rang.
4. Our team .... (win) until the others scored in the last minute.
5. It .... (rain) when I went out for a walk yesterday morning.
6. The sun .... (shine) when we left the house.

5 Choose the correct verb forms to complete the sentences.

1. I didn't know what he **meant / was meaning** about the homework. Did you understand?
2. I **thought / was thinking** about what to do when my dad called me.
3. I **heard / was hearing** the good news while I was having breakfast.
4. I didn't want to call him while he **watched / was watching** the movie.
5. I completely **believed / was believing** what that man said.
6. Jack **understood / was understanding** everything.
7. We **didn't have / weren't having** time for breakfast because Emma was waiting for us.
8. He was hiding behind a tree, so I **didn't see / wasn't seeing** him.

-ing form

6 Complete the sentences with the correct form of these verbs.

do	eat	listen	look	paint	play	say	swim	talk	think

1. .... is probably the best form of exercise.
2. Ella doesn't like .... in front of everyone else in class. She's very shy.
3. I didn't want to go to the museum – I'm not interested in .... at old things.
4. After .... my dinner, I went round my friend's house and we watched a film.
5. Without .... , I ran into the garden and rescued the cat!
6. .... to music is the most relaxing hobby.
7. You shouldn't leave without .... goodbye – it's rude!
8. My dad finished .... my room yesterday. It looks great!
9. Experts say that by .... homework, students learn to manage their time better.
10. I hate .... chess with my brother. He always wins!

7 Complete the sentences to make them true for you. Use -ing forms.

1. .... is one of my favourite activities.
2. I can't stand ....
3. I love ....
4. I don't like .... very much.
5. I sometimes watch TV after ....
6. I'm not very keen on ....
7. I hate ....
8. I never go to bed without ....

129

GRAMMAR FILE UNIT 3

REFERENCE

talking about the future

will

positive

| I/He/She/It/We/You/They | **'ll (will)** | win. |

negative

| I/He/She/It/We/You/They | **won't (will not)** | win. |

questions

| **Will** | I/he/she/it/we/you/they | win? |

short answers

| **Yes,** | I/he/she/it/we/you/they | **will.** |
| **No,** | I/he/she/it/we/you/they | **won't.** |

We use *will*:
- to talk about things we think are going to happen, based on our personal ideas and opinions.
  Perhaps we **will use** e-books for all our studies in the future.
- to make offers.
  I**'ll help** you with your homework.
- for unplanned decisions that we make at the time we are speaking.
  I feel tired. I think I**'ll go** home now.

going to

positive

I	**'m (am)**		
He/She/It	**'s (is)**	going to	leave.
We/You/They	**'re (are)**		

negative

I	**'m (am) not**		
He/She/It	**isn't (is not)**	going to	leave.
We/You/They	**aren't (are not)**		

questions

Am	I		
Is	he/she/it	going to	leave?
Are	we/you/they		

short answers

Yes,	I	**am.**
	he/she/it	**is.**
	we/you/they	**are.**
No,	I	**'m not.**
	he/she/it	**isn't.**
	we/you/they	**aren't.**

We use *going to* to talk about:
- intentions and plans for the future that haven't been arranged or agreed yet.
  I**'m going to visit** my friend in Turkey sometime next year.
- things that we expect to happen because of outside information.
  It**'s going to rain** soon. (There are big grey clouds.)

present continuous and present simple

We use the present continuous for future arrangements. These are activities that we've agreed to do with other people. We know the details such as when, where, etc.

I**'m playing** in a football match on Saturday.

We use the present simple for schedules and timetabled events.

The film **finishes** at 9.30 p.m.

advice and suggestions

advice

We use *should/shouldn't* + infinitive to give strong advice. This is an opinion about what we think is a good or bad idea.

You **should have** a nap. You look tired.

You **shouldn't cycle** so fast.

We use *should* in questions to ask for advice.

What **should** I **do**?

Where **should** we **go** to get the bus?

suggestions

We use *how about* + noun/*-ing*, *why don't you/we* + infinitive and *you could* + infinitive to make a suggestion. This is an idea for the listener to consider. We use *you could* + infinitive when different options are possible.

How about watching a film?

Why don't we go out?

We **could go** by train to the beach.

We use *shall I/we* + infinitive for suggestions and offers.

Shall I bring some crisps for the picnic?

What **shall we do** after school today?

PRACTICE
talking about the future

1 Find and correct the mistakes with future forms in six of the sentences.

1 Oh look, there's no bread left. I'm going to the shop to get some.
....
2 Jonny and I go to the cinema later.
....
3 I'm not sure why but I think the trip tomorrow is being fun.
....
4 Do we play football after school?
....
5 I'm going to start a new book tonight.
....
6 Sally's chatting online later.
....
7 The class starts at six on Monday.
....
8 The flight arrives in a few moments.
....

2 Choose the correct verb forms to complete the sentences. Where both forms are possible, choose the most appropriate one.

1 I'm **reading / going to read** a book tomorrow morning.
2 You aren't **sleeping / going to sleep** tonight after that scary film.
3 Jack and I are **playing / going to play** in the snow. Are you coming?
4 I'm **taking / going to take** the train to my grandparent's house at the weekend. I've already got my ticket.
5 It's cold outside. I'm **going to put / putting** the heating on.
6 We're **meeting up / going to meet up** at six on Friday.

3 Complete the sentences with the most appropriate future form of the verbs in brackets.

1 We .... (meet) Nick at school in five minutes.
2 I think you .... (be) tired tonight. You've been busy all day.
3 The train .... (leave) at 12.35, so we've got thirty minutes to get there.
4 My grandparents .... (come) to visit us tomorrow.
5 Watch out! The cat .... (jump) on you.
6 The dog wants to go for a walk. I .... (take) him.
7 Where .... (you/meet) your cousin tonight?
8 The concert .... (start) at 8 p.m., so don't be late.

4 Complete the predictions with *will*, *won't* or the correct form of *going to*. Decide which is the most appropriate in each case.

1 I .... enjoy the film. I don't like scary movies.
2 It's .... to rain later. I saw it on the weather report.
3 I don't think we .... win the match tonight. We've lost our best player.
4 I expect my parents .... come and pick me up later.
5 Our teacher .... be late. His car's broken down.
6 We .... finish this homework in time. The lesson starts in ten minutes.

advice and suggestions

5 What is the speaker doing in each sentence: giving advice (A) or making a suggestion (S)?

1 You shouldn't eat so many sweets! ....
2 Why don't you grow your hair long? ....
3 How about chicken for dinner? ....
4 We could cycle or walk. Which would you prefer? ....
5 Dan should apologise to his friend. ....
6 We should go out and get some fresh air. ....

6 Complete the conversation with one word in each gap.

A: ¹.................... we make a video today?
B: What about?
A: We ².................... film ourselves on our skateboards.
B: Good idea. Why ³.................... we go to the skate park and film there?
A: Everyone does that. We ⁴.................... go somewhere different. It's better.
B: Alright. How ⁵.................... the beach? We could skate near the mini-golf course.
A: Sounds good. Why ⁶.................... you message Liam and invite him?
B: OK … Done!

7 Find and correct the mistakes in four of the sentences.

1 Shall I to help you with those books?
....
2 Why aren't we go to the park after school?
....
3 We could stay at home and watch a film.
....
4 How about have some sandwiches for lunch?
....
5 What shall we get Joe for his birthday?
....
6 What should I wearing to Fiona's party?
....

GRAMMAR FILE UNIT 4

REFERENCE
present perfect

positive

I/We/You/They	've (have)	finished.
He/She/It	's (has)	

negative

I/We/You/They	haven't (have not)	finished.
He/She/It	hasn't (has not)	

questions

Have	I/we/you/they	finished?
Has	he/she/it	

short answers

Yes,	I/we/you/they	have.
	he/she/it	has.
No,	I/we/you/they	haven't.
	he/she/it	hasn't.

We use the present perfect to talk about:
- something that happened in the past and has a result in the present.
  Robert has broken his leg, so he can't play.
- a situation or an experience in our lives that is still true now.
  I've lived in this street all my life.

present perfect with adverbs of time

We use *ever* in questions and statements to refer to an event or experience which happened/didn't happen at some point in the past.
Have you **ever lived** in the USA?
We use *never* to talk about something that hasn't happened.
I've never eaten Japanese food.
We use *yet* for something we expect to happen.
I haven't finished my homework **yet**.
We use *just* for recent events.
I've just had a text from my friend.
We use *already* for something that has happened before now.
We're not hungry because we**'ve already had** lunch.
We often use *for* and *since* with the present perfect.
I haven't heard this song **for** years. (a period of time)
I've known Ian **since** I was seven. (a specific time in the past)

past simple and present perfect

We use the past simple for an action that happened at a definite time in the past.
I joined a chess club a few weeks ago.
We use the present perfect for a past action when we don't know when it happened, or when it isn't important.
We've visited this town before.
We also use the present perfect for something that happened in the past but in a period of time that is not finished, e.g. *today*, *this month*, *this year*.
I've made a lot of new friends this year.

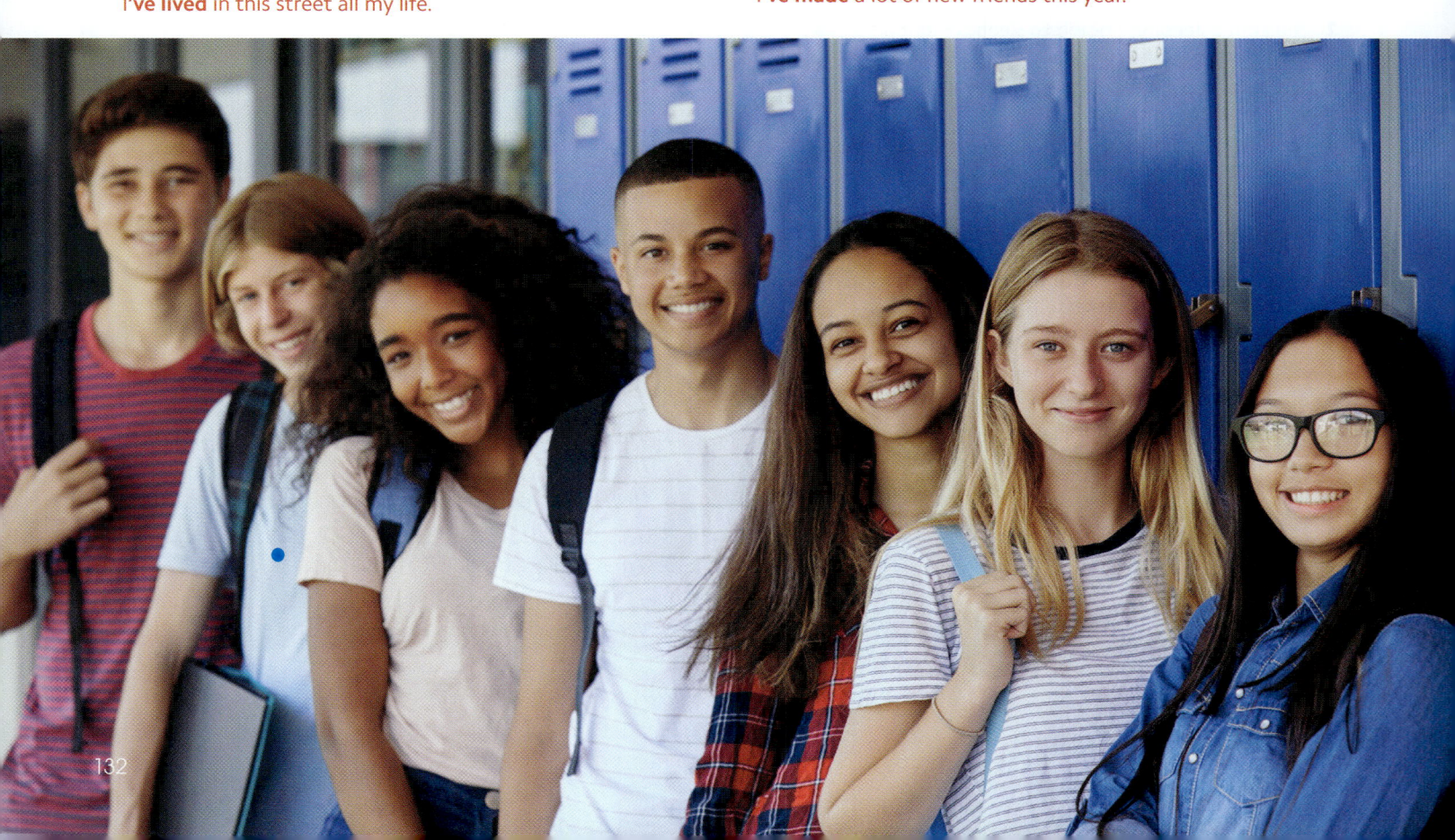

PRACTICE
present perfect

1 Complete the sentences with the present perfect form of the verbs in brackets.

1 I .... (buy) a ticket for the concert.
2 She .... (not write) her homework in English.
3 We .... (not eat) Indian food before.
4 Which sports .... (you/try)?
5 .... (you/visit) your cousins this year?

2 Complete the sentences with 'ever', 'never', 'yet', 'just' or 'already'.

1 Have your parents .... been to New York?
2 I've .... been on holiday without my parents. I'd love to go alone!
3 Marco, have you found your phone .... ?
4 She didn't want to see the film because she's .... seen it.
5 We've .... bought some cola for this evening. We got it a few minutes ago.

3 Complete the sentences with these words. Choose one word from each group for each sentence. Put the verbs in the correct form.

A	be buy meet see (x2)	B	already ever just never yet

1 .... (she) a famous footballer?
2 .... (you) the latest episode of 'Kingdom' .... ? It was on last week.
3 We .... tickets for the match. We did it online five minutes ago.
4 They .... to Florida before, so I think they'll enjoy it.
5 I don't want to watch that film. I .... it.

4 Write questions using 'how long' and the present perfect. Then complete the answers with 'for' or 'since'.

1 you / have / that tennis racquet?
   A: ....
   B: .... last year.
2 your family / live / in that house?
   A: ....
   B: .... five years.
3 they / know / that famous footballer?
   A: ....
   B: .... they were children.
4 Celia / play / the guitar?
   A: ....
   B: .... a long time.

past simple and present perfect

5 Choose the correct verb forms to complete the sentences.

1 My sister **has lived / lived** in seven different countries, so she is very well travelled!
2 We **have seen / saw** that film. We went to see it together last weekend.
3 She **has hurt / hurt** her hand the day before the match. She was really disappointed.
4 My mother **has spoken / spoke** French when she was at school.
5 I **have read / read** nine books this year! I'm really proud of myself!
6 At the weekend, my brother and his friends **have won / won** a volleyball competition.
7 **Have you seen / Did you see** Mr Sinder today? I can't find him!
8 I **haven't done / didn't do** the homework, so I got into trouble.

6 Complete the conversation with the past simple or present perfect form of the verbs in brackets.

A: Everybody was talking about the freerunning video we posted. It's all over school!
B: Yeah, a girl from my tennis class **1** .... (text) me a few minutes ago. She says 300 people **2** .... (watch) it already. That's brilliant for the first day.
A: I think we **3** .... (do) really well, don't you? I'm so glad we decided to do it!
B: Yes, it was a good idea. So, lots of people **4** .... (see) the video and liked it. It has been viewed more than 200 times!
A: Definitely! They've left some really good comments. I think that before we **5** .... (make) the video, some people at school had the wrong idea about freerunning. They didn't think it was a real sport.
B: That's right. And now the video **6** .... (show) everyone how good we are!
A: Yeah … Why don't we start a freerunning club after school? It will be good fun and perhaps we can make more videos.
B: Great idea! It was great fun making the video. I like checking how it is doing as well!
A: But it **7** .... (take) ages. The best bit for me **8** .... (be) the music.
B: I know, but next time I'd like to choose some music, too.

GRAMMAR FILE UNIT 5

REFERENCE

zero, first and second conditionals

zero conditional

if clause	main clause
if/*when* + present simple	main verb + present simple
When I **call** my friends,	I often **talk** for hours.

We use the zero conditional to talk about something that always or usually happens.

If/**When** my friend **sings**, everyone **stops** to listen.
I **don't watch** TV **if**/**when** I **have** homework.

first conditional

if clause	main clause
if + present tense	*will*/*could*/*might* + infinitive
If you **like** romantic stories,	you**'ll enjoy** this film.

We use the first conditional to talk about a possible action in the future.

If you **don't understand** the words, you **could look** them up online.
If I **have** time at the weekend, I **might practise** that new song.

second conditional

if clause	main clause
if + past simple	*would* + infinitive
If I **became** a singer,	I **would travel** around the world.

We use the second conditional:
- to talk about imaginary or unreal situations in the present.
  If I **were** a good singer, **I would be** in a famous pop group.
  If my dog **could** talk, he**'d ask** me to feed him more often!
- to talk about present or future situations that are possible but unlikely.
  If I **won** lots of money, I**'d buy** more musical instruments for my school.
  If I **met** my favourite actor, I **would ask** him how he got where he is now.
- to give advice.
  If I **were** you, I**'d have** extra music lessons.
  I **would work** harder at school **if** I **were** you.

unless, *in case*, *if I were you*

unless

We can use *unless* instead of *if not*.
I can't help you **if** you **don't tell** me your problem.
I can't help you **unless** you **tell** me your problem.
If he **doesn't pass** his music exam, Sam won't be happy.
Unless he **passes** his music exam, Sam won't be happy.
Note: We don't use a negative verb after *unless*.
Unless you ~~don't invite~~ invite him, he won't come to the party.

in case

We can use (*just*) *in case* instead of *if* when we want to stress 'to be safe or prepared'.
I'll take my coat (**just**) **in case** it gets cold.
I always have my phone (**just**) **in case** I need to call someone.

if I were you

We can use *if I were you* to give someone advice. We use it in second conditional sentences.
If I were you, I would change football teams.
I'd take my coat **if I were you**. It's freezing outside!

PRACTICE

zero, first and second conditionals

1 Choose the correct verb forms to complete the sentences.
1. If they make another 'Avengers' film, I **go / will go** and see it.
2. If a computer is not connected to electricity, it **doesn't switch / won't switch** on.
3. When people eat a lot fast food, they **have / will have** a lot of health problems.
4. If you leave water in the sun, it **disappears / will disappear** eventually.
5. If it rains this evening, I **don't go / won't go** out.
6. If there's a good movie on tonight, I **stay / will stay** home.
7. When you **mix / will mix** red and blue, you get purple.
8. If she calls me tonight, I **tell / will tell** her about the party.

2 Complete the zero and first conditional sentences with the correct form of the verbs in brackets.
1. When I .... (see) my friends, we always .... (chat) about music.
2. If you .... (meet) Eli later, you .... (be able) to tell her about the party.
3. You .... (not get) any better if you .... (not practise).
4. If I .... (become) famous, I .... (buy) a huge house!
5. When you .... (press) this key on the piano, it .... (make) a very deep sound.
6. I .... (not come) to the play if it .... (start) in the afternoon.
7. If she .... (not have to) go to school, she never .... (get up) early.
8. If you .... (ask) him nicely, I'm sure he .... (help) you.

3 Match 1–6 with A–F to make sentences.
1. If I knew the answers,
2. If I were famous,
3. I'd be able to buy a new guitar
4. No one could become successful
5. I would be nervous
6. Everyone would vote for you

A if they hadn't worked really hard.
B I'd hate all the attention.
C if I entered a talent show.
D if I'd saved more money.
E if they heard you sing.
F I'd tell you, but I don't.

4 Make second conditional sentences.
1. if / he / not stay up late, he / not feel tired in the morning
....
2. if / I / have / enough money, I / buy / an extra ticket
....
3. if / she / not like / you, she / not invite / you / to all her parties
....
4. if / we / have / some cheese, I / make / some sandwiches
....
5. if / you / be / more careful, you / not make / so many mistakes
....
6. if / he / lie / to me, I / be / very angry
....
7. if / he / work / harder, he / not fail / all his exams
....
8. if / my friends / be / here, we / have / a great time
....

unless, in case, if I were you

5 Complete the sentences with 'unless' or 'in case'.
1. I won't come .... you want me to.
2. I bought tickets early .... they run out.
3. I won't wave at you, ... it makes you nervous.
4. You won't survive in show business .... you have the right contacts.
5. He won't go on stage .... we go with him.
6. I'll stay with you, ... your parents are late.

6 Complete the advice with the correct form of these phrases.

find out why   go on holiday   practise more often
start making short films   take lessons from a family member
write a few pages each night

1. Our band is awful.
   If ....
2. I can't cook at all.
   If ....
3. I won $5,000.
   If ....
4. I want to be a director.
   If ....
5. My friend's really angry with me.
   If ....
6. I want to write a book.
   If ....

GRAMMAR FILE UNIT 6

REFERENCE

the passive: present simple and past simple

present simple passive

subject +	be (am/is/are) +	+ past participle (+ by)	
The river	is	cleaned	every year.
The bottles	aren't	used	again.
The articles	are	written by the students.	

past simple passive

subject +	be (was/were) +	+ past participle (+ by)	
The trees	were	destroyed by the fire.	
The caves	were	found by a tourist.	
The book	was	published	in 2017.

We use the present simple passive or past simple passive:

- when we want to focus on the action more than the person that does or did the action.
  The old clothes **are recycled**.
  The bridge **was repaired**.
- when we don't know or don't want to say who does or did the action, or when it's obvious who did it.
  The film **was watched** around the world.
  My phone **was stolen** at the train station.

When we know or want to mention who does or did the action, we use *by*.
The island was discovered **by a famous scientist**.

Verbs without an object (e.g. *come, go, happen, arrive*) are not used in the passive because there is no object to become the subject.

Note: When we form the passive, it is important to make sure we use the correct form of *be*. To do this, look at the subject and think about whether it is singular or plural.

The pizza was delivered by someone on a bike.
Pizzas were invented in Italy.

have/get something done

subject +	have/get +	object +	past participle	
I	have	my hair	cut	at Headlines.
We	got	our photos	taken	at school today.
I	get	my make-up	done	by Selina.

We use *have/get something done* when somebody else does something for us. We often pay them to do it for us. *Get something done* means the same as *have something done* but it is less formal. We use it when we are talking.
I **get my teeth checked** every six months.

When we want to say who does the action for us, we use *by*.
They had the food for the party made **by professional chefs**.

PRACTICE

the passive: present simple and past simple

1 Put the words in the correct order to make sentences.

1 watched / last month / the documentary / by millions / was
....

2 in the kitchen / served / each day / lunch / is
....

3 thousands of people / visited / the mountain / is / by / each week
....

4 to make the programme / were / a lot of cameras / used
....

5 some strange lights / seen / last night / in the sky / were
....

6 enjoyed / by adults and children / is / the beach
....

7 given / who leave rubbish / are / to people / on the beach / fines
....

8 was / by / written / a well-known author / the book
....

9 only given / to customers / refunds / with a receipt / are
....

10 by / was / that film / Steven Spielberg / directed
....

2 Complete the sentences with the present simple or past simple passive form of these verbs.

clean   collect   deliver   drive   film   give   make
speak   steal   waste

1 English .... all around the world.
2 These chocolates .... by hand in Belgium last week.
3 A parcel .... for you this morning.
4 Homework .... to students each day.
5 Some money .... from a wallet yesterday.
6 The classrooms .... every day by a team of cleaners.
7 Tonnes of water .... every day when people leave taps running.
8 A large amount of rubbish .... from the beach last week.
9 The movie .... on the streets of Rio de Janeiro.
10 My children .... to school by their grandmother every morning.

3 Complete the text with the correct active or passive form of the verbs in brackets.

Forest food

Last year I [1].................. (take) to an amazing restaurant for my friend's birthday. It's called The Green Forest Café and it [2].................. (locate) in a forest about thirty kilometres from my town. My friend's mum drove us to a car park nearby and then we [3].................. (walk) for about twenty minutes through the trees to get to the café.

The building [4].................. (make) from wood. It has large windows and a glass ceiling, so you really feel part of the forest around you. The food is delicious. The salad and vegetables [5].................. (grow) locally and they [6].................. (freshly/pick) every day. We [7].................. (serve) our meal by a really friendly waiter who [8].................. (explain) some of the things we could see around us. It was really interesting. We all enjoyed the experience a lot.

have/get something done

4 Choose the correct verb forms to complete the sentences.

1 We **have** / **had** our cooker repaired yesterday.
2 I think I **get** / **'ll get** my hair done next week.
3 My sister and I **have had** / **had** our teeth checked by the dentist last week.
4 We **get** / **'re getting** our post delivered every morning at about 10 a.m.
5 Most car owners **are having** / **have** their cars fixed by a mechanic these days.
6 In future, I think that we **'ll have** / **'re having** our parcels delivered by drones.
7 My mum **has had** / **had** her hair done twice this week!
8 We **have** / **'re having** our house painted at the moment.

5 Complete the sentences using 'have/get something done'.

1 My sister .... (paint/her nails) every week.
2 My cousin .... (make/all his meals) by his mum every day. He's thirty!
3 He .... (decorate/his room) next week.
4 Maggie .... (cut/her hair) yesterday.
5 My dad .... (wash/his car) by a neighbour's son.
6 My parents .... (deliver/their new car) tomorrow morning.
7 I .... (test/my eyes) once a year.
8 We .... (deliver/a takeaway) every Friday.
9 Maisie .... (fix/her washing machine) next week sometimes.
10 I never .... (clean/my room). I always do it myself.

# GRAMMAR FILE UNIT 7

REFERENCE

defining relative clauses

That's the girl	**who/that**	wants to be a pilot.
The train	**which/that**	leaves in ten minutes is full.
That's the place	**where**	we need to meet.
That's the boy	**whose**	bike was stolen.

We use defining relative clauses to describe exactly which people, things, places, etc. we mean. We use:
- *who* or *that* for people.
- *which* or *that* for things/animals.
- *where* for places.
- *whose* to show possession.

Defining relative clauses can give us information about the subject or the object of the main clause. e often use them to join two sentences.

A girl found my passport. (*A girl* is the subject.)

She was very nice.

The girl who found my passport was very nice.

I met **a girl** at the airport. (*A girl* is the object.)

She speaks four languages.

The girl who I met at the airport speaks four languages.

We can leave out the relative pronoun when it is the object of the relative clause.

The girl I met at the airport speaks four languages.

We don't use commas in defining relative clauses.

We use *whose* as the possessive form of *who*.

This is Ella, whose family I travelled with last summer.

modals of obligation, prohibition and necessity

present

| must | I **must get** a new passport. |
| | You **mustn't use** a mobile phone on the plane. |

have to	We **have to collect** the tickets from the station.
	He **has to stay** here.
	They **don't have to leave** now.
	She **doesn't have to pay** for her ticket.
	Do we **have to go** now?
	Does he **have to be** here?

past

had to	I was late, so I **had to run** to the bus stop.
	We **didn't have to walk** because the bus came.
	Did you **have to buy** another ticket?

future

will have to	We**'ll have to go** home soon.
	You **won't have to talk** to him again.
	Will she **have to find** a different flight?

We use *must* when we think it is very important or necessary to do something.

I must buy a new bag for the journey.

We use *mustn't* when it's important or necessary not to do something or when something is prohibited.

You mustn't tell him about the party.

We use *have to* to talk about something that is important or necessary, often because it's a general rule.

All passengers have to show their passports before they get on the plane.

We use *don't have to* to talk about something that isn't necessary or when there is no obligation.

You don't have to sit there if you don't want to.

We use *had to* to talk about obligation in the past.

I had to buy another ticket.

We use *will have to* to talk about obligation in the future.

You'll have to take the bus to the airport.

need to

We use *need to/don't need to* when we think something is/isn't necessary but not an obligation.

We need to see our grandparents before we leave.

PRACTICE
defining relative clauses

1 Choose the correct words to complete the sentences.
1. Is that the boy **which / who** won the singing competition?
2. The singer **that / which** I like watching most on stage is Adele.
3. The performers **which / who** we saw at the festival were great.
4. I'd like to find a flight **that / who** goes direct.
5. Do you know the name of the band **which / where** is on TV now?
6. There are some borders **where / who** it is dangerous to cross.
7. That's the man **which / who** we saw when we checked in.
8. The girl **which / who** sat next to me on the flight spoke Arabic.

2 Circle the relative pronoun if it is not necessary.
1. The house where we stayed was really expensive.
2. The boy who I sat next to at school is famous now.
3. The guidebook which she gave me was out of date.
4. We went to a restaurant where you had to cook your own food!
5. She thanked the man who found her dog.
6. Is that the song which you said won the competition?

3 **e** Read the article and for each question, write the correct answer. Write one word for each gap.

GO TO ZAKOPANE!

Last year my family and I flew to Poland. We wanted to visit some cousins **1**............................ live in Zakopane, a ski resort in the mountains. We went by car and, unfortunately, there was a long delay at the border because **2**............................ the snow. But we had a brilliant time after that. We stayed in a small house **3**............................ was at the top of a mountain. It had an amazing view! Normally, I hate activity holidays but it was nice to be somewhere **4**............................ we had friends and could enjoy the local life. **5**............................ food was really good and my cousins taught me **6**............................ to cook local dishes. And the skiing was great, too. I would definitely recommend the resort.

modals of obligation, prohibition and necessity

4 Choose the correct words to complete the sentences.
1. We **have to / need to** wear a tie to school. It's a rule.
2. We **mustn't / needn't** wear trainers. They're not allowed.
3. We **had to / must** give our homework in last Friday.
4. You **don't need to / mustn't** bring a pen. I've got one.
5. Next week we **will have to / must** practise the play.
6. You **don't have to / mustn't** sign up if you want to be in the team. It's up to you.

5 Complete the blog post with the correct form of 'have to', 'must' or 'need to'.

My advice for a school trip

On our last school trip to Lisbon I learnt a lot about travelling. And I think I've got some helpful advice for what to do when you are on a school trip.

- You **1**............................ look after all your money. Ask the group leaders to hold it for you.
- Normally, you **2**............................ allow for ten euros a day but you don't **3**............................ take more than this.
- At the airport you'll **4**............................ collect your luggage and take it to check-in. Nobody will do it for you and the check-in staff **5**............................ know it's your luggage.
- You **6**............................ write you flight number down so you're sure you're in the right place at the right time.
- You **7**............................ leave your luggage anywhere. Make sure it's always with you.
- You **8**............................ keep your passport with you at all times. Put is somewhere safe. Make sure no one can take it.

6 Complete the conversation with the correct form of 'have to', 'must' or 'need to'.

A: Are you ready for the trip?
B: No! I still **1**............................ get some money.
A: Oh goodness! Can you ask your mum?
B: I **2**............................ ask her, I suppose. And I haven't packed.
A: Oh dear! You really **3**............................ be more organised. We're leaving tomorrow.
B: Well, we're going to the beach, so I **4**............................ take any warm clothes. That's good!
A: Yes, but you do **5**............................ take a beach towel, I think. Have you got one?
B: I'll look now.
A: Oh, and you **6**............................ put any food in your suitcase. It's not allowed.

GRAMMAR FILE UNIT 8

REFERENCE

reported speech
reported statements

direct speech	reported speech
'I **take** photos of the stars.'	Liam said (that) he **took** photos of the stars.
'I **can** see it.'	Elena said (that) she **could** see it.
'I **will** do it again.'	Nathan said (that) he **would** do it again.

We use reported speech to tell somebody else what a person said.

Liam said (that) he read about the stars every night.

In reported speech, the main verb usually moves back one tense into the past.

She said, 'I **want** to be a dancer.'

She said (that) she **wanted** to be a dancer.

reported questions

yes/no questions

direct speech	reported speech
She asked me, '**Are** you **studying** Arabic?'	She asked **if** I was studying Arabic.
She asked me, '**Do** you **live** in London?	She asked me **if** I **lived** my lessons.

When we report yes/no questions, the verb is not in question form and we don't use the auxiliary verb. We use *if* instead.

wh- questions

direct speech	reported speech
She asked me, '**What's** your name?'	She asked me **what** my name **was**.'

When we report wh- questions, the verb is not in question form – we use the same structure as in statements. We repeat the question word in the reported question.

We use *say* or *tell* when reporting statements. *Tell* needs an object.

Ahmad said, 'I love photography.'

Ahmad **said** (that) he loved photography.

Lizzie told the receptionist, 'I need to collect a form.'

Lizzie **told the receptionist** (that) she needed to collect a form.

We use *ask* in reported questions. We can use it with or without an object.

'What happened?' he asked.

He **asked** what had happened.

'Where are you?' she asked me.

She **asked me** where I was.

pronouns in reported speech

In reported speech, we change subject pronouns (*I*, *you*, *he*, *she* etc.), possessive pronouns (*mine*, *yours*, *his*, *hers*, etc.) and possessive adjectives (*my*, *your*, *his*, *her* etc.) so that it's clear who or what they refer to.

Sandra said, '**My** hobby is collecting shells.'

Sandra told me (that) **her** hobby was collecting shells.

indirect questions

yes/no questions

direct question	indirect question
Is it a difficult job?	**Can you tell me if it's** a difficult job?
Do they live here?	**Do you know if they live** here?

wh- questions

direct question	indirect question
Where do you practise?	Can you tell me where you practise?
Why do you enjoy your hobby?	Can I ask why you enjoy your hobby?

In indirect questions, we use the same verb form as in statements – the verb is not in question form.

In yes/no questions, we use *if*. In wh- questions we use the question word.

Does he work here?

Can you tell me if **he works** here?

What time **does the concert start**?

Do you know what time **the concert starts**?

140

PRACTICE

reported statements

1 Rewrite the statements in reported speech.

1 'I love making cookies,' said Samir.
....
2 'That's really kind', said Ed.
....
3 Marie Alejandra said, 'I'll email later.'
....
4 Jerry said, 'I'm finishing a new project.'
....
5 'I can't come to the party,' Piotr told Adam.
....
6 'The train will arrive soon,' Jamie told Dan.
....

2 Complete the sentences with 'said' or 'told'.

1 He .... me that he was happy.
2 My sister .... that it was raining.
3 She .... that something bad had happened.
4 The teacher .... the class that there was a test that day.
5 The bus driver .... the passengers that he was running late.
6 The teacher .... that it was time to go home.

reported questions

3 Rewrite the reported questions as direct speech.

1 Renée asked what we were doing.

2 Carolina asked if we were finished.

3 My mum asked us what we would like.

4 Our teacher asked if we could help him.

5 Michiko asked if we had seen Ming.

6 The tennis coach asked what we wanted to do next.

pronouns in reported speech

4 Complete the sentences with the correct pronouns and possessive adjectives.

1 'You need to come back later,' the woman said.
   The woman said that .... needed to come back later.
2 'We need to leave,' said the man.
   The man said that .... needed to leave.
3 'You will always be safe,' Jess told me.
   Jess told .... that .... would always be safe.
4 'Your sister is my best friend,' Isabel said.
   Isabel said that .... sister was .... best friend.
5 'I've got your book,' my friend told me.
   My friend told .... that .... had .... book.
6 'The red book is yours and the black one is mine,' Jack said to his mother.
   Jack told .... mother that the red book was .... and the black one was ....

indirect questions

5 Choose the correct words to complete the sentences.

1 John asked **when / if** I was ready.
2 Suzanne asked **which / if** book was mine.
3 Keiko asked **what / if** my sister liked classical music.
4 My teacher asked **what / if** I was doing later.
5 The lady asked **where / if** I could help her.
6 Martin asked **where / if** I was.

6 Complete the indirect questions.

1 Can you see the stage?
   Could you .... ?
2 Will you be at the show?
   Can I .... ?
3 When do you want we get tickets?
   Can I .... ?
4 What time does the show end?
   Do you know .... ?
5 Is Sebastian playing the lead part?
   Do you know .... ?
6 Does this bus stop at the cinema?
   Could you .... ?

GRAMMAR FILE UNIT 9

REFERENCE

past perfect

positive

I/You/He/She/It/We/They	**'d (had)**	**finished**.

negative

I/You/He/She/It/We/They	**hadn't (had not)**	**finished**.

questions

Had	I/you/he/she/it/we/they	**finished**?

short answers

Yes,	I/you/he/she/it/we/they	**had**.
No,		**hadn't**.

We use the past perfect to talk about something that was completed at an earlier point in the past.

I got a lovely surprise on my birthday. My parents **had organised** a party.

past perfect and past simple

We use the past perfect with the past simple to show that one action happened before another in the past. The past perfect simple describes the action that happened first and the past simple describes the action that happened second.

past ——————×——————×—————— now
       The party **had finished**   when Ben **arrived**.

(First, the party finished. Then, Ben arrived.)
We can also say:
When Ben **arrived**, the party **had finished**.

We use many of the same time expressions that with use with the present perfect. We use adverbs of time, e.g. *already, ever, just* and *never*.

She offered us a snack but we'd **just** had lunch.
Mark was funny. I'd **never** met anyone quite like him.
I didn't want any more surprises. I'd **already** had enough!

We use time linkers (e.g. *after, before, by the time, once, until, when*) to talk about two actions in the same sentence.

After they had seen the concert, they went to bed.
I had done my homework **before** I went out.
By the time we got to school, the first lesson had started.
Once it stopped raining, we went for a walk.
My parents had left for work **when** I got up.

used to

positive

I/You/He/She/It/We/They	**used to**	**collect** comics.

negative

I/You/He/She/It/We/They	**didn't use to**	**have** any hobbies.

questions

Did	I/you/he/she/it/ we/they	**use to**	**have** any hobbies?

We use *used to* to talk about something that happened regularly in the past, but does not happen now. We use it to refer to past habits or states.

He **used to enjoy** drama at school, but he doesn't do it now.
I **didn't use to watch** horror films, but I like them now.
You speak French well. **Did** you **use to live** in France?

We often use *used to* with *never*.
I **never used to like** curry but I do now.
Jack **never used to be** so tall.

We don't use *used to*:
- to talk about an action which happened only once or twice.
- with a time expression that tells us how many times an action happened.
- with a time expression that tells us when an action happened.

I ~~used to swim~~ **swam** in the sea a few times when I was young.
We ~~used to go~~ **went** swimming last August.

We don't use *used to* to say how long a **state** lasted. But we can use it to talk about how long a repeated or regular past **action** lasted.

They ~~used to live~~ **lived** here for ten years.
I ~~used to like~~ **liked** this song for about two years but I don't now.
We **used to play** in the tree house for hours.

PRACTICE
past perfect

1 Find and correct the mistakes in the sentences.
1. I couldn't call her because I left my phone at home.
2. After we'd finished the match, we got changed and went home.
3. I had eat too much for lunch, so I didn't want any dinner.
4. I was tired when I went to bed. It been a busy day.
5. Fay's phone had no battery because she'd forgotten to charge it.
6. My mum bought me a book that I already read.
7. School closed early because the heating break down.
8. I couldn't read what I'd wrote in my notebook.

2 Choose the correct verb forms to complete the sentences.
1. I **just fell / had just fallen** asleep when my sister **woke / had woken** me up.
2. We **played / had played** a game of cards which I **never played / had never played** before.
3. I **was / had been** tired because I **only slept / had only slept** for about five hours.
4. Brett **handed / had handed** in the essay that he **wrote / had written** the night before.
5. The lesson **started / had started** five minutes before we **arrived / had arrived**.
6. When we **got / had got** to the concert, we found that the first band **already started / had already started** playing.
7. I **offered / had offered** to wash up but my dad **already did / had already done** it.
8. Greg **wasn't / hadn't been** very happy because he **dropped / had dropped** his mobile phone again.

3 Complete the text with the past simple or past perfect form of the verbs in brackets.

A bad start to the day

Jen decided to take the bus to school. Her dad's car ¹............... (break down) the day before, so he couldn't take her.

She ²............... (just/get) there when the bus arrived. She got on and ³............... (reach) into her bag to get her purse and realised she ⁴............... (leave) it at home.

Walking was her only option but it was raining and she ⁵............... not bring an umbrella. Still, she started to walk. After a few minutes, a car ⁶............... (drive) really fast past her and ⁷............... (hit) a huge puddle. The water ⁸............... (fly) up in the air and ⁹............... (land) on Jen. She looked like she ¹⁰............... (just/get) out of the bath!

used to

4 Complete the sentences with the correct form of 'used to'.
1. I .... like coffee but I love it now.
2. .... (you) spend a lot of time outdoors when you were young?
3. Liam .... make model aeroplanes but now he's into other things.
4. .... (Miriam) live next door to you?
5. My family and I .... go skiing every winter but we don't now.
6. .... (your brother) have longer hair?
7. Sara .... say much in class but she's much chattier these days.
8. I .... be interested in history but now I quite like it.

5 Complete the sentences with the correct form of 'used to' and these verbs.

borrow   do   enjoy   know   live   own   play   tidy

1. We .... in a big house by the sea but then we moved to the city.
2. My parents .... a car but they bought one last year.
3. .... (you) a lot of sport when you were younger?
4. I .... watching football but I do now.
5. My sister .... my clothes without asking but she's stopped now.
6. .... (Mark) the piano?
7. My friends and I .... all the words to One Direction songs.
8. .... (you) your room yourself when you were younger?

6 Choose the correct verb forms to complete the sentences. Sometimes both are possible.
1. My sister **annoyed / used to annoy** me but now we're great friends.
2. My uncle **made / used to make** me laugh a lot last weekend.
3. We **lived / used to live** in a bigger house than this for a few years.
4. I **enjoyed / used to enjoy** doing sports when I was younger.
5. For years, my family and I **went / used to go** camping.
6. Rebecca **hated / used to hate** getting up early every single morning.
7. Dan **was / used to be** a postman for a long time.
8. My parents and I **visited / used to visit** the art gallery one summer.

EXTEND VOCABULARY

Unit 1
personality adjectives
amusing
anxious
brave
careless
intelligent
modern
nervous
old-fashioned
polite
reliable
sociable
sweet

adjective + preposition collocations
affected by
afraid of
angry with
different from
famous for
impressed with/by
positive about
unhappy about

Unit 2
Language and communication
accent (*n*)
comment (*n*)
complaint (*n*)
excuse (*n*)
explanation (*n*)
greeting (*n*)
interrupt (*v*)
out loud (*adv*)
translation (*n*)

Unit 3
phrasal verbs
break down (e.g. for a car)
break up (a relationship)
carry on (doing something)
carry out (an activity)
check out (a fun website)
cross out (a mistake)
deal with (a problem)
end up (doing something)
find out (something)
get back (home)
get rid of (rubbish)
give up (a hobby)
hand in (your homework)
hand out (a worksheet)
run out (battery)

Unit 4
sport
athlete (*n*)
badminton (*n*)
canoeing (*n*)
captain (*n*)
champion (*n*)
contest (*n*)
cup (*n*)
cycling (*n*)
fan (*n*)
fencing (*n*)
final (*n*)
golf (*n*)
ice hockey (*n*)
jogging (*n*)
judo (*n*)
medal (*n*)
skiing (*n*)
squash (*n*)
stadium (*n*)
water polo (*n*)

Unit 5
entertainment
animation (*n*)
author (*n*)
ballet (*n*)
DJ (disc jockey) (*n*)
exhibition (*n*)
fiction (*n*)
film-maker (*n*)
folk art/dance (*n*)
gallery (*n*)
journalist (*n*)
musician (*n*)
performer (*n*)
poem (*n*)
poet (*n*)
recording (*n*)
reporter (*n*)
studio (*n*)
video clip (*n*)

Unit 6

the natural world
cave (n)
coast (n)
continent (n)
farmland (n)
flood (n)
grass (n)
hill (n)
lake (n)
rainforest (n)
space (n)
sunrise (n)
sunset (n)
valley (n)
wildlife (n)
wood (n)

adjective + noun collocations
bright star
calm sea
clear sky
frozen lake
green grass
heavy snowfall
high cliff
humid weather
icy river
narrow path
rough/smooth rocks
sandy beach
strong waves
thick fog

Unit 7

travel
boarding card (n)
book (v)
border (n)
brochure (n)
camping (adj)
charter (n, adj)
cruise (n)
currency (n)
departure (n)
fare (n)
guide (n)
guidebook (n)
hitchhiking (n)
information centre (n)
luggage (n)
package (adj)
passenger (n)
reception (n)
reservation (n)
route (n)
subway (n)
suitcase (n)
touring (adj)
vacation (n)

types of accommodation
bed and breakfast (n)
campsite (n)
full board (n, adj)
guesthouse (n)
hotel (n)
self-catering (n, adj)
youth hostel (n)

Unit 8

personal qualities
calm (adj)
charming (adj)
cheerful (adj)
gentle (adj)
have a good sense of humour (phr)
honest (adj)
professional (adj)
romantic (adj)
sweet (adj)
talented (adj)

getting better
achieve (v)
attempt (v)
check (v)
deal with (phr v)
defeat (v)
get on (phr v)
lead (v)
succeed (v)
try (v)

Unit 9

adjectives to describe feelings
afraid
angry
anxious
ashamed
depressed
mad
miserable
negative
positive
proud
sad
strong
stupid
tired
weak

EXAM FILE: SPEAKING

SPEAKING FILE

You take the Speaking test with a partner, and there are two examiners. One examiner speaks to you and the other examiner just listens. There are two parts to the Speaking test. Each part has two phases. The whole test takes 8–10 minutes.

Part 1: Interview (2–3 minutes)

Task overview
The examiner asks you and your partner some general personal questions about where you live, your daily routines, your likes and dislikes, etc. You speak to the examiner, not to your partner.

Example task
- What's your name?
- Where do you live?
- Tell me about the people you live with.
- How do you get to school every day?
- What did you do last weekend?

Exam help
- Try not to feel nervous at the start of the test. The questions are easy to understand.
- Listen to the questions carefully. Ask the examiner to repeat if you don't understand.
- Speak clearly and try to sound natural.
- Don't give one-word answers. Include reasons and examples as often as possible.

> **useful language**
> **giving personal information**
> I'm from (a small town near) …
> I have (two brothers and a sister).
> I usually (walk to school).
> We have English lessons at my school.
> On Sunday I (saw my friends / played basketball).
> I enjoy history **because** it's interesting.
> My sister and I are twins, **so** we're very close.
> I like going out with my friends, **for example** to the cinema.
> I don't like the winter. **One reason is** (**that**) it's too cold to go outside.

Part 2: Long turn (2–3 minutes)

Task overview
You and your partner take turns to describe one photo each. You each speak for about one minute. You just listen while your partner speaks.

Example task
Here is your photo. It shows people spending time as a family. Tell us what you can see in the photo.

Exam help
- Describe the people and activities in your photo in as much detail as possible.
- Start by introducing the idea in the photo, then include information about the place, what the people look like, what they are doing, the weather and how you think the people are feeling.
- Try to use connectors (e.g. *but, so, because*) to link your ideas.
- If you aren't sure what something is or can't remember the word, describe it or say what you think it might be.

---

useful language

describing what you see
It's a photo of / The photo shows a family.

I guess that this photo was taken in a park because there are a lot of trees.

There are six people in this photo.

The boy is wearing …

The man is cooking.

saying where things are
On the left / On the right …

At the front / At the back …

It's/They're in / on / under / next to / near / in front of / behind / between …

making guesses
He/She/It/They look(s) (happy/bored / about fourteen).

He/She/It/They might (be/have) …

Maybe he/she/it/they …

He/She/It/They is/are probably …

I'm pretty sure (that they are a family).

explaining words you don't know
It looks like a / a kind of…

It's a type of …

It looks like a kind of …

It could/might be …

Perhaps/Maybe it's …

I can't remember what this is.

It's something you use to/for …

SPEAKING FILE

Part 3: Collaborative task (2–3 minutes)

Task overview
The examiner gives you and your partner a situation. You talk together about a picture showing different objects or activities and try to agree which one to choose. You speak together for 2–3 minutes.

Example task

A friend wants to get fit quickly so she can go on a mountain-climbing trip with her friends. Here are some things she could do. Talk together about the activities and say which would be the best one.

Activities the girl could do

Exam help

- Have a conversation with your partner and take turns to speak. If your partner is quiet, ask questions to encourage him/her to say more.
- Discuss most or all of the different options. Compare the options and explain why you think each one is good or bad.
- Give your own opinion and ask for your partner's opinion. Agree or disagree politely.
- Make suggestions and respond to suggestions that your partner makes.
- When you have talked about most or all of the options, try to agree which one is best. It doesn't matter if you can't agree, but you must try.

useful language

taking turns to speak
Sorry, go ahead.
Do you agree?
What do you think?

making and responding to suggestions
What about …?
What do you think about …?
Would … be a good idea?
Why don't we recommend …?
Shall we suggest …?
Let's look at the first …
What/How about suggesting …?
That's a good / great idea!
That sounds great!
I don't think so.
I'm not sure about that.
I'd rather / I'd prefer to choose …

giving and asking for opinions
I (don't) think (that) …
In my view, / In my opinion, …
For me, …
Do you agree?
What do you think?
What's your view?

agreeing and disagreeing
Yes, I agree with you.
Yes, you're right.
That's right/true.
No, I disagree.
I can't agree.
I'm not sure about that because …
That's a good point but …

comparing options
I think … is better / more sensible because …
I think that's the best idea because …

reaching agreement
I would choose …
My choice would be …
Shall we choose …?
Let's choose that one.

Part 4: Discussion (3 minutes)

Task overview
The examiner asks you four or five questions connected to the topic that you talked about in Part 3. You and your partner answer individually.

Example task
- Do you have any hobbies?
- What else do you do in your free time?
- Which free time activity would you like to try? Why?
- What is the most exciting free time activity you have ever tried?

Exam help
- Try to give longer answers to these questions.
- Talk about your own experiences.
- Give your own opinions and add examples to support them.

useful language

giving your opinion
I think … For me, …

adding examples
For example, … One example of this is …

EXAM FILE: WRITING

WRITING FILE

Part 1: Email

Task overview

You **must** do the task in Part 1. You read an email with notes on it and write a reply. You have to include four main points in your email and write about 100 words.

Example question

> Read this email from your English teacher, Mrs Edwards, and the notes you have made.
>
> Write your **email** to Mrs Edwards using all the notes. Write about **100 words**.
>
> From: Mrs Edwards
> Subject: End-of-term trip
>
> Dear Class,
> I'd like our class to go on a weekend trip to celebrate the end of term. — *great!*
> We could either go to the countryside or to a town or city in our area. Which would you prefer? — *say which I prefer*
> What sort of activities should we do on the trip? — *suggest*
> What kind of accommodation do you think we should stay in on Saturday evening? — *tell Mr Miller*
> Please reply soon!
> Mrs Edwards

Example answer

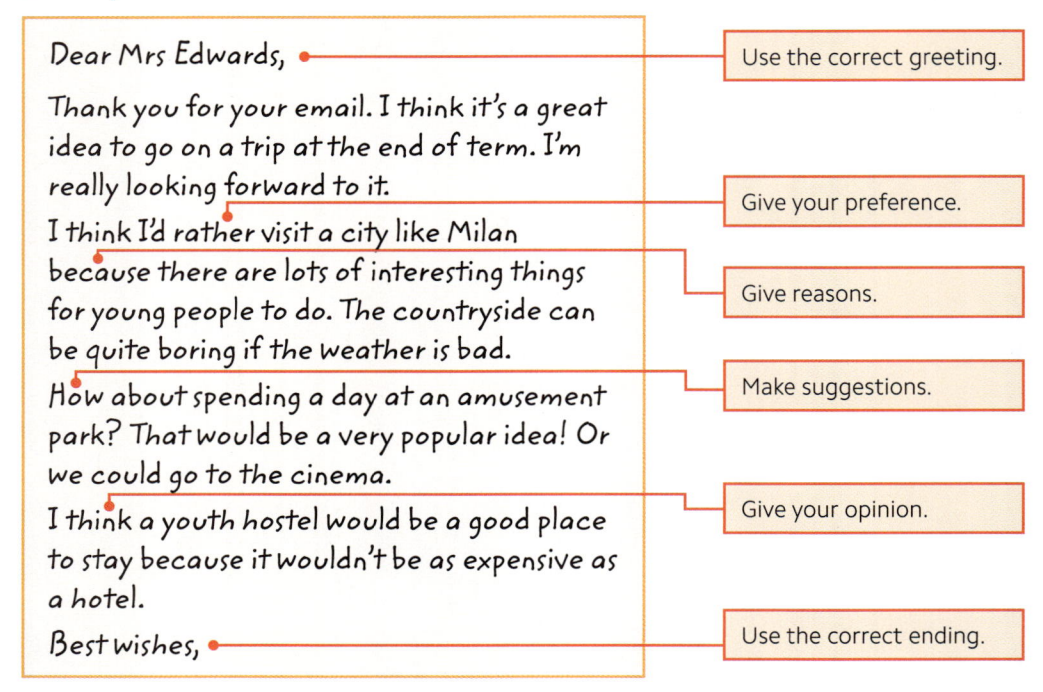

> Dear Mrs Edwards, — *Use the correct greeting.*
>
> Thank you for your email. I think it's a great idea to go on a trip at the end of term. I'm really looking forward to it. — *Give your preference.*
>
> I think I'd rather visit a city like Milan because there are lots of interesting things for young people to do. The countryside can be quite boring if the weather is bad. — *Give reasons.*
>
> How about spending a day at an amusement park? That would be a very popular idea! Or we could go to the cinema. — *Make suggestions.*
>
> I think a youth hostel would be a good place to stay because it wouldn't be as expensive as a hotel. — *Give your opinion.*
>
> Best wishes, — *Use the correct ending.*

Over to you

Read this email from your English-speaking friend Jo and the notes you have made.

Write your **email** to Jo using all the notes. Write about **100 words**.

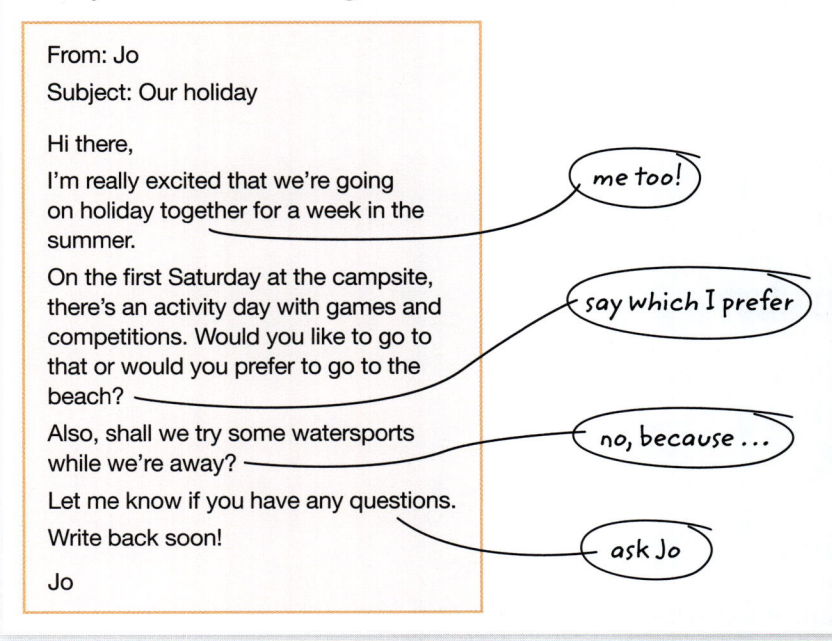

> From: Jo
> Subject: Our holiday
>
> Hi there,
> I'm really excited that we're going on holiday together for a week in the summer. — *me too!*
>
> On the first Saturday at the campsite, there's an activity day with games and competitions. Would you like to go to that or would you prefer to go to the beach? — *say which I prefer*
>
> Also, shall we try some watersports while we're away? — *no, because …*
>
> Let me know if you have any questions. Write back soon! — *ask Jo*
>
> Jo

Exam help
- Read the task, including the notes, carefully so that you understand what you need to write. Think about who is going to read your email.
- Begin and end the email with a suitable phrase.
- Make sure that you include all four points from the notes. Give some extra information about each point.
- Think about the language you need for each idea in the notes. Use a variety of phrases for accepting an invitation, giving advice, making suggestions, etc.
- Write about 100 words. Check your work for grammar or spelling mistakes.

useful language

greetings and endings
Dear (Mrs Edwards), / Hi (Jo), / Hi there,
Best wishes, / Write back soon. / Please reply soon. / Bye for now. / See you (soon / next week).

accepting an invitation
Thank you for / Thanks so much for …
I'd love to (come with you).
(An activity day) sounds good.

making suggestions
Why don't we (try sailing)?
How about (going to the beach)?
Shall we (make some food)?
We could (go swimming).

giving a preference
I'd rather (watch a film).
I'd prefer to (play basketball).

giving an opinion
I think it would be good to (invite the class).
I don't think we should (stay in a hotel).
It would be fun to (go to a concert).

inviting someone
Would you like to (come to the cinema with me?)

giving advice
I think you ought to (invite Sam).
You could (ask your parents for help).

WRITING FILE

Part 2: Article

Task overview
You choose **one** of the tasks in Part 2. You can choose **either** an article **or** a story. For an article, you read a notice from a magazine or website asking for articles. The notice gives the topic of the article and includes some questions. You write your article on that topic. You have to answer the questions and write about 100 words.

Example question

> You see this notice on an English-language student website.
>
> **Articles wanted!**
>
> **A restaurant in my town**
>
> Tell us about a restaurant you have been to in your town or city.
>
> What was good about it?
>
> Was there anything that wasn't so good?
>
> Would you recommend it to other people?
>
> Write an article answering these questions and we will publish the most interesting articles on our website.
>
> Write your **article** in about **100 words**.

Example answer

Do you like Italian food? I love it, so I was delighted when my parents took me to Fratelli's restaurant last weekend.

The good thing about Fratelli's is that there's plenty of choice. You can either have pizza or pasta, or a meat or fish dish. Everything is delicious, except the salads, which aren't very exciting.

The only bad thing about the restaurant is that there's no music, so it's very quiet! But on the whole, I would recommend it, and I'm sure you'd love the food. Do you think I should ask them to put some music on next time I go?

- Ask an opening question to make your reader feel involved.
- Answer all the questions in the task. You can choose the order in which you include the information.
- Use connectors to link ideas.
- Use adjectives to make your writing more interesting.
- This answers the second question.
- This answers the third question.
- Invite other people to give their opinions.

Over to you

You see this notice in an English-language magazine.

Articles wanted!
A good day out

What makes a good day out?

Is it the people you go with, the activities, the weather – or all of these things?

Tell us about a good day out that you have had and what made it so special.

Write an article answering these questions and we will publish the most interesting articles in our magazine.

Write your **article** in about **100 words**.

Exam help
- Read the task carefully so that you understand what you need to write. Think about who is going to read your article.
- Answer all the questions in the task.
- Use connectors (e.g. *but*, *so*, *because*, *either*, *or*) to link your ideas.
- Use adjectives to make your writing more interesting.
- When you are describing something, give positive and negative points about it.
- You can start with an opening question, to interest your readers.
- Invite other people to give their opinions.
- Write about 100 words. Check your work for grammar or spelling mistakes.

useful language

linking ideas
and / but / so / because
either … or …
as soon as
except
so that
although

giving your opinion
I think …
For me, …
In my opinion, …

opening questions
Have you ever …?
Do you like …?
How important is it for you to …?

inviting other people to give their opinions
Do you think (that) …?
What do you think of this idea/plan?
Have you got any suggestions / good ideas?

making positive comments
The good thing about …
The best thing is …

describing problems
The … can sometimes be poor.
The only bad thing is …

making a recommendation
If you watched/saw/tried this, you'd love it.
On the whole, I would/can recommend this (concert/TV show/restaurant/film).

WRITING FILE

Part 2: Story

Task overview
You choose **one** of the tasks in Part 2. You can choose **either** an article **or** a story. For a story, the writing task gives you the first line of the story and you have to write about 100 words.

Example question

> Your English teacher has asked you to write a story. Your story must begin with this sentence:
>
> 'I woke up and got my things ready for the big day.'
>
> Write your **story** in about **100 words**.

Example answer

I woke up and got my things ready for the big day. I had booked my first surfing lesson, and I was really excited.
Soon, I was standing on the beach with my surfing instructor. First, he showed us how to lie on our boards. Next, we practised standing up, but on the beach, so it was quite easy. Eventually, we went into the sea, to try surfing in real waves. I was really terrible at first!
I kept on falling over while I was trying to stand up! But finally, I did it! It was absolutely brilliant!
After a long and tiring day, I could surf!

- Give a clear beginning and explain the situation.
- Use the past simple, past continuous and past perfect to show the order of events.
- Use time expressions to order the actions in the story.
- Use strong adjectives and adverbs to make your writing more interesting.
- Give a clear ending.

Over to you

Your English teacher has asked you to write a story. Your story must begin with this sentence:

'I got on the train and sat down.'

Write your **story** in about **100 words**.

Exam help
- Use the opening sentence and don't change it.
- Plan your story to include a clear beginning, middle and end.
- Use the past simple, past continuous and past perfect and a variety of time expressions to tell your story and show the order of events.
- Use interesting language (e.g. strong adjectives and adverbs).
- Write about 100 words. Check your work for grammar or spelling mistakes.

useful language

time expressions to order the actions in a story
First, I …
After that / Then / Next, …
When (we) had finished, …
While I was (waiting), …
Before …
Half an hour later, …
After a (long/tiring/brilliant) day, …

strong adjectives to create interest

awful	furious
brilliant	hilarious
delicious	huge
disgusting	terrible
fantastic	wonderful

creating interest with adverbs

how
walk slowly/quickly/carefully
speak loudly/quietly/slowly
look at someone angrily
laugh happily
explain something carefully/clearly

when

suddenly	immediately
eventually	finally

adverbs to use with adjectives
really kind
very big
extremely dangerous
absolutely brilliant/fantastic/hilarious

giving a clear ending
In the end, …
I realised that …
After a great day / scary experience, …
I'll never forget my … / what happened.

ACTIVITY FILE

Unit 1 Speaking, page 15, Ex 8
Student A

You and Student B are going to ask and answer questions about your life. Follow these steps.

1. Ask Student B for the information to complete your fact file.
2. Imagine you are a famous star or sportsperson. Answer Student B's questions.

Fact file

Name:	....
Town/City:	....
Free time:	....
	....
	....

Unit 2 Speaking, page 27, Ex 5
Student A

Unit 4, Speaking, page 51, Ex 6
Student A

1 You and Student B will take turns to talk about a photo. You begin. Look at your photo and use these questions to help you prepare your answer. Talk about your photo.

1. Who is in the photo?
2. Where are they?
3. What are they doing?
4. What are they wearing?
5. How are they feeling?
6. What do you think about this activity?

2 Now listen to Student B describing his/her photo. Does he/she talk about these things? Take notes while you are listening.

- activity
- feelings
- place
- clothes
- person/people

ACTIVITY FILE

Unit 3, Speaking, page 39, Ex 6

A company is thinking of creating a new kind of robot. Here are some ideas for things a robot might do. Talk together about the different kinds of robot they could make and which would be the most useful.

Things a robot might do

Unit 4, Speaking, page 51, Ex 6
Student B

1 You and Student A will take turns to talk about a photo. Student A begins. Listen to him/her describing his/her photo. Does he/she talk about these things? Take notes while you are listening.
- activity
- feelings
- place
- clothes
- person/people

2 Now look at your photo and use these questions to help you prepare your answer. Talk about your photo.
1. Who is in the photo?
2. Where are they?
3. What are they doing?
4. What are they wearing?
5. How are they feeling?
6. What do you think about this activity?

ACTIVITY FILE

Unit 6, Grammar, page 72, Ex 6
Student A

Complete the sentences with the correct passive form of the verbs in brackets.

1 In 2016, a lake .... (discover) at the bottom of the ocean.
2 Ninety percent of the world's water is drinkable. Three percent of that .... (freeze) in the Antarctic.
3 Water .... (first/purify) for drinking by The Romans.
4 A living shark .... (recently/find) in Greenland which is between 270 and 500 years old.
5 Around 2,500 litres of water .... (use) to make the last burger you ate.
6 The Earth .... (inhabit) by around 8.7 billion different types of animals.

Unit 6, Grammar, page 72, Ex 7
Student B

Answers
1 True 2 False (It's a half.) 3 True
4 False (It's under the ocean.) 5 True 6 True

Unit 8, Reading, page 94, Ex 4
Student A

Read your notes and close your book. Ask Student B questions to find the missing information from your notes. Then turn to to page 94 and complete the task.

The marshmallow test

Purpose: to test patience
Age: 4 years old
Materials: a .... with one marshmallow and ....
Method: Offer the child one marshmallow. Explain that they can eat it, but if they can wait a few minutes, they can have two marshmallows to eat.
Conclusion: Children who can .... have shown two important qualities.

Unit 5, Speaking, page 63, Ex 4
Student A

Student B

ACTIVITY FILE

Unit 1 Speaking, page 15, Ex 8
Student B

You and Student A are going to ask and answer questions about your life. Follow these steps.

1. Imagine you are a famous star or sportsperson. Answer Student A's questions.
2. Ask Student A for the information to complete your fact file.

Fact file

Name: ....
Town/City: ....
Free time: ....
....
....

Unit 6, Grammar, page 72, Ex 7
Student A

Answers

1 True 2 False.(Three percent is drinkable. Ninety percent of that is frozen in the Antarctic.) 3 False (It was the Egyptians.) 4 True 5 True 6 True

Unit 8, Reading, page 94, Ex 4
Student B

Read your notes and close your book. Ask Student A questions to find the missing information from your notes. Then turn to to page 94 and complete the task.

The marshmallow test

Purpose: to test patience
Age: .... years old
Materials: a plate with one marshmallow and some extra ones
Method: Offer the child one marshmallow. Explain that they ...., but if they can wait a few minutes, they .... to eat.
Conclusion: Children who wait for the second marshmallow have shown two important qualities.

Unit 6, Speaking, page 75, Ex 6

Your school wants to become more eco-friendly. The school headmaster is wants to encourage students to be more eco-friendly and save fuel and energy. Here are some ways he could encourage people to be more actively eco-friendly. Talk together about the different ways and say which would be best.

Think about these things:
- Will it be cheap/expensive?
- Will it be easy to understand?
- Will it be popular?
- Will people remember it?
- Will people see it?
- Will people take action?

Ways to encourage people to save electricity

ACTIVITY FILE

Unit 8, Speaking, page 99, Ex 4

Your school is going to put on a talent show. Here are some of the students' suggestions for things they could do in the talent show. Talk together about the different things they want to do and say which you think would be the most popular with the audience.

★ **Acts for the talent show** ★

Unit 9, Vocabulary, page 109, Ex 6

Are you an **optimist** or a **pessimist**?

1 You have to attend a family event that you don't usually enjoy.
   A You're **relaxed / relaxing** about it. It'll be nice to see your relatives.
   B You're angry. It'll be really **bored / boring** and you'll hate every minute.

2 The queue in the shop is really long.
   A You feel **relaxed / relaxing**. The queue will soon go down.
   B You feel really **annoyed / annoying**. Why does this always happen to you?

3 You've planned a big outdoor event with friends.
   A You're looking forward to it. It'll be really **excited / exciting**.
   B You can't look forward to it. The weather forecast makes you **worried / worrying**.

4 You have the opportunity to go on a huge water slide.
   A You're **satisfied / satisfying**. It'll all be fine and you'll enjoy it.
   B You're **frightened / frightening**. It'll all go wrong and you'll hate it.

5 You have the chance to talk to a famous person.
   A It's **amazed / amazing**! You can't wait to speak to them.
   B The whole situation is **embarrassed / embarrassing**. Why would they want to speak to you?

Results

Mostly As: You're definitely an optimist. You always look on the bright side of life.

Mostly Bs: You're a bit of a pessimist. Your glass is usually half empty and not half full.

ACTIVITY FILE

Unit 10, Speaking, page 121, Ex 5

Read the information below and talk together about the situation for two to three minutes.

Holiday activities

A group of friends are really busy over the holiday and only have one day to meet up. Here are some activities they could do. Talk together about the activities and say which would be the most fun.

AUDIOSCRIPTS

S.1
1. It was my first time in a lake. It was so cold but felt great when I got to the other side!
2. Honestly, I didn't really like it. It was much too sweet for me.
3. I spent hours just looking at all the buildings and the views over the river were wonderful! I couldn't speak the language, though.
4. All of my family were there – my aunts, my uncles and my cousins. I think we got through about a hundred burgers by the end of the evening.
5. It's fairly simple, but I was on my computer for days after I tried it. I think I'm going to look to see if they have any new updates for it.
6. Well, I know the summer probably isn't the best time for skiing lessons, but it was at an indoor centre and it was really quiet, so nobody saw me fall down.
7. Well, I have about a hundred new selfies on my phone and I already put most of them online.
8. I saw a lot of birds, and mostly farm animals, but we hiked fifteen kilometres every day.

1.1 and 1.2
S = Speaker

S1: On Tuesdays I do a commercial dance class and on any other day I come home and do my homework and then just watch TV.
S2: In the evenings I play sport, such as tennis or football, and I also play video games.
S3: I usually have my dinner and then start getting cosy and ready for bed and watch some TV.
S4: On Wednesdays, I play netball or go to the park with my friends and play basketball or tennis.
S5: In the evenings I usually watch YouTube.
S6: In the evenings I usually play on my Playstation or talk to my friends online.
S1: I'm looking after my friend's cat because her and her family are on holiday.
S7: As it's the winter season, I'm playing hockey every Friday night for my local club.
S8: In my free time I play football. And I do it on Tuesdays and Saturdays.
S9: I'm watching a film a day to learn more about acting styles.
S10: At the moment I'm studying hard for my exams that I have in, like, the next couple of months.
S2: At the moment I am playing a sport called racquets, which is similar to squash but played on a larger court and the racket head is smaller, and so is the ball.
S6: At the moment I am doing gymnastics to practise for a show.
S11: On Tuesdays I often play my guitar, but I can't if I have homework. Every Saturday I play rugby for school. I do the same on Sunday.
S3: I'm doing a lot more dancing because I've got a dance competition, a choreographics competition, coming up, so I'm learning my solo.

1.4 and 1.5
1
A: Oh it's such a horrible day today, isn't it?
B: Yes! I hate autumn – it's always so windy. And the wind goes round the tall buildings and gets even stronger.
A: Mind you, it's good it's not the same weather all the time.
B: Oh I don't know. I wouldn't mind it being sunny all year! The wind makes me so cross.
A: You need to move somewhere else! But it's true that the weather is really annoying here!
B: Too right! I'd love to live in California – sunshine every day!

2
A: Hi, Lucia. How are you getting on? Do you like the city?
B: Oh yes. I thought all cities were the same, but they're not. I was in Manila before and it was much bigger. But people usually said 'hello' and talked to you more than here.
A: Yeah, we are smaller but maybe we don't have such a mix of people. Still, there's loads to see and do here. I hope you're finding that?
B: Yeah, it's great there's so much choice – I never know what to pick.
A: Well, the good thing is there's always enough people interested in doing something.
B: Yeah, it's amazing.

3
A: Ali, where would you like to go for a holiday?
B: Not sure. My parents are deciding now. I'd like to go to Istanbul. It's got an amazing history.
A: Yeah, I read about it – it sounds wonderful. But I'd like to go to Paris. It's so romantic; and I love museums.
B: Really? I'd rather walk round and get the feel of a city.
A: You know where else sounds good? Singapore. It's so busy and exciting.
B: Oh my aunt went there. She said it was quite noisy.
A: Well, I hope you get your wish!
B: Me too!

4
A: Grandad, what was this place like when you were young?
B: Oooh very different from now! It was all old buildings when I was young. Now there are so many new ones – they're not all lovely, though!
A: I love the modern architecture. It makes the city feel really exciting.
B: They've improved the transport because the city has grown, but it's too busy for me. But when I was young everything was more the same. Now we've got people from all over you can get all kinds of things and food, which is more interesting.
A: Yes, you don't have to leave to travel the world!

5
A: Hey, what did you get up to at the weekend?
B: We went to my grandparents in the country. I enjoyed myself – nice change from the city.
A: Not sure I could live there. I can't relax when it's so quiet!
B: No, I don't think I could live there – I like having all my friends close by me. But it was a nice change.
A: Yes, it's easier to see them.
B: But I think I'm not as serious in the country. The life is easier.
A: Yeah. I don't think I laugh as much here. Maybe it's because we're not on holiday! But I still prefer it.

6
A: Hey, Rocco. How's it going?
B: Fine. I'm enjoying living here now I know where everything is.
A: How do you get to school? On the bus? I haven't seen you.
B: No, I come on the train – it's faster.
A: Yeah, but you have to change trains, so I'm not sure it is. Why don't you come on the bus? Then you can read or sit and chat to friends.
B: Oh yeah, I didn't think of that. Hmm … I might do that. I was going to walk because I like looking at things as I walk round. It's a good way to get to know the city.
A: Not in the winter!

1.6
1
A: Elsa, where do you live?
B: I live in the town centre.
A: And where do you come from?
B: I come from England.

2
A: Where do you come from, Chen?
B: I'm from Guanzhou. It's a very big city in China, but it's not the capital. I live near the main square.
A: Where do you live?
B: I don't live in China. I live in the United States. But I like to visit China.

1.7
1
A: What do you enjoy doing in your free time, Chen?
B: Er, I like swimming. I go swimming once a week. I also enjoy basketball. It's fun and I'm in the school team.

2
A: Elsa, what do you enjoy doing in your free time?
B: Well, I enjoy lots of different things. For example, I'm keen on music, so I have singing lessons twice a week. I love listening to music on my music player. At the moment I'm learning to play the piano, too. And I do karate because I think it's important to keep fit.

1.9
1 A: What? Why are you laughing? What's so funny?
B: You are! You look really funny in those shoes!
2 A: Do you always visit your grandparents at the weekend?
B: Yes. Every Sunday.
3 A: Jason doesn't want to come with us today.
B: Really? Why not?

4 A: Can you stop that noise? I'm trying to revise for my test.
B: Sorry!
5 A: I don't think that's a very good idea.
B: Hmm … maybe you're right.
6 A: What happened? Why is Ella crying?
B: No idea. Come on, let's ask her.

2.1 and 2.2
S = Speaker
S1: At six o'clock last night I was watching television and I was about to go for dinner.
S2: Last night at six o'clock I was walking to my nan's house, which took me two hours.
S3: I was cleaning my room about a week ago and I got a phone call from my nan saying that my dog broke his leg.
S4: Last night I was out with my friends at the park taking photographs for my school project.
S5: Last weekend I was eating breakfast and I got a text from my friend that I haven't seen in a year to meet up, so we made plans to meet up.
S6: I was playing hockey and, afterwards, I came home and had some food.
S3: At six o'clock last night I was getting a Chinese takeaway with my family.
S7: I was watching a film with my family and it was very funny.
S5: Around six o'clock I was watching the West Side Story with my friends.
S8: At six o'clock last night I was having dinner with my mum.
S6: I was running and I overheard that my favourite football team had scored a goal.
S9: At six o'clock last night I was coming home from my friend's house.
S10: I was practising my drama lines for my drama exam and my mum called me saying my cousins were coming round this weekend.
S1: I was watching TV, and then my sister came in my room and she told me that we might be getting another dog.
S11: I was out shopping with my friend when I heard there was a sale in my favourite shop.
S9: The best thing that happened to me this week was that I was doing my homework and my auntie rang to tell us that she had her baby.
S2: I was loading the dishwasher when my mum came in and said my dog just jumped out of the window.

2.4–2.6
Last summer I went to summer camp, but it was a bit different to other camps. It was an app camp. We did all the usual sports but we were also learning how to develop apps for smartphones. Applying takes time – it's a popular camp. So, although camp didn't start until 1 August, I had to do my application by 5 May at the latest and then I was waiting for a whole month! I finally knew I had a place on 8 June.

They were running three app courses: one for beginners, an intermediate and an upper intermediate – but no advanced. Because I'd never written an app before, I joined the lowest level course. But that was OK. We did some really cool stuff and there were only twelve of us. I made some good friends. The app I created is called RoundEmUp – that's all one word. You spell it R–O–U–N–D–E–M–U–P. It's an app that makes it easier to communicate with your friends because it puts people in different groups on your phone and means you don't end up forgetting to text someone. I first had the idea when I was organising a basketball match. But I use it to now for study groups and for organising my social life.

Anyway, at the end of the week the camp leader, Mr Saunders, looked at all the apps and decided which were the top three in each group. The prize for first place was fifty dollars! Mr Saunders loved my idea and I was second. My prize was a T-shirt – it's really cool.

On the last day of camp we did a trip to a museum, but not to see natural history or art; this was all about computing – right from the earliest machines to the latest tablets. It was awesome!

2.7
Well, this photo shows a typical shop scene. Erm, there's a woman who is buying something. She's with her daughter. I, er … I think they are both happy.

2.8 and 2.9
1 Something that is very popular is **fashionable**.
2 I've got this great **app** on my phone that translates words from Spanish to English.
3 News from the area where you live is **local** news.
4 The stars come out at night and when day comes, they **disappear**.
5 English is an **international** language. People in all countries speak it.
6 If you don't have enough information for your project, you can look **online**.

3.1 and 3.2

S = Speaker

S1: In the future I think people will listen to music the same way as they do now.

S2: At the moment I listen to pop music but in the future I think it will change to opera because you … because when you're older, you develop – like, your ears develop to like different sounds.

S3: I'm not sure, so I'll probably watch TV with my family.

S4: I listen to musical theatre and I don't think my music taste will change.

S5: I really like listening to hip-hop, but I think I will change my style of music in the future.

S6: I'm meeting my uncle for lunch and we're going to a Turkish restaurant.

S7: I think people will start listening to vinyls again as I've heard they're going back into fashion.

S8: Tonight I am going to go out with my friends to the cinema.

S9: I'm meeting a friend for lunch in town and then we're going to watch a film at the cinema.

S1: Tonight I am going to iron my clothes and get ready for playing sport tomorrow.

3.4 and 3.5

N = Narrator

1

N: What does the girl decide to buy?

A: My mum's given me some money to buy a mobile but now I'm not sure if that's the best thing. What should I buy?

B: You ought to get a tablet. It's got a bigger screen than a mobile.

A: Yeah, but I won't be able to carry it around with me very easily. I could get a smart watch.

B: My sister's got one. She'll know if it's a good idea. Shall I ask her?

A: Maybe. I don't think it'll work without a mobile phone, though, which I don't have.

B: Oh yeah.

A: To be honest, I think I'll just stay with my first idea. It's the best thing to do.

2

N: What has a music player in it?

A: Hey, Emilio! I see you've got a new sweatshirt! Was it a birthday present?

B: No, my dad bought it for me a few weeks ago. My cap was a present, though. Do you like it?

A: Yes, it's cool, but what are those black things in your ear? Are they earphones?

B: Yes, but they're part of my sunglasses, not my cap. I can listen to songs when I wear them! Listen … it's great! You should get some.

3

N: Which book would the girl like?

A: Mr Jones, I'd like to read a story in English. Have you got 'Marley and Me'?

B: Yes, we've got it in the library, but someone borrowed it yesterday. There are some great stories here, though. Do you want a book or do you want to download a digital version?

A: I'd like a book, please. Oh, this one looks good. Has anyone read it yet?

B: No, it's new – you're the first. Do you need to borrow a dictionary, too?

A: Er, no, thanks. I use one online.

4

N: What app does the boy decide to download?

A: Hey, Bruno. I'd like to download a funny app. Got any ideas?

B: Yes, listen to this!

A: It sounds like a cat.

B: It is. You can make a song with cat sounds.

A: Sounds annoying!

B: Why don't you get this photo app? You could upload a photo of us and it puts your face on my body and my face on your body.

A: That might be fun.

B: Or how about this one, where you make your voice sound really, really high?

A: Hmm … the voice one sounds funny but I think I'll get the photo app.

5

N: What does the boy want?

A: Mum, are you going to go into town today?

B: Yes, we need something for dinner. There's nothing in the fridge! Why? Do you want anything?

A: Yeah, can you get me a games magazine, please? I want to read about a new game.

B: Can't you find out about it online?

A: Yeah, but Liam uses the laptop most evenings and my phone's not working.

B: OK, fine – I'll get it later.

6

N: Which of the boy's things has stopped working?

A: Why does something stop working just when you really need it?

B: What happened? Has your guitar stopped working again?

A: Not this time. That was my fault, though. I forgot to plug it in.

B: So, what is it then?

A: I have to hand in my photography homework to the art teacher tomorrow. I borrowed my dad's camera last week and took some great photos. I'm really proud of them. But when I was printing them out, the printer just went off for no reason. Now it won't switch on.

B: You could present them on the camera. I'm sure that'll be OK.

7

What does the girl collect these days?

A: Do you collect anything, Maddy?

B: I used to collect DVDs. You know, when I was younger. I think I only had about twenty but that's quite a lot when you're eight!

A: I guess it is.

B: My parents have a big CD collection. Over 200, but they seem so old-fashioned these days.

B: True.

A: I've started buying records. I saved up my pocket money and bought myself a record player. I've got some really cool second-hand music as well as more up-to-date stuff. The sound quality is much better than CDs and MP3s in my view.

3.6 and 3.7

A: In my opinion, the robot pet would be useful. People could play with it without having to clean it or feed it, or take it for walks.

B: That's true, but it's not the same as a real pet, is it? You can love a real pet but in my view, you couldn't really love a robot pet.

A: I disagree. I think that a lot of robots are very cute, so it's easy to think they're real.

B: Really?

A: Yeah. I think a robot pet would be great for some people. People who can't have a real pet because it's too expensive or because they're too busy to look after it.

B: That's a good point. Also, people who can't look after one. Older people, for example.

A: Yes, that's right.

B: OK, so maybe they would be useful for some people. What's your view on the robot doctor?

A: Hmm. I don't think this would be a good idea. You couldn't trust it. It's better to speak to a human.

B: I'm not sure. Maybe the robot could find out what's wrong with us faster and better?

A: Really? But it could only check our bodies. I'd say that's a problem.

B: That's a good point. Maybe robot doctors and humans could work together. Shall we talk about the robot cleaner?

A: OK. For me, a robot that cleans my room would be really useful.

B: You're right. I hate cleaning my room. It's so boring!

A: I don't think anyone likes doing housework. My parents hate it.

B: A robot like this would be really helpful. They'd give people more time to do other things.

A: Yes, good point. People could spend more time on their hobbies.

B: And families could spend more time together, perhaps.

AUDIOSCRIPTS

A: OK, so do we think the robot that does housework would be the most useful?
B: Yes, I think so.

3.8
1. You put clothes in it so you can clean them.
2. You put water in it so you can make a cup of tea.
3. You use it to change the channel on the television.
4. You use it to make a cup of coffee.
5. It keeps your food cool or freezes it.
6. You can stream films or watch TV shows live on it.
7. It cleans your dirty plates and pans.
8. It heats up your food quickly.

4.1 and 4.2
S = Speaker
S1: I've danced since I was three and I've played netball for the last two years.
S2: In hockey I've already played for my region but in the future I would like to play for my nation.
S3: I have swum with dolphins but I still haven't had a chance to surf yet.
S4: I've played for the school football team for a year and we have won some tournaments.
S5: I've played basketball since I was ten years old.
S6: I've played netball for five years – I really like it because it's fun and I play wing-attack.
S2: I've played racquets for five years but I've never played snooker.
S4: I've never played tennis but I would like to try it because it seems fun.
S7: I have swum in the ocean with sharks, I have been to the largest rainforest in Australia, I have visited different continents such as Australia, North America, Europe, Asia; I haven't been to Antarctica yet but I hope to go some day.
S1: I've never played any individual sports but I'd like to try skiing.
S8: I've been skiing since I was three and then last year I decided I wanted to start snowboarding.
S9: I've swum in the sea but I haven't swum in a river or lake.

4.4–4.5
I = Interviewer   E = Elena
I: Hi, Elena. Thanks for doing this interview for the school radio. We want to talk to you because a few years ago you didn't enjoy sports. But now you do?
E: Hi. Yes, and I think it's because I stopped trying to be good at it. You think you have to be good at a something to enjoy it, but you don't!
I: Oh. I know you do a lot of running. Do you do competitions?
E: I've been a runner for years but I don't enter competitions. They're hard work. It can take lots of preparation. Before the race, you have to run the same distances but you also need rest days. Sometimes, for myself, I run the same distance as in a competition, but I don't compete and I don't try to run it in a short time.
I: So why do you enjoy running then?
E: I know it's unusual that I don't like competing. People think if you do something a lot, you should compete. I started running because my friends recommended it. I like to be in the open air most days. It helps me think and I enjoy the time on my own. Competitions make me depressed, not happier!
I: And have you done any other sports?
E: When I was younger, I wanted to play rugby. But at school we played netball and I hated it. I've always liked rugby – not for the competition but because I actually enjoy all the pushing and pulling! I'm too slow to be good at it, though.
I: So what would you say to students who are not good at sports then?
E: Don't worry. You don't need to get better – just enjoy it for what it is at the time that you are doing it. And it may even help you become fitter, and that can make you feel happier.
I: And do you prefer individual or team sports?
E: I think it's better to play in a team. And not because I can have rest moments during a match! I enjoy being with lots of others – we have more fun.
I: Do you believe that competition stops a lot of people doing sport then?
E: Well, in a sport that's very competitive, like football, for example, maybe people don't want you to play when you're not very good. Then choose something different that's less popular! Go off on your own and find something that not many people do. You can always take a friend along.
I: Great! I'm sure that's helped other students!

4.6
Well, the photo shows some friends. Six are sitting on a sofa and one is standing. There's a white wall behind them. Most of them are wearing jeans and a shirt or T-shirt. I think they're watching a match on TV. They are all happy and excited. They're celebrating because their hands are in the air.

4.7
1. They've started a new gym class.
2. Have you bought some new trainers?
3. Jack hasn't seen the match yet.
4. We've played tennis a lot this summer.
5. The team hasn't had a good practice.
6. Well done! You've won the competition.
7. She's taken part in three races this year.
8. Emily has been in our team for three years.

5.1 and 5.2
S1: If I meet my friends after school, we go to the shop and buy loads of sweets.
S2: If I meet my friends after class, we usually go on social media or listen to music.
S3: If my social media became really popular, I would be happy but I would also not be happy because you would have no privacy.
S4: If I meet my friends after class, we usually walk to the bus stop and on the way there we go get some food.
S5: I'd be really happy if my social media account became popular.
S4: If I met my favourite actor, Emma Watson, I would ask her what age she started acting.
S6: If I meet my friends after school, we usually go into town and we look at the shops and usually go to a restaurant to eat food.
S7: If I met my favourite actor, I would ask him how he got to where he is now.
S1: If my social media account became really popular, I'd be happy because I would get loads of money.

5.3
1
A: You had a happy time at school. When did you start writing songs?
B: Well, I was ten when I wrote my first song. It wasn't very good.
2
A: Laura, can you do that again, please? We want to add some more guitar to it.
B: OK, OK. La, la, la …
3
A: Hi, I'm phoning about the play that's on …er, on Saturday? It's for me and two friends.
B: Yes, of course. We've only got seats in row B and C left.
A: That's fine. How can I pay?
4
A: Why didn't you tell me?
B: I tried but you weren't listening. I'm so sorry.

5

Behind me is the house where the famous musician, Mozart, was born. He lived here for twenty-six years until 1773. Mozart often performed for his friends. The house became a museum in 1880 and many of his instruments …

5.4

1 It's a group of people and they sing together. What are they?
2 Go to the back and there's a big red door with a sign on it. What is it?
3 There aren't any seats in that one. Go to the one behind. What is it?
4 More than two hundred people came to see the show. Who were they?
5 Her dress and shoes were amazing. She looked like a real queen. What type of clothes were they?
6 It was high, so we could see everything very well. What was high?
7 It's a big group of people and they play different musical instruments. Who are they?

5.5

A: So, how do you find out about new music?
B: I usually listen to a lot of music on the bus in the mornings. Everyone does. The other kids on the bus share their favourite songs, and I often hear really good ones that I don't know. I also hear some new songs on the local radio station, but they're usually only by well-known artists, so that's not as good. How about you?
A: I have a music site that I'm registered with and they keep a record of all the music I listen to and make suggestions for songs. Some of my mates send me links to new songs, and they're usually the ones I end up playing all the time, so I also think that's the most useful way, really.

5.6 and 5.7

N = Narrator

1
N: You will hear a girl talking about her new music lessons.
A: How was your new guitar lesson?
B: I was so lucky to get that particular teacher. There's a waiting list of people who want to take lessons with her.
A: Did it take long to get to the top of the list?
B: Well, actually, I was able to take the four o'clock lesson because I have maths in the same building and I can get there straight after the bell. Only a couple of us could make it at that time.
A: Who's paying for the lessons?
B: Luckily, my uncle offered to pay, otherwise I wouldn't be able to afford it.

2
N: You will hear two friends talking about a band.
A: Who's your favourite band?
B: I really love AeroDome.
A: Didn't they do that song for an advert?
B: Yeah, the song on the advert was really calm, and the voices were quiet. It was really different from the rest of their work.
A: I wasn't a fan, to be honest.
B: You should listen to their album. They always manage to write such amusing lines and nice tunes to go with them. Of course, that I means that listening to them while I try to do my homework isn't the best option. I can't concentrate on what I'm doing.
A: Maybe I should try.

3
N: You will hear a boy telling his friend about a rock concert he went to.
A: How was the concert?
B: It was brilliant. Well, to be honest, we paid so much for the tickets I expected us to be right at the front. I could hardly see the stage unless I stood up.
A: That's normal, though.
B: I guess you're right. I can't wait to see how my friends react when I post the pictures I took.
A: I wonder if it's worth trying to get tickets for their concert next year. I'd like to see them, too.
B: I think they've already sold out. I'd go with you if I could.

4
N: You will hear two friends talking about singing on stage.
A: I agreed to sing at the school concert.
B: You'll be fine.
A: No, *you* would be fine. I'm just totally nervous.
B: Well, I know you've done enough practice.
A: I doubt any more would help now.
B: I guess not. I imagine your mum and sister have had enough already.
A: That's true.
B: If I were you, I'd work on your body language, and where you put your arms. Pick a singer you like and try and copy how they move on stage.
A: I hadn't thought of that.
B: Your voice is great. That's the only thing you need to work on.

5
N: You will hear two friends talking about playing the guitar.
A: I'm so glad my mum made me take guitar lessons when I was kid.
B: Me too. I mean, when it was all those soft, slow romantic songs at the beginning. It's better now we do rock.
A: I like that style. I find playing a beautiful piece of music helps me to deal with the stress of studying and passing exams.
B: I always go and play my guitar with the headphones on whenever I have an argument. It helps me relax.
A: Don't the neighbours complain about the noise?
B: No, but I think they're looking forward to me moving out.

6
N: You will hear two friends talking about a competition they entered.
A: That's the competition over for another year.
B: Time to start practising for next year. I think they picked the best choir in the end, though. Some of the entries were quite weak.
A: Well, I thought it was tough to choose a winner among them. They were all excellent. But I think they got it right.
B: I really liked being in that concert hall, too. The sound travelled around the space so well it made everything sound so much better.
A: I was disappointed. It wasn't as large as the place last year and they only let us have two tickets each.

5.10 and 5.11

1 Susan has a lovely voice. She is in the choir and they are going to sing in a concert.
2 He is a very successful singer. He is going to record a new album this summer.
3 If you could interview your favourite singer, what would you ask him or her?
4 I didn't enjoy the film. The people in the row behind us were talking all the way through.
5 We are here to entertain you. So relax and enjoy the show.
6 The performance hasn't finished. Don't clap yet!
7 There was a wonderful orchestra with violins, drums and wind instruments.
8 I really want to see that play. I'm going to book tickets for it now.

5.12 and 5.13

1 What would happen if video games were real? Well, in the ones I play, if you fell off a building, you'd be able to stand up again. That really doesn't happen in real life. You can even run off afterwards.
2 I love playing that game where you try and cut up the fruit. If you had a sharp knife, you'd be able to cut fruit in mid-air, but I'm pretty sure nobody can do that in real life.

AUDIOSCRIPTS

3 I love games where you discover things. I wish it was as easy in real life! You'd find diamonds if you made a deep hole. Wouldn't that be great? Easier than studying for exams and trying to get a good job!

4 I love those games where you race around objects. Wouldn't it be cool if those games were real? I mean, imagine that: if you hit a mushroom, it would give you coins. Cool, huh?

5 I think I'd be pretty good at driving a car, based on my gameplay. If racing games were real, though, you'd drive at twice the speed if you went over a special part of the track. Really, you need a better engine for that in real life.

6.1

I = Interviewer   M = Man   W = Woman

1

I: I'm trying to find out how well we know our own planet. Can I ask you some questions?
M1: Sure.
I: Earth was formed how many billions of years ago?
M1: Oh, er … I've got no idea. Two?
W1: No idea. Five?
M2: I could guess. Maybe thirty?
M3: I don't know. Ten?
W2: Ah, I've studied this, so I know. It was formed about four and a half billion years ago.
I: You're right.
W2: The oldest rocks were found in Canada, apparently.
I: You know more than me!

2

I: The world's water is divided into how many major oceans?
W3: It's seven, isn't it?
M1: Seven, I think. Oh no, is that seas? Seven seas. Hmm … I'm not sure now.
M3: Er … six?
W4: I think it's four. Let's see: the Pacific and the Atlantic; the … er … Indian Ocean and the … um … Arctic Ocean. Yeah, four.
M4: What about the ocean around the Antarctic?
W4: Oh yeah. What's that called? The Antarctic Ocean?
I: Actually, yes. Or the Southern Ocean.
W4: Five then. So, I was almost right!

3

I: How many people inhabit the Earth?
M2: It's billions, isn't it? Five billion?
W3: Ten billion?
M5: It's around seven billion, I think.

W4: No idea. Three billion? Or is that how many people live in China? I can't remember!
M6: I think it's about seven billion people now but it's going up all the time.
I: It's almost seven and a half billion.
M6: So, I wasn't too far away then.
W3: I was nowhere near then.
W4: Really? Wow, that's a lot of people!

4

I: What percentage of the earth is covered in water?
M1: Um … I don't know. Fifty percent?
W1: Er … I know it's a lot … Sixty?
M2: I don't know. Forty?
M3: I know this one. Seventy percent!
I: You're right!
W2: Yeah, it's seventy percent. And that's how it got the name 'the blue planet'. Yeah, when astronauts first saw the Earth from space, it looked … well … it looked blue!

5

I: The highest temperature on Earth was recorded in what country?
W3: Um … Ethiopia? I know it's one of the hottest places on Earth.
M1: Er … uh … I've got no idea.
M3: I think it was Libya in North Africa?
I: Well, that was the second highest temperature ever recorded.
M3: Oh. Uh … I don't know.
W4: Ah, I recently saw a documentary about this, so I know: it was in Death Valley, California, USA. In 1913, I think.
I: Correct! It was recorded on 10 July 1913 and it was fifty-eight degrees!
M1: Fifty-eight degrees?! Wow! That's hot!

6.2–6.5

I = Interviewer   H = Holly

I: Today I'm joined by Holly Jones, a local teenager who created a recycling app for young people in her area. Holly, when did you first become interested in recycling?
H: Well, my mum used to show me newspaper stories about problems with rubbish but I never cared much about those. Then one day I saw a documentary on TV about how much plastic is wasted. That was when I started paying attention to the issue. Later I went to a conference to hear other young people talk about the topic.
I: Your app encourages young people to recycle things. What makes it successful?
H: Well, it's a game where teenagers get points when they recycle things. They then use those points to buy things in the real world – like a coffee or cinema ticket. I thought people would like it because

it's a simple game and enjoyable to play but, actually, users tell me it's because they feel happy when they use it because they're doing something good.
I: What was the most challenging thing about creating this app?
H: Finding someone to create the app for me for free was really hard. The idea for the game came to me quickly, so that wasn't a problem, and neither was telling people about the app. I just use social media.
I: What's your goal? What do you hope to achieve with this app?
H: None of my friends think much about the environment. They throw plastic bottles away after one use. They get pizza delivered and throw away the boxes. I want to persuade young people to think differently about the environment – this might lead to even bigger changes beyond recycling.
I: You must be very busy doing school work and running your app. What do you do to relax?
H: I do spend a lot of time working on my project. Last weekend I had my picture taken by a well-known photographer for a magazine! But I do have free time too. I should use it to update my website but I forget. I spend the time drawing.
I: What are your plans for the future?
H: I'm going to university, so my little brother's going to start running the app. I hope to learn from some brilliant technology professors because I want to help clean up our oceans. There's a Dutch guy called Boyan Slat who started a company to do that when he was just nineteen. I'd love to go and work for him.
I: Thank you very much, Holly, and good luck!

6.6

A = Abi   S = Sam

A: It's really important to look after the environment. I mean, we need it to live, so of course we must look after it.
S: I agree. It's …
A: When we don't look after it, problems occur – like, for example, air pollution and rubbish in the oceans.
S: Yes.
A: Er, these cause problems. Um, air pollution causes health problems and, er, rubbish in the seas affects sea life.
S: That's true.
A: But I think people are becoming better at thinking about the environment. We understand more than in the past and that's a good thing.
S: That's true. Some …
A: People understand now how important it is.

172

6.7 and 6.8

A = Abi   S = Sam

A: Without a healthy environment, we can't really live, so it's really important that we look after it. What do you think?

S: I agree with you. It's …

A: When we … Sorry, go on.

S: It's the most important thing to worry about.

A: Why do you say that?

S: I mean, we need animals, plants and clean water to live. We need clean air to breathe. So I think taking care of those things is more important than other problems. Do you agree?

A: Yes, you're right. It probably is the most important thing. We need to reduce pollution if we can. I try to turn off lights when I leave a room. … What do you do?

S: Oh, er … I'm not very good at that, actually, but I like recycling things.

A: Me too. I often shout at my dad for forgetting to put plastic in the recycling bin!

6.9 and 6.10

1 It's so dark outside. We need some sunshine.
2 The sand on some beaches is black, not brown or white.
3 It's a really clear day. There's not a cloud in the sky.
4 Don't go too near the edge of the cliff. It's a long way down to the beach!
5 Look at that star up there. It's really bright. Do you think it's a planet?
6 Don't walk through that field. The farmer won't be very happy.
7 I don't think you should go in the sea. The waves are too strong.
8 I can hardly see anything outside. The fog is really thick.

7.1 and 7.2

P = Presenter   D = Dan   E = Ella

P: Welcome to todays' general knowledge quiz. We have Dan and Ella here with us. Let's make a start. Dan, what is the very fast train which runs in Japan?

D: The bullet.

P: Ella, who is the famous explorer who went to the Arctic?

E: Matthew Henson.

P: Which is the country which is furthest south in the world?

D: Chile.

P: What is the name of the city where you can take the Underground?

E: London.

P: What do we call a person who flies a plane?

D: A pilot.

P: Who was the man who went to the South Pole?

E: Captain Scott.

P: OK, they each got three right, so we have to wait for tomorrow to see who wins!

7.3

1 Rome is a beautiful city that's very popular with tourists.
2 Do you know the student that spoke to you?
3 They enjoyed sightseeing at the old castle that's in the mountains.
4 We're going to see our cousins that live near the lake.
5 I love travelling on trains that go fast.

7.4

1 destination: the place you are travelling to
2 flight: a journey in a plane
3 land: move from the air down to the ground
4 motorway: a wide road where cars travel very fast
5 abroad: in a foreign country
6 border: the line that separates two countries
7 check in: go to a desk at an airport or hotel to say you are there
8 delay: make someone or something late
9 passport: a small book with your photo which you show when you cross a border
10 sightseeing: visiting interesting places as a tourist
11 take off: move from the ground up into to the air
12 traffic jam: a long line of cars moving very slowly

7.5–7.7

Hi, I'm Sarah. You know, I've been traveling the world with my parents and my twin brother for six years! Yes, we don't have to go to school! My parents decided that we needed to travel to really find out how the world works. They said we mustn't just study from books but that we must learn subjects like geography and history and sciences from the real world and all the living things surrounding us.

We set off on the road when I was ten but we didn't travel abroad until two years later, when I was twelve. I remember because our first trip abroad was on my birthday! At the start we travelled around Australia quite a lot, enjoying the nature and beauty of our own country. We had to sell our house before we could go overseas, but then, with only a couple of suitcases, we boarded a plane to the southern states in the USA and after two weeks went on to Mexico and central America. And now we've been everywhere! We've travelled to six continents and forty-one countries; but all places which are hot – we don't like the cold! We've had tons of adventures and experiences, and learned such a lot!

And what's been great about this time? Well, I enjoy travelling with a passion; I love reading stories – rather than maps or travel guides – about the places I'm in and I especially like writing about my experiences. I love walking in nature – and pretty much anything to do with beautiful beaches or the water. I really love swimming in the sea or ocean. I know many people think I've missed school but in fact, I've learnt more. I've met a lot of amazing, interesting people and, most of all, I value the friends I've made. Soon we'll have to go home. It's been nice not being in school but, like everyone else, I have to do my exams!

7.8 and 7.9

B = Boy   E = Examiner   G = Girl

B: I was on a plane last year, when the captain made an important announcement. He told us there were some animals on board but they were safely in the cargo hold with the baggage. However, about half an hour later, there was another announcement. One of the crocodiles had escaped! The flight attendants told us to keep calm but people were scared. One lady screamed! Fortunately, it was a short flight and we landed without seeing the crocodile. It turned out that it was only sixty centimetres long anyway. It was a baby!

E: What about you, Molly?

G: That's never happened to me! It's unbelievable! I once went to Rome with my parents. We were walking down the road when I saw someone I went to primary school with in a completely different country. That was surprising!

AUDIOSCRIPTS

8.1 and 8.2
S = Speaker

S1: This morning I asked my brother if I could borrow his phone charger.
S2: The last person I spoke to was my drama teacher and she told me to learn my lines.
S3: The last time I asked a question was when I asked my friend if I could borrow a pen.
S4: I last asked a question to my mum. I asked her if she could drop me into town.
S5: The last person I spoke to was my dad and he said, 'Have a good day at dance rehearsals.'
S6: The last time I asked someone a question was yesterday, when I asked my uncle what time he was going to arrive in my village.
S7: The last person I spoke to was my mum and she said, 'Don't forget your school bag.'
S4: I last spoke to my dad and he said, 'Have a fun day.'
S8: I last spoke to my sister. She told me to get out of her bedroom.
S6: The last person I spoke to was my cousin and she said she was going to leave at two o'clock to come and see my family.

8.3
A: OK, so who's coming?
B: Well, Jane said she could come after eight o'clock.
A: That's a bit late. What about Ed?
B: Ed said he would bring some snacks.
A: Great! And Chris?
B: Chris said he couldn't come because he was sick.
A: Oh dear! Is Melanie coming?
B: Yes, Melanie said she loved rehearsing after school.
A: She always does! How about Simon?
B: Simon said he was going to be late. He said he hadn't left the house yet.
A: He'll get here. OK, so the last one is Lizzie.
B: Lizzie said that she really wanted to try on the new costumes.
A: Great!

8.4
1 OK, is everybody ready? Big smiles now!
2 [someone playing the guitar]
3 OK, with the music, everybody! Here we go: arms up, arms down, and to the left …
4 [someone playing an online game]
5 Shh, everybody. Can we do that again, please? OK, Ellie, you walk on now …
6 That's it. I've finished. I think I'll wear it tonight for the party.

8.5
1 one point five
2 four pounds fifty-seven pence
3 twelve and a half million
4 twelve thousand five hundred
5 the twenty first of January, two thousand and nineteen
6 nine hundred and ninety-nine
7 seventy percent
8 four euros fifty-seven cents

8.6–8.8
1
A: Have you got everything you need for the course, Tom?
B: I think so. I've already put the camera in my backpack and, luckily, I found the case for my camera that I'd lost. Oh I know: have you got any batteries? The teacher said that I should take some extra ones for the camera.
A: I think so. Can you tell me what kind you need?
B: Those small ones. Thanks, they're perfect.

2
A: What's the weirdest hobby you've heard of, Max?
B: Um, well, one time I read about a man who spent all his time making giant bubbles.
A: Bubbles?! Do you know if he made them from chewing gum?
B: No. Actually, he used soap in a recipe with other secret ingredients. He said he practised for twenty years. Eventually, he made the world's biggest bubble.
A: Really? How big was this huge bubble?
B: It was six metres wide.
A: No way!

3
I started gaming when I was eight and I've been playing professionally for about a year now. I play for an e-sports team that's been in an international league since 2010, and we've got a sponsor, team colours, a logo and everything! My mum and dad were a bit worried about the hobby at first, but these days it's all quite physical. You actually have something like a bat in your hand that you have to hit the ball with. It develops your self-control and teamwork and so they support me.

4
A: Our first caller today is Bethany. Hi, Bethany. So, tell us about your unusual collection.
B: Yeah, er, I collect 'Star Wars' objects – action figures, T-shirts, posters, you know.
A: Right. And could you tell us how many objects you've got?
B: I knew the exact answer to that when I used to keep them in my bedroom, but now I've got around thirteen thousand and I've had to move them to the garage.
A: That's unbelievable! Most people have a few toys in their attic, but not that many.
B: If I tried to keep them all there, the ceiling would fall down!

5
A: Your jewellery's beautiful, Liz. How do you make it?
B: I use things I find. I recycle old stuff, mainly.
A: What's this necklace made of? Are these plastic buttons?
B: No, they aren't. Guess again!
A: Er, are they plastic bottle tops?
B: Nope. They're plastic 'coins' from a Monopoly game.
A: Plastic money? You mean toy money?
B: Yes, that's right! I glue them together and paint them to make necklaces.

6
B: I've always enjoyed cooking and my family think I'm pretty good at it, so last year I decided to go in for a cooking competition on a local TV channel. I wasn't sure what to make. My mum said I should make a really special cake, my brothers told me to make pizzas, but in the end I decided to make my speciality: tomato bread. Luckily, the judges loved it – they gave me a score of nine point five out of ten – and I won!

7
A: Come on, Lucy. It's four forty-five – you're going to be late for class!
B: I don't care. I don't want to go.
A: What do you mean? You love drama class. And today they're going to tell you what part you've got. You said you wanted to be the astronaut in the play.
B: They've given that part to Jane.
A: So they've announced them all then. Which one did you get?
B: The donkey!
A: Never mind. You'll always be a princess in my eyes!

9.1 and 9.2
A few summers ago, I saw a TV programme about orienteering. Orienteering is a kind of outdoor adventure sport where you run from one place to another and then another along a course, usually in the countryside somewhere. You find each place using an old-fashioned map and compass. No mobile phones allowed! I hadn't heard of it before, but I thought it looked exciting. I really wanted to try it because I had spent a lot of time at the park as a child and I love the outdoors.

So, I persuaded my mum to take me orienteering and run with me. She'd recently run a half-marathon, so I knew she was the right teammate. She's also much better at map-reading than my dad! Anyway, it was a Sunday morning in August. We got up early and after we'd put our boots and stuff in the car, we drove to a nearby forest. There were lots of people there, including young kids and older people too. Mum and I started the race quite slowly but once we'd worked out the quickest way to complete the course, we ran faster. We found each location quite easily and were pleased when we got to the finish line. We had a drink while we watched the other teams arrive. And then, when they announced the winners, we found out that we had won! We couldn't believe it. We were so happy but I think it was probably beginner's luck!

9.3–9.6

1
- **A:** Hey, Jen. Apparently, we all have to do a week's work experience next month.
- **B:** I know. The school deals with organising it.
- **A:** Yeah, but we have to choose the type of work. I have no idea.
- **B:** You ought to do something you'll like doing. It'll be more fun.
- **A:** Sounds good.
- **B:** Some people are choosing things they want to do when they leave school but that's a long time away. I don't think that's important. And don't go for something too simple. It'll be boring.
- **A:** Good point. Maybe I could do something at a gym.

2
- **A:** What are you doing over the weekend?
- **B:** I'm not sure yet. Do you want to hang out?
- **A:** I'm going climbing with a local club. You could come with me.
- **B:** I'm not sure.
- **A:** I know you don't like high places, so I won't say you'll love it but you'll be really proud of yourself when you get to the top.
- **B:** Is it safe?
- **A:** Yes, you don't have to worry about that. There are really experienced climbers there that make sure everyone's OK.

3
- **A:** Hey, Nathan. How was your summer?
- **B:** It was good, thanks. I went to a sci-fi festival.
- **A:** What's that?
- **B:** You know, where people dress up as their favourite science fiction characters and watch films together and things.
- **A:** Oh right. How was it?
- **B:** Well, it was actually really crowded and difficult to move about.
- **A:** That's a shame.
- **B:** Yeah, I'd been really looking forward to it but it wasn't what I expected at all. It was all quite stressful. I had to play three hours of video games afterwards just to calm down!

4
- **A:** I really enjoyed that trip. Did you?
- **B:** Yeah, it was great to be without the parents for a while.
- **A:** Actually, I missed my dad's cooking. The hotel food was awful.
- **B:** My favourite thing was going up to the top of the mountain. I'd never done anything like that before.
- **A:** I hadn't either. And I liked that the most too. You could see for miles.
- **B:** The research project was interesting.
- **A:** Really? I didn't understand what we were supposed to do, so I didn't really take part in it.

5
- **A:** I sent you a message last night telling you how annoying my sister is.
- **B:** I didn't get it.
- **A:** I know. I sent it to my sister by mistake.
- **B:** Oh no! That wasn't good.
- **A:** No. That wasn't the worst thing though. I then wrote you a second message asking you what I should do about the first message. But I sent that one to my sister too.
- **B:** I thought it was bad when you called our history teacher 'dad' but at least you learnt from that mistake and didn't do it again!

6
- **A:** I helped out at the local children's hospital last weekend. There was a special party there.
- **B:** That sounds great! I used to help at a home for elderly people. It was hard but I always went home feeling pleased that I'd done it.
- **A:** I felt the same last weekend.
- **B:** I didn't use to like speaking to new people, so it gave me more confidence.
- **A:** Did you use to do it every weekend?
- **B:** Sure, until I got too much homework.
- **A:** Well, I'll definitely do it again next year.

9.7 and 9.8

E = Examiner   A = Anna   B = Bert

- **E:** Do you prefer to do the same things or try new things?
- **A:** I absolutely love trying new things. I like to challenge myself. I can't stand doing the same things all the time. For example, last month I tried go-karting at a local club. I didn't win the race but I came third. I was pleased. I'd love to do more of it.
- **E:** What about you, Bert?
- **B:** Hmm, it depends what it is. I'm not keen on going to big events where there are lots of people but I don't mind trying new things with a few friends. For example, last summer a small group of us made a short film and uploaded it online. It got lots of likes. That was fun.

9.9

1. The concert wasn't as good as I'd expected.
2. I was very surprised when I heard about Tom. In fact, I couldn't believe it.
3. Kate doesn't seem happy. I think she wants everything that Becky has.
4. Helen broke a chair at the party but didn't say anything. She feels bad about it.
5. My cat hasn't been home for three days now. I keep thinking that something bad has happened.
6. I worked hard on my maths homework and I got a B. I wanted an A but I was OK with a B.
7. When the man shouted, I didn't get angry or feel afraid or anything. I was quite cool.
8. I'm a bit angry with Alex. He's left wet towels all over the bathroom floor.

AUDIOSCRIPTS

10.1 and 10.2

Hi. I know many of you are thinking about what you can do that's useful over the summer. Have you thought about being a lifeguard at your local swimming pool? I know some of you tried to do this when you were thirteen or fourteen but now you're fifteen you can apply. The only thing is, before you do this, you need to make sure that you've taken all the relevant water safety exams to get the certificates you'll need to give to the pool. Once you have those, you can find a part-time job.

So what do you have to do? Well, when I started, I only worked on Saturdays, then I worked Sundays as well and now I do ten hours a week. You do lots of things. For example, guards are responsible for cleaning the pool daily, so we take turns and do it once a week. But your main job will be making sure that all the children are safe. We all have to do this and sometimes there are more than fifty in the pool at the same time – and that's scary. But you get used to it.

Now, we don't get very much money so what are the benefits? Well, first of all, it gives you the opportunity to learn about being a leader. And if you spend a lot of your time swimming, you'll already know some of the things you have to do because the role allows you to put into practice the things you know as part of your hobby. Of course, I realise swimming may not be for everyone but I think it's a good idea to try and do some work over the summer if you can.

10.3 and 10.4

P = Presenter   K = Kat

P: Hi and welcome to 'Job Spot', where we find out about different jobs you might want to try in the holidays. Today I'm talking to Kat Sparkes, who is training to be a makeup artist. Kat, what does a make-up artist do?

K: Well, a make-up artist works mainly with people's faces. Sometimes that means making them look their best, for weddings or parties, but I'm not keen on doing that. I'm more into making people look very unusual or different. I think it's because I studied art and design at school.

P: And did you have to practise a lot?

K: Oh yes. When I was at college, I used my brother and sister as models! I painted their faces with kids' paint. I made my brother look like a monster, with green and black paint. And I made his hair untidy and wild. Once I glued hundreds of tiny plastic beads on my sister's face. She looked amazing! Sometimes my whole family helped. They've been very patient!

P: In fact, at college you did lots of different things, didn't you? What did they teach you to do that really helped you?

K: Yes, I enjoyed experimenting with paint, string, beads and other objects. The best thing was when we had projects where we had to look at a particular artist's work first and then develop our own ideas based on that. It made you try different styles.

P: What are the good things about your job?

K: Well, a lot of make-up artists don't make much money. Often companies only want you to work for a few days and then you have to find the next job. But sometimes you meet famous actors if you work on a film. That's cool.

P: And are you working at the moment?

K: Yes, but I'm not earning any money. It's a chance to work as a professional with a large, well-known company. I get lots of training and experience, so I can become an expert at my job. Lots of my friends are doing this. When I start looking for a 'real' job next year, other companies will be more interested in me.

P: So, if our young listeners are interested in becoming make-up artists, what can they do?

K: Um, I know a lot of people try out their ideas at home and that's great. But I suggest finding out about someone whose work you think is wonderful and maybe ask if you can help for a bit over the summer. Practice is more important than knowledge!

P: Thanks, Kat!